First World War
and Army of Occupation
War Diary
France, Belgium and Germany

61 DIVISION
Headquarters, Branches and Services
Commander Royal Engineers
1 July 1918 - 31 July 1919

WO95/3041/2

The Naval & Military Press Ltd
www.nmarchive.com
Published in association with The National Archives

Published by

The Naval & Military Press Ltd

Unit 10 Ridgewood Industrial Park,

Uckfield, East Sussex,

TN22 5QE England

Tel: +44 (0) 1825 749494

www.naval-military-press.com

www.nmarchive.com

This diary has been reprinted in facsimile from the original. Any imperfections are inevitably reproduced and the quality may fall short of modern type and cartographic standards.

© **Crown Copyright**
Images reproduced by permission of The National Archives, London, England, 2015.

Contents

Document type	Place/Title	Date From	Date To
Heading	WO95/3041/1		
Heading	61st Division C.R.E 1918 July-1919 Jly		
Heading	War Diary Of H.Q 61st (S.M) Div R.E For The Month of July 1918 Vol XXVII		
War Diary	P.1.a.4.5	01/07/1918	01/07/1918
War Diary	O.6.b.8.4	02/07/1918	11/07/1918
War Diary	M.5.c.7.3 Ham	12/07/1918	21/07/1918
War Diary	A.6. Wardrecques	22/07/1918	31/07/1918
Heading	Routine Orders By C.R.E		
Miscellaneous	Routine Orders Issued By Lieut-Colonel G.E.J. Durnford D.S.O. R.E. Commanding 61st (South Midland) Divisional Royal Engineers	12/07/1918	12/07/1918
Miscellaneous	Routine Orders Issued By Lieut-Colonel G.E.J. Durnford D.S.O. R.E. Commanding 61st (South Midland) Divisional Royal Engineers	13/07/1918	13/07/1918
Miscellaneous	Routine Orders Issued By Lieut-Colonel G.E.J. Durnford D.S.O. R.E. Commanding 61st (South Midland) Divisional Royal Engineers	15/07/1918	15/07/1918
Miscellaneous	Routine Orders Issued By Lieut-Colonel G.E.J. Durnford D.S.O. R.E. Commanding 61st (South Midland) Divisional Royal Engineers	16/07/1918	16/07/1918
Miscellaneous	Routine Orders Issued By Lieut-Colonel G.E.J. Durnford D.S.O. R.E. Commanding 61st (South Midland) Divisional Royal Engineers	18/07/1918	18/07/1918
Miscellaneous	Routine Orders Issued By Lieut-Colonel G.E.J. Durnford D.S.O. R.E. Commanding 61st (South Midland) Divisional Royal Engineers	19/07/1918	19/07/1918
Miscellaneous	Routine Orders Issued By Lieut-Colonel G.E.J. Durnford D.S.O. R.E. Commanding 61st (South Midland) Divisional Royal Engineers	20/07/1918	20/07/1918
Miscellaneous	Routine Orders Issued By Lieut-Colonel G.E.J. Durnford D.S.O. R.E. Commanding 61st (South Midland) Divisional Royal Engineers	26/07/1918	26/07/1918
Miscellaneous	Routine Orders Issued By Lieut-Colonel G.E.J. Durnford D.S.O. R.E. Commanding 61st (South Midland) Divisional Royal Engineers	27/07/1918	27/07/1918
Heading	War Diary Original July 1918 C.R.E 61st Div Move & Relief Orders By C.R.E		
Miscellaneous	Warning Order	06/07/1918	06/07/1918
Operation(al) Order(s)	61st Divisional R.E Order No. 103	09/07/1918	09/07/1918
Miscellaneous	Table"A" Issued with 61st Division R.E Order No. 103	09/07/1918	09/07/1918
Miscellaneous	Orders For Move Of R.E.N.O	11/07/1918	11/07/1918
Miscellaneous	Notes By C.R.E 61st Divn	12/07/1918	12/07/1918
Miscellaneous	Machine Gun Emplacement		
Miscellaneous	List Of Maps Handed Over		
Miscellaneous	61st Divisional R.E Order No. 104	22/07/1918	22/07/1918
Miscellaneous	61st Division R.E Order No. 104	22/07/1918	22/07/1918
Operation(al) Order(s)	R.E Order No. 104	22/07/1918	22/07/1918
Miscellaneous	Reference Warning Order No. 24	29/07/1918	29/07/1918
Operation(al) Order(s)	61st Divisional R.E Order No. 106	29/07/1918	29/07/1918

Miscellaneous	March Table To Accompany 61st Divisional R.E Order 106	30/07/1918	30/07/1918
Operation(al) Order(s)	61st Divisional R.E Order No. 107	30/07/1918	30/07/1918
Heading	Work Orders & Instructions		
Miscellaneous	Notes Of Conference	04/07/1918	04/07/1918
Miscellaneous	Notes On Conference Held At R.E.H.Q 8.7.1918	06/07/1918	06/07/1918
Miscellaneous	Notes On Conference Held At R.E.H.Q	14/07/1918	14/07/1918
Miscellaneous	Minutes of Meeting of Recreation Committee held 10 a.m. 20.7.1918	20/07/1918	20/07/1918
Miscellaneous	476 Field Co		
Miscellaneous	478 Field Co. Copy To 476 Field Co	27/07/1918	27/07/1918
Heading	War Diary Original July 1918 C.R.E 61st Div Nominal Rolls		
Miscellaneous	Nominal Roll Of Unit	01/07/1918	01/07/1918
Miscellaneous	61st (S.M) Divisional Royal Engineer		
Heading	War Diary 6 Original July 1918 C.R.E 61st Divn Defence Schemes & Instructions		
Miscellaneous	Defence Scheme	06/07/1918	06/07/1918
Miscellaneous	Defence Scheme 61st Div R.E. Appendix A	06/07/1918	06/07/1918
Miscellaneous	Defence Scheme 61st Div RE Appendix B	07/07/1918	07/07/1918
Miscellaneous	Appendix C Prepared Demolitions.	07/07/1918	07/07/1918
Diagram etc	Appendix D		
Miscellaneous	Gas Defence	07/07/1918	07/07/1918
Miscellaneous	Hostile Attack Heavy Enemy Bombardment Or Orders To Man Battle Station	06/07/1918	06/07/1918
Miscellaneous	Reference 61st div R.E Defence Scheme	06/07/1918	06/07/1918
Miscellaneous	Defence Scheme 61st Div R.E Appendix B	25/07/1918	25/07/1918
Miscellaneous	61st Div R.E Defence Scheme (Appendix F)	24/07/1918	24/07/1918
Miscellaneous	Herewith Appendix F	27/07/1918	27/07/1918
Miscellaneous	Defence Scheme 61st Div R.E Appendix F	27/07/1918	27/07/1918
Miscellaneous	Defence Scheme 61st Div R.E Appendix F	24/07/1918	24/07/1918
Heading	War Diary Of H.Q 61st Div R.E For The Month of August 1918 Vol XXVIII		
War Diary	Ham M.5.c.7.3	01/08/1918	06/08/1918
War Diary	I.20.a.5.7	07/08/1918	30/08/1918
War Diary	Croix Marraisse J.21.c.5.3	31/08/1918	31/08/1918
Heading	War Diary Original Augt 1918 C.R.E 61st Div Routine Orders By CRE		
Miscellaneous	Routine Orders By Lieut-Colonel G.E.J Durnford D.S.O. Commanding 61st (South Midland) Divisional Royal Engineers	02/08/1918	02/08/1918
Miscellaneous	Field Coy R.E Saluting		
Miscellaneous	Routine Orders Issued By Lieut-Colonel G.E.J. Durnford D.S.O. R.E. Commanding Divisional Royal Engineers	03/08/1918	03/08/1918
Miscellaneous	Routine Orders Issued By Lieut-Colonel G.E.J. Durnford D.S.O. R.E. Commanding 61st (South Midland) Divisional Royal Engineers	06/08/1918	06/08/1918
Miscellaneous	Routine Orders By Lieut-Colonel G.E.J. Durnford D.S.O. R.E. Commanding 61st (South Midland) Divisional Royal Engineers	06/08/1918	06/08/1918
Miscellaneous	Routine Orders By Lieut-Colonel G.E.J. Durnford D.S.O. R.E. Commanding 61st (South Midland) Divisional Royal Engineers	26/08/1918	26/08/1918
Miscellaneous	Routine Orders Headquarters 61st Divisional R.E	30/08/1918	30/08/1918

Miscellaneous	War Diary Original Augt 1918 C.R.E 61st Div. Move & Relief Orders By C.R.E		
Miscellaneous	A Form Messages And Signals.		
Operation(al) Order(s)	R.E Order 108	04/08/1918	04/08/1918
Operation(al) Order(s)	61st Divisional R.E Order No. 109	05/08/1918	05/08/1918
Miscellaneous	Table A Issued With 61st Divisional R.E Order No. 109		
Miscellaneous	Ref. Relief Of 5th Div. By 61st Div	04/08/1918	04/08/1918
Miscellaneous	Orders For Move Of 61st Div. R.E Headquarters	06/08/1918	06/08/1918
Miscellaneous	Reference R.E Order 110	07/08/1918	07/08/1918
Operation(al) Order(s)	R.E Order No. 110	07/08/1918	07/08/1918
Operation(al) Order(s)	R.E Order No. 111	09/08/1918	09/08/1918
Operation(al) Order(s)	R.E Order No. 112	10/08/1918	10/08/1918
Operation(al) Order(s)	R.E Order No. 113	20/08/1918	20/08/1918
Operation(al) Order(s)	R.E Order No. 114	20/08/1918	20/08/1918
Operation(al) Order(s)	R.E Order No. 115	21/08/1918	21/08/1918
Operation(al) Order(s)	61st Divisional R.E Order No. 117	23/08/1918	23/08/1918
Operation(al) Order(s)	61st Divisional R.E Order No. 116	23/08/1918	23/08/1918
Miscellaneous	470 Field Co	30/08/1918	30/08/1918
Heading	Work Orders & Instructions Notes on Conferences Reconnaissance		
Miscellaneous	Notes On Conference Held At R.E.H.Q	01/08/1918	01/08/1918
Miscellaneous	Extracts from Proceeding of a Conference held by The Cheif Engineer	11/08/1918	11/08/1918
Miscellaneous	257 Tunnelling Co RE		
Miscellaneous	Method Of Repair		
Miscellaneous	476 Field Co	12/08/1918	12/08/1918
Miscellaneous	Notes On Conference At H.Q. 479	14/08/1918	14/08/1918
Miscellaneous	Employment Of 1/5 D.C.L.I (Pioneers) From 20.8.1916	19/08/1918	19/08/1918
Miscellaneous	Reconnaissance Of Bridge Over River Bourre on 20th August 1918	20/08/1918	20/08/1918
Miscellaneous	A.D.M.S 61st Divn	21/08/1918	21/08/1918
Miscellaneous	ADMS 61Div	22/08/1918	22/08/1918
Miscellaneous	1/5 D C.L.I Copies To 476 Field Co	25/08/1918	25/08/1918
Miscellaneous	Water Supply Report	23/08/1918	23/08/1918
Miscellaneous	61st Division "Q"	28/08/1918	28/08/1918
Miscellaneous	O.C. 479 Field Co	30/08/1918	30/08/1918
Miscellaneous	O.C. 479 Field Co	31/08/1918	31/08/1918
Miscellaneous	61st Division "G"	31/08/1918	31/08/1918
Heading	Nominal Rolls		
Miscellaneous	Nominal Roll Of Unit	01/08/1918	01/08/1918
Heading	Defence Schemes & Instructions		
Miscellaneous	Defence Scheme, 51st Div. R.E. Appendix F	01/08/1918	01/08/1918
Miscellaneous	476 Field Co. App 6	28/08/1918	28/08/1918
Miscellaneous	C.R.E 61st Division	27/08/1918	27/08/1918
Heading	War Diary Of HQ 61st Div R.E. For Month of September 1918 Vol XXIX		
War Diary	Croix Marraisse J.21.c.5.3	01/09/1918	07/09/1918
War Diary	L.27.d.8.4	08/09/1918	30/09/1918
Heading	War Diary Original For September 1918 C.R.E 61st Div Routine Orders By C.R.E		
Miscellaneous	Special Order Of The Day Issued By:- Lieut-Colonel G.E.J. Durnford D.S.O. R.E. Commanding 61st (South Midland) Divisional Royal Engineers T.F.	07/09/1916	07/09/1916
Miscellaneous	Routine Orders By Lieut-Colonel G.E.J Durnford D.S.O. Commanding 61st (South Midland) Divisional Royal Engineers	18/09/1918	18/09/1918

Miscellaneous	Routine Orders By Lieut-Colonel G.E.J Durnford D.S.O. Commanding 61st (South Midland) Divisional Royal Engineers	19/09/1918	19/09/1918
Miscellaneous	Routine Orders By H.B Louis M.C Commanding 61st (S.M) Divisional RE	23/09/1918	23/09/1918
Miscellaneous	Routine Orders By H.S Davis M.C Commanding 61st (S.M) Divisional Royal Engineers	29/09/1918	29/09/1918
Miscellaneous	Routine Orders By Major H.S Davis M.C. Commanding 61st Divisional Royal Engineers	29/09/1918	29/09/1918
Heading	Move & Relief Orders By C R E		
Miscellaneous	A Form Messages And Signals.		
Operation(al) Order(s)	R.E Order No. 118	03/09/1918	03/09/1918
Operation(al) Order(s)	61st Divisional R.E Order No. 119	11/09/1918	11/09/1918
Miscellaneous	A Form Messages And Signals.		
Operation(al) Order(s)	R.E Order No. 120	11/09/1918	11/09/1918
Operation(al) Order(s)	R.E Order No. 121	13/09/1918	13/09/1918
Operation(al) Order(s)	R.E Order No. 122	18/09/1918	18/09/1918
Operation(al) Order(s)	R.E Order No. 123	20/09/1918	20/09/1918
Operation(al) Order(s)	R.E Order No. 124	27/09/1918	27/09/1918
Operation(al) Order(s)	R.E Order No. 124	01/10/1918	01/10/1918
Operation(al) Order(s)	R.E Order No. 125	28/09/1918	28/09/1918
Heading	War Diary Original For Sept 1918 C.R.E 61st Div Work Orders & Instructions		
Miscellaneous	A Form Messages And Signals.		
Miscellaneous	476 Field Co	01/09/1918	01/09/1918
Miscellaneous	476 Field Co	02/09/1918	02/09/1918
Miscellaneous	Reconnaissance Report	02/09/1918	02/09/1918
Miscellaneous	476 Field Co.	04/09/1918	04/09/1918
Miscellaneous	A Form Messages And Signals.		
Miscellaneous	476 Field Co	05/09/1918	05/09/1918
Miscellaneous	A Form Messages And Signals.		
Miscellaneous	61st Division Instructions No.1	06/09/1918	06/09/1918
Miscellaneous	476 Field Co	06/09/1918	06/09/1918
Miscellaneous	OC 257 Tunnelling Co RE	09/09/1918	09/09/1918
Miscellaneous	Bridging Programme	11/09/1918	11/09/1918
Miscellaneous	479 Field Co	13/09/1918	13/09/1918
Miscellaneous	61st Divisional Instructions No.4	15/09/1918	15/09/1918
Miscellaneous	61st Divisional Instructions No.5	15/09/1918	15/09/1918
Miscellaneous	182 Inf Bde 61st Div Art	15/09/1918	15/09/1918
Miscellaneous	Tank Minefields N.W. Of St. Quentin	15/09/1918	15/09/1918
Miscellaneous	476 Field Co	16/09/1918	16/09/1918
Miscellaneous	Reference XI Corps Q.J.4	17/09/1918	17/09/1918
Miscellaneous	Maintenance of Brigades, etc	19/09/1918	19/09/1918
Miscellaneous	Nominal Rolls		
Miscellaneous	Nominal Roll Of Unit	01/09/1918	01/09/1918
Heading	R E Stores & Dumps		
Miscellaneous	476 Field Co.	02/09/1918	02/09/1918
Miscellaneous	476 Field Co	04/09/1918	04/09/1918
Heading	App 6 Drawings Issued During Month		
Diagram etc	Sketch Showing Site For Above Bridge		
Map	Map Shewing Bridge Situation		
Diagram etc	Splinter Proof Shelter Made In A Ruined Village		
Miscellaneous			
Diagram etc	German Contact Mine In Trench		
Diagram etc	German Railways		

Type	Description	Start	End
Heading	War Diary HQ 61st (S.M) Div R.E For Month of October 1918 Vol XXX		
War Diary	L.27.d.8.4	01/10/1918	02/10/1918
War Diary	La Lacque	03/10/1918	05/10/1918
War Diary	Doullens	06/10/1918	08/10/1918
War Diary	Sht 57c Lagnicourt C.24.c.2.2	09/10/1918	10/10/1918
War Diary	Lagnicourt	11/10/1918	12/10/1918
War Diary	Noyelles Sur L' Escaut	13/10/1918	18/10/1918
War Diary	Rieux	19/10/1918	22/10/1918
War Diary	Sht.51a. St Aubert	23/10/1918	23/10/1918
War Diary	St Aubert & Montrecourt	24/10/1918	24/10/1918
War Diary	Montrecourt Vendegies	25/10/1918	25/10/1918
War Diary	Vendegies	26/10/1918	31/10/1918
Heading	War Diary (Original) For October 1918 C.R.E 61st Divn		
Miscellaneous	Routine Orders By Major M. Whitwill D.S.O. M.C. Commanding 61st Divisional Royal Engineers	02/10/1918	02/10/1918
Miscellaneous	Routine Orders By Lieut Colonel G.E.J. Durnford D.S.O. R.E. Commanding 61st (South Midland) Divisional Royal Engineers	11/10/1918	11/10/1918
Miscellaneous	Routine Orders By Lieut Colonel G.E.J. Durnford D.S.O. R.E. Commanding 61st (South Midland) Divisional Royal Engineers	20/10/1918	20/10/1918
Miscellaneous	Routine Orders By Lieut Colonel G.E.J. Durnford D.S.O. R.E. Commanding 61st (South Midland) Divisional Royal Engineers	30/10/1918	30/10/1918
Heading	Move Relief & Operation Orders By C R E		
Miscellaneous	List Of Document And Maps Handed Over		
Operation(al) Order(s)	61st Divisional R.E Order No. 126	02/10/1918	02/10/1918
Miscellaneous	Table A Issued With 61st Div R.E Order 120	02/10/1918	02/10/1918
Miscellaneous	Handing Over Report To C.R.E. 59 Divn from C.R.E. 61 Divn	02/10/1918	02/10/1918
Miscellaneous	Orders For Move of R.E.H.Q	08/10/1918	08/10/1918
Operation(al) Order(s)	R.E Order No. 127	10/10/1918	10/10/1918
Operation(al) Order(s)	R.E Order No. 128	22/10/1918	22/10/1918
Miscellaneous	Movement Tanks R.E Order No. 198	22/10/1918	22/10/1918
Operation(al) Order(s)	R.E Order No. 129	23/10/1918	23/10/1918
Miscellaneous	Reference R.E Order No. 129	23/10/1918	23/10/1918
Operation(al) Order(s)	R.E Order No. 130	28/10/1918	28/10/1918
Operation(al) Order(s)	R.E Order No. 131	29/10/1918	29/10/1918
Miscellaneous	Table A Issued With R.E Order no.131	29/10/1918	29/10/1918
Miscellaneous	Reference R.E Order No. 131	29/10/1918	29/10/1918
Miscellaneous	O.C. Detachment 178 T. Co. R.E	30/10/1918	30/10/1918
Heading	Work Orders & Instructions By C R E		
Miscellaneous	C.E XI Corps	14/10/1918	14/10/1918
Miscellaneous	C.E XI Corps.	16/10/1918	16/10/1918
Miscellaneous	C.R.E 24th Division	27/10/1918	27/10/1918
Miscellaneous	C.R.E 61st Div No.23/2/1	27/10/1918	27/10/1918
Miscellaneous	Summary Of Information Obtained From Reconnaissance	28/10/1918	28/10/1918
Miscellaneous	Work Order For 29th Oct	28/10/1918	28/10/1918
Miscellaneous	Reference C.E 321 Dated 27.10.18	31/10/1918	31/10/1918
Miscellaneous	61st Division Royal Engineers	01/11/1918	01/11/1918
Heading	Nominal Rolls		
Miscellaneous	Nominal Roll Of Unit	01/10/1918	01/10/1918
Heading	Appendix 4		

Miscellaneous	Nominal Roll Of Unit	01/10/1918	01/10/1918
Miscellaneous	Special Order Of The Day By Major-General F.J. Duncan, C.M.G. D.S.O. Commanding 61st Division	07/10/1918	07/10/1918
Map	App 6		
Map	Map Showing Defences Of Vendegies		
Miscellaneous	Appx 6		
Heading	War Diary Of H.Q 61st (S.M) Div R.E For The Month of November 1918 Vol XXXI		
War Diary	Vendegies	01/11/1918	02/11/1918
War Diary	St Aubert	03/11/1918	07/11/1918
War Diary	Vendegies	08/11/1918	13/11/1918
War Diary	Rieux	14/11/1918	14/11/1918
War Diary	Cambrai	15/11/1918	24/11/1918
War Diary	Bernaville	25/11/1918	30/11/1918
Heading	Routine Orders Issued By C R E		
Miscellaneous	Routine Orders Issued By Lieut-Colonel C.E.J. Durnford D.S.O. R.E. Commanding 61st (South Midland) Divisional Royal Engineers	09/11/1918	09/11/1918
Miscellaneous	Routine Orders Issued By Lieut-Colonel G.E.J. Durnford D.S.O. R.E. Commanding 61st (South Midland) Divisional Royal Engineers	13/11/1918	13/11/1918
Miscellaneous	Routine Orders Issued By Lieut-Colonel G.E.J. Durnford D.S.O. R.E. Commanding 61st (South Midland) Divisional Royal Engineers	16/11/1918	16/11/1918
Miscellaneous	Routine Orders Issued By Lieut-Colonel G.E.J. Durnford D.S.O. R.E. Commanding 61st (South Midland) Divisional Royal Engineers	29/11/1918	29/11/1918
Heading	Move Relief & Operation Orders By C R E		
Operation(al) Order(s)	R.E Order No. 132	01/11/1918	01/11/1918
Miscellaneous	March Table Issued With R.E Order 132	01/11/1918	01/11/1918
Heading	Work Orders & Instructions By C R E		
Miscellaneous	Summary Of Information Obtained From Reconnaissance	01/11/1918	01/11/1918
Miscellaneous	The Following Message Received From The Divisional Commander	03/11/1918	03/11/1918
Heading	War Diary of C.R.E 61st Division From Dec 1st To Dec 31st 1918 Vol XXXII		
War Diary	Bernaville	01/12/1918	07/12/1918
War Diary	St Riquier	08/12/1918	31/12/1918
Miscellaneous	Routine Orders By C.R.E		
Miscellaneous	Routine Orders Issued By Lieut-Colonel C.E.J. Durnford D.S.O. R.E. Commanding 61st (South Midland) Divisional Royal Engineers	09/12/1918	09/12/1918
Miscellaneous	Routine Orders Issued By Lieut-Colonel G.E.J. Durnford D.S.O. R.E. Commanding 61st (South Midland) Divisional Royal Engineers	28/12/1918	28/12/1918
Heading	War Diary Of C.R.E 61st Divn January 1919 Vol XXXIII		
War Diary	St Riquier	04/01/1919	31/01/1919
Miscellaneous	Routine Orders Issued By Major H. Humphreys Commanding 61st (South Midland) Divisional Royal Engineers	24/01/1919	24/01/1919
Heading	War Diary Of C.R.E 61st Division February 1919		
War Diary	St Riquier	03/02/1919	28/02/1919
Heading	Routine Orders By C R E		

Miscellaneous	Routine Orders Issued By Lieut-Colonel C.E.J. Durnford D.S.O. Commanding 61st (South Midland) Divisional Royal Engineers	04/02/1919	04/02/1919
Operation(al) Order(s)	R.E Order No. 132	12/02/1919	12/02/1919
Miscellaneous	Routine Orders Issued By Lieut-Colonel C.E.J. Durnford D.S.O. R.E. Commanding 61st (South Midland) Divisional Royal Engineers	17/02/1919	17/02/1919
Miscellaneous	Routine Orders Issued By Lieut-Colonel G.E.J. Durnford D.S.O. R.E. Commanding 61st (South Midland) Divisional Royal Engineers	28/02/1919	28/02/1919
Heading	War Diary Of C.R.E 61st Division March 1919 Vol XXXV		
War Diary	St Riquier	03/03/1919	26/03/1919
War Diary	Ailly-Le-Haut-Clocher	27/03/1919	31/03/1919
Heading	Orders Received & Issued		
Operation(al) Order(s)	R.E Order No. 133	22/03/1919	22/03/1919
Operation(al) Order(s)	R.E Order No. 134	25/03/1919	25/03/1919
Operation(al) Order(s)	R.E Order No. 135	29/03/1919	29/03/1919
Heading	Routine Orders By C R E		
Miscellaneous	Routine Orders Issued By Lieut-Colonel C.E.J. Durnford D.S.O. R.E. Commanding 61st (South Midland) Divisional Royal Engineers	03/03/1919	03/03/1919
Miscellaneous	Routine Orders Issued By Lieut-Colonel C.E.J. Durnford D.S.O. R.E. Commanding 61st (South Midland) Divisional Royal Engineers	14/03/1919	14/03/1919
Miscellaneous	Routine Orders Issued By Lieut-Colonel G.E.J. Durnford D.S.O. R.E. Commanding 61st (South Midland) Divisional Royal Engineers	29/03/1919	29/03/1919
Heading	War Diary Of C.R.E 61st Division April 1919 Vol XXXVI		
War Diary	Ailly-Le-Haut-Clocher	02/04/1919	30/04/1919
Heading	Routine Orders By C R E		
Miscellaneous	Routine Orders Issued By Major H. Humphreys Commanding 61st (South Midland) Divisional Engineers	09/04/1919	09/04/1919
Heading	Orders Received & Issued		
Operation(al) Order(s)	R.E Order No. 136	03/04/1919	03/04/1919
Miscellaneous	Special Order Of The Day By Lieutenant-General G.E.J. Durnford D.S.O. Commanding Royal Engineers 61st Division	07/04/1919	07/04/1919
Miscellaneous	Board Of Officers	12/04/1919	12/04/1919
Heading	War Diary Of C.R.E 61st Division May 1919 Vol XXXVII		
War Diary	Ailly-Le-Haut-Clocher	07/05/1919	31/05/1919
Heading	Routine Orders By C.R.E		
Miscellaneous	Routine Orders Issued By Major H. Humphreys Commanding 61st (South Midland) Divisional Engineers	16/05/1919	16/05/1919
Heading	Orders Received & Issued		
Operation(al) Order(s)	R.E Order No. 137	18/05/1919	18/05/1919
Operation(al) Order(s)	R.E Order No. 138	25/05/1919	25/05/1919
Heading	War Diary Of C.R.E 61st Div June 1919 Vol XXXVII		
War Diary	Ailly-Le-Haut-Clocher	01/06/1919	10/06/1919
War Diary	Abbeville	11/06/1919	30/06/1919
Operation(al) Order(s)	R.E Order No. 139	05/06/1919	05/06/1919
Heading	War Diary Of C.R.E 61 Div July 1919 Vol 39		

War Diary   Abbeville Sheet 14   01/07/1919   31/07/1919

WO 95/304/1/1

61ST DIVISION

C. R. E.

~~JAN 1918 JLY 1919~~

1918 JLY — 1919 JLY

Confidential

Vol 27

WAR DIARY
OF
HDQRS. 61ST (S.M.) DIV. R.E.

For the month of

JULY 1918.

Vol XXVII

Army Form C. 2118.

WAR DIARY
or
INTELLIGENCE SUMMARY

(Erase heading not required.)

HEADQUARTERS.
61st. DIV. ROYAL ENGINEERS.
Vol. XXVII
Page 1.

Place	Date	Hour	Summary of Events and Information	Remarks and references to Appendices
	JULY. 1918.		Sheet 36a. 1/40000 FRANCE.	
			Nominal Roll of Unit	Appx 4.
P.1.a.4.5.	1st.	10.30 am.	Received advice that 1 section 439 Field Co (74th. Divn) will move to ST. VENANT asylum for work under 61st. Division. G.S.O.1. telephoned to say that the XI Corps disapproves of move of D.H.Q. and 476 Field Co should discontinue building the new camp. Telephoned "Q" who said that work should be stopped pending return of G.O.C. who is out and "Q" will send orders to 476 Field Co to stop work. C.R.E. visited forward area with O's. C. 478 and 479 Field Cos General GRANT, C.E. Fifth Army called and informed us that we are in Fifth Army from today.	
0.6.b.8.4.	2nd		R.E. Headquarters moved to late H.Q. of 476 Field Co. Captain J.K. RENNIE (R.A.M.C) rejoined R.E.H.Q from hospital. Captain HUMPHREYS assumed Command of 479 Field Co vice Major O.S. DAVIES, D.S.O. C.R.E. visited forward area. During the evening C.R.E. and Adjutant developed P.U.O - Most of our officers are down with it now.	
	3rd.		30 men from Labour Corps were attached to 478 Field Co for cutting crops in forward area. Lieut-Colonel G.E.J. DURNFORD, D.S.O (C.R.E) went to hospital with P.U.O. and Major M. WHITWILL, D.S.O., M.C. assumed temporary command of Divisional R.E.	
	4th.		Issued Notes on Conference held today. 30 men of Labour Corps rejoined their unit as a result of their lodging objection to working in the forward area.	Appx 3.

Army Form C. 2118.

WAR DIARY
or
INTELLIGENCE SUMMARY.
(Erase heading not required.)

HEADQUARTERS.
61st. DIVNL. ROYAL ENGINEERS.
Vol XXVII

JULY. 1918.

Page 2.

Instructions regarding War Diaries and Intelligence Summaries are contained in F. S. Regs., Part II. and the Staff Manual respectively. Title pages will be prepared in manuscript.

Place	Date	Hour	Summary of Events and Information	Remarks and references to Appendices
0.5.b.8.4. FRANCE. Sht. 36a. 1/40000	5th	1 pm.	Received 61st. Divisional Order 174 re relief of 183 Brigade by 184 Brigade, and this was cancelled later owing to Divisional relief which is shortly to take place. G.S.O.1. called.	
	6th.		Received 184 Brigade Order 190 re relief of 183 Brigade 9/10th, but this was cancelled later owing to Divisional Relief Issued Divisional R.E. Defence Scheme and Appendices	Appx 5
	7th.	1 pm. 2.45pm	Received 183 Brigade Order 224 re relief by 184 Brigade, and this was cancelled owing to relief Received 183 Brigade Order 223 re relief raid by East Lancs at 11 p.m. Received report on action of 61st. Division April 10th-30th 1918 (61 Div G.C. 40/5)	
	8th. pm 6.30 7 pm.		C.E. XI Corps called and stated that relief of 61 by 74 Divn will commence on 10th. inst. C.R.E. 74 Division called and discussed relief. Received 61 Div Order 175 warning re relief of Division Issued Warning order 24/2/1 to Companies re relief of Division by 74 Division Issued Notes on Conference held 5 p.m. today Lce/Corporal E.G. ANGELL (our draughtsman) went to hospital with P.U.O.	Appx 2 Appx 3

Army Form C. 2118.

WAR DIARY
or
INTELLIGENCE SUMMARY

(Erase heading not required.)

HEADQUARTERS.
61st. DIV. ROYAL ENGINEERS.
Vol. XXVII   Page 3

Instructions regarding War Diaries and Intelligence Summaries are contained in F.S. Regs., Part II. and the Staff Manual respectively. Title pages will be prepared in manuscript.

Place	Date	Hour	Summary of Events and Information	Remarks and references to Appendices
O.6.b.8.4. FRANCE. Sht. 36a. 1/40000. JULY 1918.	9th.	am 8.30	~~Breakfast~~ Received 61 Div Order 176 re relief of 61 Div by 74 Div 10th-14th inst Issued R.E. Order 103 re relief of 61 Div R.E by 74 Div. R.E. Received 74 Div Order 22 re relief of 61 Div R.E. Received 183 Brigade Order 225 re Div. Relief Received A.D.M.S. order re Medical Arrangements on relief Adjutant went to HAM via "Q" office to arrange for the billeting of the whole Divisional R.E in that village, and called in on the way back at 476 Field Co to arrange for their Company to move to HAM tomorrow morning. Lieut-Colonel G.E.J. DURNFORD, D.S.O. rejoined from hospital and resumed command of Div. R.E Captain J.K. RENNIE (R.A.M.C) proceeded on one months special leave and was relieved by Captain TOBIAS (R.A.M.C)	Appx 2
	10th		G.S.O.1. called. XI Corps maintains that the Divisional R.E must administer the supply of all R.E. stores required by the Division when in the back area training. This attitude was strongly contested and ultimately Divisional Headquarters took the matter up with the result that all requirements of units will be attended to by area commandants.	
	11th		Issued orders for move of R.E.H.Qrs tomorrow to ~~HAMXXX~~ HAM. C.R.E. 74 Division called and was taken round the line by Major WHITWILL, D.S.O, M.C. (478 Field Co). He brought his stores officers up and he is to remain with us until the relief	Appx 2

Army Form C. 2118.

WAR DIARY

HEADQUARTERS. 61st. DIVN. ROYAL ENGINEERS.

INTELLIGENCE SUMMARY.

Vol. XXVII.   Page 4

JULY 1918.

Place	Date	Hour	Summary of Events and Information	Remarks and references to Appendices
FRANCE. Sht. 36a. 1/40000				
M.5.c.7.3. HAM	12th		R.E. Headquarters moved to HAM after handing over to C.R.E. 74th. Division. Issued Routine Orders 85 - 90 G.O.C. called at R.E.H.Qrs HAM.	Appx 2 Appx 1
	13th		Issued Routine Orders 95 - 98 Companies spent the day improving their billets and preparing for vigorous training to commence on MONDAY.	Appx 1
	14th	9.30am	Church Parade. Issued Notes on Conference held at 11 a.m. today. Corporal F.L. PENNY proceeded on leave to U.K. Received notification that Division (less 183 Brigade) is in G.H.Q. Reserve at 24 hours notice and 183 Brigade at 8 hours notice. C.R.E. reconnoitred various training grounds and rifle ranges.	Appx 3
	15th		Issued Routine Orders 96 and 97 re training Received 61 Div Order 177- 184 Brigade to exchange billeting accomodation with 183 Brigade -the former will now be at 8 hours notice	Appx 1

Army Form C. 2118.

HEADQUARTERS,
61st. Divisional ROYAL ENGINEERS.

Page 5.

WAR DIARY
of
INTELLIGENCE SUMMARY.

(Erase heading not required.) Vol. XXVII.

Instructions regarding War Diaries and Intelligence Summaries are contained in F.S. Regs., Part II. and the Staff Manual respectively. Title pages will be prepared in manuscript.

JULY 1918.

Place	Date	Hour	Summary of Events and Information	Remarks and references to Appendices
M.5.c.7.3. HAM.	16th.	—	FRANCE, Sheet 36a. 1/40,000. Issued Routine Orders 98 & 99: Lieut. GIBBS struck off strength – Received 183 Inf. Bde. Order No.226 re exchange of billets with 184 Bde. –	Appx.1 Appx.2
	17th.	—	All Companies training as usual.	
	18th.	— 11.15am	Issued orders to Companies re formation of Brigade groups in case of necessity – Issued Routine Orders Nos. 100 – 102 re Bounds, Inspection, Dress and Equipment. Received 61st.Divisional Order No.178 re move of 184 Inf.Bde. to new area –	Appx.5 Appx.1 Appx.2
	19th.	—	Issued Routine Orders No.103/4 – re Recreation and Standardization of transport. C.R.E. inspected Field Companies on parade. G.O.C. Division called.	Appx.1.
	20th.	—	Issued Routine Order No.105 re Church parade – Issued Minutes of meeting of Recreation Committee –	Appx.1. Appx.3.
	21st.	10am 9 pm	Church Parade. Received 184 Bde. Defence Instructions – Received intimation that Division will move tomorrow to unknown destination and advised Companies accordingly.	

Army Form C. 2118.

WAR DIARY

HEADQUARTERS,
61st.(S.M.)Divl. R.E.

INTELLIGENCE-SUMMARY.

(Erase heading not required.) Vol. XXVII.

Page 6.

JULY 1918

Instructions regarding War Diaries and Intelligence Summaries are contained in F.S. Regs., Part II. and the Staff Manual respectively. Title pages will be prepared in manuscript.

Place	Date	Hour	Summary of Events and Information	Remarks and references to Appendices
A.6. WARDRECQUES.	22nd.	3.12am.	FRANCE, Sheet 36a. 1/40,000. Received 61st.Div.Order 179 re transfer and move of Division from XI Corps to XV Corps today.	
			Received 183 Bde. Order 227 re move of Brigade -	
		9.30am.	Issued R.E.Order No.104 re move of Div. R.E. -	Appx.2.
		4 p.m.	R.E.H.Q. move to WARDRECQUES.	
			Received instructions from Division to send one Field Co. and one Company 1/5 D.C.L.I.(Pnrs.) to EECK HOUT CASTEEL for work on EAST HAZEBROUCK Line under orders of C.E. XV Corps -	
		11.15pm.	Issued R.E. Order No.105 re move of 476 Field Co. and one Coy.1/5 D.C.L.I.	Appx.2.
	23rd.		C.R.E., with G.O.C. and G.S.O.1, reconnoitred Army Line.	
	24th.		Issued Appendix F (Part 1) to 61st.Div.R.E. Defence Scheme - C.R.E. and Adjutant visited 476 Field Co. and returned via HAZEBROUCK and XV Corps H.Q.	Appx.5.
	25th.		Issued Appendix E to 61st.Div.R.E. Defence Scheme - Issued Appendix F (Part II) to 61st.Div.R.E. Defence Scheme - Received 61st.Div. Order No.180 re move of one Brigade 61st.Div.art - Received 183 Inf.Bde. Defence Instructions -	Appx.5. Appx.5.
		9 am		
	26th.		Issued Routine Orders Nos. 106 - 108 re G.O.C. Inspection - C.R.E. and Adjutant visited C.E. XV Corps and Corps dump at RENESCURE, and 476 Field Co.	Appx.1.
	27th.		Issued instructions to Field Companies to reconnoitre the whole of the Corps front - Issued Routine Order No.109 - Cancelling G.O.C. inspection - C.R.E. attended Divisional Confe-rence at 9 a.m.	Appx.3. Appx.1.

HEADQUARTERS, Army Form C. 2118.

WAR DIARY
or
INTELLIGENCE-SUMMARY.

61st.Divisional ROYAL ENGINEERS.

JULY 1918.

Page 7.

Instructions regarding War Diaries and Intelligence Summaries are contained in F.S. Regs., Part II. and the Staff Manual respectively. Title pages will be prepared in manuscript.

(Erase heading not required.) Vol.XXVII.

Place	Date	Hour	Summary of Events and Information	Remarks and references to Appendices
A.6. WARDRECQUES.	28th.		Issued Appendix F (Part I) to 61st.Div.R.E. Defence Scheme - Instructed 478 Field Co. to collect pontoons of 476 Field Co. working forward under C.E. XV Cps. C.R.E. with G.O.C.; G.S.O.1 and O.C. Machine Gun Battalion reconnoitred 9th.Div. Area. C.E. II Army called.	Appx.5. Appx.3
	29th.		C.R.E. with G.S.O.1 and O.C. 479 Field Co. continued reconnaissance of the forward area, including the village of METEREN. Lieut. G.H. SIMMONS, M.C. joined R.E.H.Q. for duty. Received 61st.Div. Warning Order G.C.31/1 re move of Division back into XI Corps and advised Companies - Gave Field Companies details of probable moves -	Appx.2. Appx.2.
		11.40pm	Issued R.E. Order 106 re move of 476 Field Co. from EECK HOUT CASTEEL to LES BRUNERES -	Appx.2.
	30th.		476 Field Co. moved from EECK HOUT CASTEEL to LES BRUNERES today. Received 61st.Div.Order No.181 re move of Division back into XI Corps -	Appx.2.
		1 pm	Issued Order for move of Field Coys. back into HAM (BLESSY), XI Corps 31st./1st.Aug.	
		4.15pm	Received 183 Bde. Order No.228 re move of Division - Nominal Roll of Officers -	Appx.4.
	31st.	11pm.	Field Companies and R.E.H.Q. transport left LES BRUNERES (BANDRINGHEM) and WARDRECQUES, respectively marching to HAM, and 476 Field Co. dismounted to MARTHES under verbal instructions from 61st.Div."Q". Remainder of R.E.H.Q. will move to HAM at 10 a.m. tomorrow.	

Capt.
Adjutant,
for C.R.E. 61st.Division.

WAR DIARY
ORIGINAL.
JULY 1918.
C.R.E. 61ST DIVN.

APPENDIX 1

ROUTINE ORDERS BY CRE

ROUTINE ORDERS.

Issued by:- Lieut.-Colonel G.B.J. DURNFORD, D.S.O., R.E.
Commanding:- 61st. (South Midland) Divisional ROYAL ENGINEERS.

R.E.H.Q. 12th.July 1918.

85. SANITATION.

(a) The village of HAM is divided into areas for which Field Companies are responsible for general sanitary work, including cleaning of roads, viz:-
  476 Field Co. - from 476 Officers mess eastwards.
  478 Field Co. - from 476 Officers mess to where the village green widens out.
  479 Field Co. - from the Village Green (inclusive) westwards, including the incinerators and latrines on the green.

(b) 476 Field Co. will complete the construction of the latrine on the Green.

(c) All refuse will be sent to the incinerators on the green and 479 Field Co. will detail a sanitary man to take charge of the incinerators.

86. GUARDS, etc.

The R.E. guard room will be at the shed next to R.E.H.Q.
It will consist of -
  1 N.C.O.   ) Dress:- Marching order with steel helmets.
  7 Sappers.)
  (2 sentry groups and one spare man).
  2 cyclist orderlies for R.E.H.Q. - Dress:- rifles, equipment and soft haps.
  2 regimental police - Dress:- walking out dress.

Guard mounting will be at 9 a.m. at which time C.S.M's. will hand over to the R.S.M. who will change the guard.
Guards will be found by Companies in turn in the order 476, 478, 479; the first guard mounting at 9 a.m. Sunday the 14th. instant.
One sentry will be posted on R.E.H.Q. and one sentry on the bridging wagons parked on the Green.
Cyclist orderlies and Regimental Police will sleep in their ordinary billets.

87. BOUNDS.

No man will leave the R.E. billetting area without wearing a belt nor without a pass bearing his Company orderly-room stamp.

88. ROUTINE.

All men will be in billet by 9.30 p.m. Lights out at 10 p.m.

89. CHURCH PARADE.

There will be Church Parade in the Park at 9.30 a.m. next Sunday.
Dress - Soft caps, stripped belts with side arms (or bandeliers)
One Officer and one marker per Company will meet the Adjutant at the Park at 9.15 a.m.
Companies will march on to their markers at 9.25 a.m.

90. TRAINING.

Field Companies are at the disposal of O's.C. until Monday, 15th.inst. when training hours will be laid down by this office.

--o-- -- -- -- -- -- -- -- -- -- --

(Sd.) M.E.FITZGERALD.
Capt. - Adjutant.

ROUTINE ORDERS.

Issued by:- Lieut.-Colonel G.E.J. DURNFORD, D.S.O., R.E.
Commanding:- 61st.(South Midland) Divisional ROYAL ENGINEERS.

R.E.H.Q.   12th.July 1918.

---

95. REMUSTERINGS.

Approval is given for the following remusterings :-
478 Field Co.
    No.420035 C.S.M. HICKMAN, E.J. remustered as a
                                                    "Pattern Maker".
    No.158945 L/Cpl. FOX, G. remustered as a "Cabinet Maker".
    No.494906 Sapper CLARKE, H. remustered as a "Bricklayer".

96. POSTING.

Approval has been given for the following posting:-

"Lieut.H.G. ROBINSON, 478 Field Co. R.E. to be second-in-Command of that unit, vice Lieut.(A/Capt.) H. Humphreys, O.C. 479 Field Co."

(Authority: A.G. No. 65/3327 (O) dated 8.7.1918).

97. PROTECTION AGAINST BOMBS.

D.R.O. No. 1937 dated 9.7.18 is republished for information.

"Owing to the move to the back areas, special attention is directed to the Circular issued with Fifth Army Routine Orders, dated 6th.July, 1918.
Paras.1 to 4 of Circular referred to are republished below:-

1. All possible steps will be taken forthwith to minimise casualties from aircraft bombs.

2. LIGHTS. A number of lights shown in the Army area are likely to serve as guides to hostile aircraft. For the safety of the troops, civilian inhabitants, railways, and factories, etc., engaged on work for the armies, it is essential that such lights shall cease to be shown.

3. All lights will, therefore, be extinguished or completely shaded one hour after sunset.

4. This order is to be repeated in the orders of all formations down to units, and all ranks will assist the Police and Gendarmes, both by complying with the order themselves and bringing to notice any infringement of the order. O's C. units will ensure that this order is carried out by periodical inspections of billets occupied by troops under their command."

98. LEAVE.

The undermentioned Officers proceeded on leave on the dates shown:-

    Capt. B. LONG, 14 days from 15.6.18.
    Lieut.G.S. HIGDEN, " " 27.6.18.
    " H.P. ROBERTS, " " 3.7.18.
    " G.H. SIMMONS, " " 13.7.18.
    " R.F. BOARD, " " 13.7.18.

(Sd.) M.E. FITZGERALD,
Capt.,
Adjutant.

ROUTINE ORDERS.

Issued by:- Lieut.-Colonel G.H.J.HURFORD, D.S.O., R.E.,
Commanding:- 61st. (South MIDLAND) DIVISIONAL ROYAL ENGINEERS.

R.E.H.Q. 15th.July 1918.

96. HOURS OF TRAINING:-

6.45 to 7.30 a.m. - Physical exercise, preceded by cup of tea and biscuits.
9.am to 12.50 p.m.- General training, including drill and route marches.
2 pm to 4 p.m. - Range practices, technical training, lectures, judging distance, map reading, etc.

On Mondays and Saturdays training will continue up to 1 p.m. when it will cease for the day.

Sunday mornings will be devoted to check parade, company conservancy and (when ordered) Church parade. The afternoons will be free for recreation.

97. INFANTRY TRAINING 1914.

Attention is called to amendments published in A.O. 275 dated 1st. August 1916. Companies who are not in possession of these amendments will report the fact to this office.

(Sd.) H.B.FITZGERALD,
Capt.,
Adjutant.

ROUTINE ORDERS.

Issued by:- Lieut.-Colonel G.E.J. DURNFORD, D.S.O., R.E.
Commanding:- 61st. (South Midland) Divisional ROYAL ENGINEERS.

R.E.H.Q. 16th.July, 1918.

---

98. **DRESS and EQUIPMENT.**

The following points on dress and equipment are laid down for the Divisional R.E.

(a) **Officers.**

To be worn on the Right side (slings over left shoulder)
Ammunition pouch, Field glasses (in front of pouch).
Haversack, compass, steel helmet (over shoulder when not worn).

To be worn on the Left side (slings over right shoulder)
Revolver, water-bottle (level with and behind elbow).
Box respirator.

To be carried on the horse:
Mess tin (near side), saddle blanket.
Surcingle pad (under belly), 4 shoes if possible.

To be carried on transport:
Horsebrush, Rubber, Bucket, Haynet.

Headropes to be white hemp or cotton; buckle facing near side.
(Leather headropes may be worn off parades).

(b)
Marching Order, other ranks.
Steel helmet normally on back of pack with straps crossed below only - badge to the left.
Breech cover on the rifle.
Waterproof sheet over top and down back of pack, and under the large flap but not under side flaps.
F.S. cap on top of pack and under all flaps.
Mess tin on top of pack *with cover towards the man*
S.A.A. - 50 rounds - 1 clip in each pouch.
All brass work on equipment cleaned when not "in the line".
Loose end of belt turned in.

(c) **Battle Order, other ranks.**
Contents of haversack: cardigan, iron ration, one pair socks, holdall, towel.
Unexpended ration in mess tin.
S.A.A - 100 rounds normally.

99. **APPOINTMENT.**
Lieut. G.M. GIBBS. M.C., 479 Field Co. is struck off strength today on assuming duties as G.S.O. 3rd.Grade, Headquarters, Fifth Army.
(Authority: A.G. No. Appts./3886 dated 15.7.18).

(Signed) M.E.FITZGERALD,
Capt.,
Adjutant.

ROUTINE ORDERS.

Issued by:- Lieut.-Colonel G.E.J. BURNFORD, D.S.O., R.E.
Commanding:- 61st. (South Midland) Divisional ROYAL ENGINEERS.

R.E.H.Q. 18th.July 1918.

---

100. BOUNDS.
The following will be added to R.E.R.O. 87:
"Men may go into BLESSY without a pass".

101. INSPECTIONS.

(a) Field Companies will be inspected tomorrow the 19th.inst. by the C.R.E.

(b) Strength: as strong as possible.

(c) Dress: Marching order.

(d) All inspections will be in HAM Park; Os.C. 476 & 478 arranging that their parade grounds do not clash.

(e) Times of Inspection will be as follows :-

　　476 Field Co. - 10 a.m.
　　478 Field Co. - 11 a.m.
　　479 Field Co. - 3 p.m.

(f) A note of any deficiencies in equipment will be added to parade states.

102. DRESS AND EQUIPMENT.

The last line of para. (b) of R.E.R.O. 98 dated 16.7.18 will be amended to read as follows :-

"Stripped belts will have the loose end turned in. On all other occasions the loose end will be turned outwards and doubled back".

(Sd.) M.E.FITZGERALD,
Capt.,
Adjutant.

ROUTINE ORDERS

Issued by Lieut-Colonel G.E.J. DURNFORD, D.S.O, R.E

Commanding:- 61st. (South Midland) Divisional Royal Engineers

R.E.H.Q. July 19th, 1918.

---

103. **RECREATION.** A committee consisting of the Second in Command of each Field Company and the Adjutant will meet at R.E.H.Q. at 10. a.m. tomorrow the 20th.
The agenda will include:-

    Games,
    Sports,
    Musical entertainments.
    Officers mess dinner.

104. **STANDARDIZATION OF TRANSPORT.**
Each Company will park one of each of the following vehicles near 476 Field Compy orderly room in the park:-

    Water cart,
    Tool cart
    R.E. Limber
    G.S. Limber.

Vehicles will be packed as for marching order but teams will not be present.

Each Company will also send a pack mule in marching order.

O's C. Field Company will meet the C.R.E on the spot at 11.30 a.m. tomorrow 20th to inspect these vehicles.

The mounted Sergeant of 476 Field Co has been shown where and how vehicles are to be parked.

                (Sd) M.E.FITZGERALD.
                Capt. Adjutant 61 Div R.E

ROUTINE ORDERS.
--by--
Lieut.-Colonel G.E.J.HURSFORD, D.S.O., R.E.
Commanding:- 61st. (South Midland) Divisional ROYAL ENGINEERS.

R.E.H.Q. 20th.July 1918.

---

105. CHURCH PARADE.

There will be Church Parade in the Park at 10 a.m. tomorrow (Sunday) the 21st. inst.

Dress - Soft caps, stripped belts with side arms (or bandoliers).

One Officer and one marker per Company will meet the Adjutant at the Park at 9.45 a.m.

Companies will march on to their markers at 9.55 a.m.

(Signed) M.E.FITZGERALD.
Capt.,
Adjutant.

ROUTINE ORDERS
by
Lieut.-Colonel G.E.J. DURNFORD, D.S.O., R.E.
Commanding:- 61st. (South Midland) Divisional ROYAL ENGINEERS.

R.E.H.Q.
26th. July 1918.

106. CHURCH PARADE.

There will be Church Parade for 478 and 479 Field Companies at 2.30 p.m. next Sunday, near 478 Field Co. H.Q. O.C. 478 Field Co. will arrange the parade. (The Chaplain is called for at 478 H.Q. at 2.15 p.m.)

107. PARADE.

The Divisional R.E. less 476 Field Co., will parade at 10.30 a.m. at A.16.b. tomorrow the 27th. inst.
One Officer per Company, with markers, will meet the Adjutant at 476 Field Co. H.Q. at 10.30 a.m.
Companies will be prepared to march on to markers at 11.00 a.m.

Dress: Marching order, as for inspection.
Steel helmets worn.
Breech covers off.
Officers valises not packed.

Strength: as strong as possible.

Parade states: as usual.

R.E.H.Q. (less L/C. Skinner) will parade at C.R.E's mess at 10.15 a.m. and move off under Sergt. Featherstone.

108. INSPECTION.

There will probably be an inspection of all Companies and presentation of decorations by the Divisional Commander on Monday next, the 29th. inst. Orders will be issued later.

(Signed) E.E. FITZGERALD,
Capt.,
Adjutant.

ROUTINE ORDERS
by
Lieut.-Colonel G.N.J. DURNFORD, D.S.O., R.E.
Commanding:- 61st. (South Midland) Divisional ROYAL ENGINEERS.

R.E.H.Q. 27th. July 1918.

No 9. PARADE AND INSPECTION.

Reference R.E.O. 107 & 108, the Parade and G.O.C. Inspection are indefinitely postponed.

(Signed) M.E.FITZGERALD,
Capt.,
Adjutant.

War Diary
ORIGINAL.
JULY 1918.
C.R.E. 61ST. DIVN.

APPENDIX 2

MOVE & RELIEF ORDERS BY C.R.E.

SECRET.

476 Field Co.
478 Field Co.
479 Field Co.
    Copy to 1/5 D.C.L.I.
         " 61st.Div."G".
         " C.R.E. 76th.Div.

WARNING ORDER.

1. The 61st.Division is being relieved by the 76th. Division - relief commencing on the 10th.instant.

2. 478 Field Co. (Left Section) will probably be relieved on the 11th.inst. by the 5th.Company, R.A.R.E., who will send an advance party of 2 officers and 4 N.C.O's. up on the 9th.inst.

3. 479 Field Co. (Right Section) will probably be relieved on the 12th.inst. by the 5th.Company, R.M.R.E..

4. 476 Field Co. will probably be relieved on the 13th. inst. by 439 Field Co. now at THEISENNES.

5. 1/5 D.C.L.I. (Pioneers) will probably be relieved on the 10th.inst. by 1/12th.L.North.Lancs.(Pioneers) now at J.19.C.

6. Relieving Sappers for Bridge guards will probably arrive 24 hours before time of relief.

8th.July 1918.   Capt. - Adjutant,
                                              for C.R.E. 61st.Divn.

SECRET.   Copy No. 10

61st. Divisional R.E. ORDER No. 103.

9th. July 1918.

1. The 61st. Division is being relieved by the 74th. Division.

2. The 61st. Divisional R.E. will concentrate at HAM (M.5. Sheet 36a.), moves taking place according to Table "A" overleaf.

3. R.E. Headquarters will be at M.5.c.7.3.

4. Maps and documents which will be useful to relieving units and R.E. materials in dumps will be handed over and copies of receipts for same will be sent to this office.

5. 61st. Divisional R.E. Defence Scheme will not be handed over but spare copies of the Appendices to same are circulated to Field Companies herewith for inclusion in their handing over reports.

6. Spaces to be maintained on the march are as follows :-

   Between Companies and units and their transport
   and the transport of units where brigaded - 100 yards.

   Between Sections of 6 vehicles - - - - - 50 yards.

7. Relieving units are sending forward advance parties and units of 61st. Division will ensure that units of 74th. Divn. are in possession of all information they require: if necessary, rear parties will be left behind.

8. Billetting accommodation at HAM is inadequate and will be supplemented by tents and trench shelters. The billetting scheme is in the hands of O.C. 476 Field Co. to whom separate instructions have been issued.

9. The Senior R.E. Officer present will assume command of troops at HAM until arrival of R.E.H.Q.

10. All billets will be disinfected before they are left and certificates that billets and horse lines were left in a clean and sanitary condition will be sent to this office.

11. Field Companies to ACKNOWLEDGE.

R.E.H.Q.   Capt. - Adjutant,
Issued at 8 p.m.   for C.R.E. 61st. Div.

Distribution :-

Copy No. 1 to 476 Field Co.   Copy No. 7 to 1/5 D.C.L.I.
 "   2 to 478 Field Co.   "   8 to C.R.E. 74 Div.
 "   3 to 479 Field Co.   "   9 to C.E. XI Corps.
 "   4 to 61st. Div. "G".   "   10 to War Diary.
 "   5 to 61st. Div. "Q".   "   11 to   do.
 "   6 to 61st. Signals.   "   12 to File.

TABLE "A"
Issued with
61st.Div.Signal R.E.Order No.103.

Serial No.	Date.	Unit.	Present position (Sheet 36.A)	By whom relieved.	Route.	Remarks.
	JULY					
1.	10th.	476 Field Co.	O.13.d.7.9	439 Field Co.	MAZINGHEM – ROMBLY – VLETTERNESSE – BLESSY.	To be clear of OBIOIS at 9 a.m.
2.	11th.	472 Field Co.	P.1.a.3.4.	5th. R.A.R.E.	Bridge at O.11.b.4.5 – MOLINGHEM – then as in Serial No.1.	
3.	12th.	473 Field Co.	P.8.b.3.2.	5th. R.M.R.E.		To be South of CANAL D'AIRE by 9 a.m.
4.	12th.	51st.R.E.H.Q.	O.6.b.8.4.	74th. R.E.H.Q.		

M Fitzwald
Capt. – Adjutant,
for C.R.E. 61st.Div.

9th.July 1918.

10.

ORDERS FOR MOVE OF R.E.H.Q.

1.   R.E.H.Q. will move tomorrow 12th. inst. to HAM
route for horse transport - R.E.F. billet (C.11.b.7.9)
fascine wood and timber bridge (C.11.b.4.5. - MOLLIEHEM
HASINGHEM - DOMBLY - VIETRHEUSE - BLENCY - HAM.

2.   On completion of move

   (a) Officers mess and O.R.E. office will be at K.5.c.7.3.

   (b) Transport lines will be in the park at K.5.c.9.7.
       as set out by O.C. 476 Field Co.

3.   The following party will move off at 6a.m under
the R.S.M.

         R.S.M.   with R.C's horse
         Dr. Lorton with G.S. Limber and Spr. TALBOT.
         Dr. DAVIES with Medical Cart.
         Sappers ELIESON, COLLIER (476), MULLEN (478)
         and Driver KING - each with a cycle.

4.   The following will travel by motor lorry in charge
of the Medical officer -   Sergt. FEATHERSTONE will be
in charge of loading:-

         Medical Officer
         Interpreter and cycle
         Sgt. FEATHERSTONE.
         Cpl. BERRY.
         L/Cs SKINNER, BANCRAFT, HUNT
         Sappers BENTON, BULLARD.
         Drivers CROUCHY, PATTEN
         1.D.C.L.I.

5.   O.R.E and Adjutant will be riding.

6.   Motor lorries attached to O.R.E will rejoin the
61st. M.T. Co during the afternoon of the 12th. inst.

7.   The 5 men underlined above will rejoin their units
on arrival at HAM and Field Companies will detail runners
to keep touch with R.E.H.Qrs.

                                      Capt. Adjutant.
11.7.1918.   61st. Div R.E.

Copy 1. to O.R.E.   6   476 Field Co.
     2. to Adjutant   7   475 Field Co.
     3. to M.O.   8   479 Field Co.
     4. to R.S.M.   9   1/5 D.C.L.I.
     5. to N.C.O   10 & 11 War Diary.
        i/c lorries

NOTES by C.R.E. 61st. DIVN

on handing over to C.R.E. 74th. DIVN. 12.7.1918.

DEFENCES GENERALLY.

These consist of:-

(a) Forward system defences. e.g. Front, support and Reserve Line.

(b) AMUSOIRES - HAVERSKERQUE System, consisting, except on the extreme right where there are only two lines, of a front, support and reserve line with a switch protecting each flank, i.e. LALEAU switch on the right and BRIDGEHEAD switch on the left.

GENERAL POLICY.

This has been to develope the defences from the rear forward. Under this policy the AMUSOIRES system has been developed under the C.R.E who, till recently, gave the Brigades a small amount of assistance only in the Forward system. For the past three weeks however, all available labour and material has been transferred to the Reserve Line, the development of which is now under the C.R.E. entirely.

All concrete available for the Division has been put into concrete M.G.E's working on the same policy. The programme for the AMUSOIRES line is now complete and work in connection with concrete M.G.E's for the Reserve Line is in progress.

BREASTWORKS.

In practically the whole area the water level during the winter months is very near the surface. In April, when work commenced, it varied from 1'.0" to 2' 0" below the surface. Consequently breastworks are unfortunately essential. The general policy with these have been to construct posts with revetted parapets and parados and about 4' 6" command. On completion of essential posts, others are interpolated and joined up by lateral communication to be eventually turned into breastwork. Owing to shortage of material it has not been practicable to adhere to a standard revetment. The eventual heightening of all breastworks to about 6' 0" command has to be borne in mind.

Copy of recent instructions to Coys is attached marked A

SWITCHES.

(a) <u>Reserve Line (forward system)</u>

Where this line passes through the close country on the CALONNE Road on the right and in the neighbourhood of ST FLORIS on the left the policy has been to develope a second line on to which to fall back should the Reserve Line in these neighbourhoods be penetrated. The alternative line on the right is the CARVIN SWITCH running from Q.13.c.15.50 to Battn H.Qrs at CARVIN. This switch has not been developed south of CARVIN as the interval between that place and the AMUSOIRES system is covered by the M.G.E at CARVIN and P.24.c.85.25.

The alternative line on the left is the ST FLORIS SWITCH running from P.12.b.30.75 to the LYS CANAL at J.36.c.20.25. This switch includes Company H.Qrs which have been worked on to make them strong points or keeps.

A progress map (1/2500) of the Reserve Line is handed over.

(b) <u>Connecting forward</u>

(2)

(b) **Connecting Forward system and AMUSOIRES System (AMUSOIRES SWITCH)**

In certain eventualities it might become necessary to reorganise the defences on the flank of the Fifth Army (see copy of XI Corps G.S. 9/270 marked B)

To enable the new Line of Resistance to be taken up this switch is under construction from the CARVIN SWITCH at P.18.d.50.40 to the AMUSOIRES system at P.18.c.20.60.

(c) **Switch connecting XIII Corps forward system and XI Corps AMUSOIRES System (ROBECQ SWITCH).**

See XI Corps G.S. 9/184 marked C

The junction of this switch from where it terminates at P.30.b.7.4. to the AMUSOIRES system at P.30.central is under construction.

(d) **AMUSOIRES SYSTEM.**

RIGHT. "LALEAU SWITCH" running from AMUSOIRES to the AIRE Canal at P.28.d.30.55 and providing an alternative defence line in the event of the loss of ROBECQ.
LEFT. "BRIDGEHEAD SWITCH" running from J.34.d.95.20 to the LYS CANAL at P.4.a.0.75 and providing an alternative defence line in the event of penetration of the defences N. of the Divisional sector

JUNCTION OF DEFENSIVE LINES WITH DIVISIONS ON RIGHT & LEFT.

Forward system. Front line. Joins on both flanks.
Support Line. Joins on right - not on left
(Flank rests on LYS CANAL.
Reserve Line. Joins on both flanks.

ST FLORIS SWITCH. No junction with Division on the left.
Flank rests on LYS CANAL.
AMUSOIRES SYSTEM. Joins with a single line only on both flanks.
Both our flanks are turned however to rest
on the right on the AIRE CANAL and on the
left on the LYS Canal (BRIDGEHEAD SWITCH)
LALEAU SWITCH Does not connect with Division on our
right, the flank resting on the AIRE Canal.

CONCRETE M.G.E's.

All concrete allotted to the Division from the Concrete Factory, AIRE has gone into the line in the form of Machine Gun Emplacements.

A statement marked D is attached showing emplacements completed, under construction, and proposed. This list also includes any emplacements of brick construction with concrete roofs.

The list contains all present proposals for M.G's and on completion, further concrete would probably have been put in in the form of infantry shelters, shelters for Battn. H.Qrs, R.A. O.P's etc. A programme of further requirements should be prepared.

Up to date, two sections of 250 Tunnelling Co, R.E have been at disposal of the Division to assist in concrete work. One section has recently been withdrawn and No.4. section is in charge of all the work (see list of locations)

A party of 1 officer and 30 O.R. Pioneers has been attached to each section to assist in the work.

Allotments of concrete are consigned to me from the factory to BERGUETTE Station. On arrival at latter place an unloading party has to be provided (M.G. Btn is a suitable unit for this).

Thence it is taken by lorry either direct to site of work or to an intermediate dump under arrangements by O.C. 250 (T) Co. Any horse transport to take material to the site is provided by the Division, O.C. 250 T. Co reporting his requirements to me.

Emplacements are handed over by 250 Tunneling co fit for occupation, i.e. they put in muzzle pivot mountings. The Machine Gun crews then build traverses to entrances, and if the emplacement is in a house, they strip out all inflammable material etc. The Field Company concerned completes with gas curtains, paints the pill box and does any necessary concealment of loopholes, strengthening of camouflage etc.

M.G.E's in Centre of RESERVE LINE.

It is impracticable to erect pill boxes here. Consequently it is proposed to erect concrete shelters for the guns and crews, the gun to be fired over the roof of the pill-box.
Construction on this type is just commencing. A speciment has been erected at H.Q. No. 1. Section, 250 Tunnelling Co.

LADDERS UP PILL BOXES.

In many cases the crops have grown to such an height as to obscure the field of fire from the loophole Ladders are therefore being fixed on such pill-boxes as may be effected to enable the gun to be fired from the roof in emergency.

TRACKS TO PILL BOXES.

Considerable precautions have been taken to prevent tracks showing up to pill boxes erected in the open and also to ensure, pill boxes erected under trees not showing up on aeroplane photos. It is necessary to keep an eye on these arrangements periodically so that necessary repairs can be quickly carried out.

N.B. All pill boxes so far erected have walls and roof 2' 3" thick not 3' 0". This was decided on so as to get as many pill boxes erected as possible in the shortest time with the material and transport available, as it was considered that an attack might be expected at any time

WIRE GAUZE FOR DISGUISING LOOPHOLES.

I have done everything possible to obtain supplies but with no success. Corps Camouflage officer has promised to try and purchase some at BOULOGNE or elsewhere. He will probably require reminding.

MOIR PILL-BOXES.

These are now available (4 allotted to us at Corps dump). As we have got so far ahead with reinforced concrete emplacements it is doubtful if we shall require many.
It is proposed seeing whether they are adaptable to breastworks by putting one in the BUSNES - STEENBECQUE Line near these Headquarters at p.2.b.5.3. C.E. XI Corps has approved.

ROADS.

The line of demarkation between Corps and Divisions is shown

-4-

is shown on a Sheet 36a (1/40000) marked E

With one exception however no road maintenance has been undertaken by the Division as it has not been urgent.

The exception is the road from Cross Roads P.2.c.4.0 to HAMET BILLET which is a very important lateral communication. The Corps were unable to do any maintenance and I have been hauling 4 loads of stone daily from LALACQUE and dumping.

LIGHT RAILWAYS.

The original Corps proposals etc are shown on Sheet 36a (1/40000) marked F but this is not up to date and I have no definite information as to development.

A light railway is under construction however to connect my dump with Corps dump.

TRENCH TRAMWAYS.

The Division has recently submitted proposals for running a trench tramway up to the Reserve Line to feed the centre of the Divisional sector. Here no roads exist. The provision of this will save large carrying parties. It is understood that Corps have no labour to assist in this. Proposals will be found in my 7/2 dated 6.7.1918 marked G

Any such system will require to be linked eventually to the Light Railway system behind.

BACK AREA DEFENCE LINES.

These are shown on Sheet 36a (1/40000) PROVISIONAL dated 9.5.1918 and marked H

The Division however is not responsible for anything W. of the AMUSOIRES - HAVERSKERQUE - LA MOTTE LINE.

BRIDGES and BRIDGE DEMOLITIONS.

The position of bridges over the AIRE and LYS CANALS and how they are prepared for demolition is given in the Bridge Map (1/20000) marked J and in Appendix "C" of 61st. Div R.E. Defence Scheme marked K

The policy is to destroy permanent bridges and the two syphons with explosives for which R.E. personnel is required. Temporary bridges to be destroyed by fire by infantry on the spot.

The guards on the permanent bridges each include one sapper who is responsible for the maintenance of the charges. In addition, each of the forward Companies details a bridge patrol for the AIRE CANAL and the left Company a patrol for the bridges on the LYS CANAL.

On "MAN BATTLE STATIONS" sappers are re-inforced up to 2 per demolition by the Field Co concerned. Each Company also detailing one officer to supervise the demolitions

Standard arrangements are being introduced for firing mobile charges on the permanent bridges in the event of the normal charges failing.

N.B. The brick arch bridge at ROBECQ mill p.29.b.6.4. is prepared for demolition and the right brigade furnish a guard. A sapper is stationed here. There is a private arrangement - not detailed by Division, as the latter have only catered for permanent canal bridges in their orders.

Locations of Units...

LOCATIONS OF UNITS.

These are shown in Appendix A 61st. Div. R.E
Defence Scheme marked L

O.P's.

Two brick tower O.P's are under construction for the Artillery. One at MT BERNENCHON near the Church (this is in 4th. Division area) and one at P.6.c.4.5.

The work is being done by R.A. personnel with sapper assistance from the Field Companies.

Details will be handed over by Field Coys concerned.

BUSNES RIVER – Flooding of.

A report marked M is attached with reference to flooding in the neighbourhood of O.28.d. – O.29.d.– O.35.a and through BUSNES owing to the rapid growth of weeds. No action has been taken. There are sluice gates on the River at about P.16.b.5.3. The raising of these might assist.

R.E. MATERIALS.

(a) No.11 R.E. Park, is at ESTREE BLANCHE M.28.a.8.6 and issues most materials on C.R.E's authority.

(b) XI Corps R.E. dump is at I.32.a.5.3 LA LACQUE and issues to you only on authority of C.E. XI Corps.

(c) Camouflage material is supplied to all arms direct by the Corps Camouflage Officer. He is on the telephone and is located in AIRE.

(d) Concrete Blocks and Beams are supplied from the concrete works at H.23.b.1.9, AIRE. The quantities are allotted by C.E. XI Corps and sent by train to BERGUETTE station. Divisions have to unload the trains and we have done so by arranging direct with the M.G. Battalion to find working parties. The unloading and subsequent handling of the material has been supervised by the 250 Tunnelling Co. who are on the telephone. The Tunnelling Co. moves the material from BERGUETTE forward by lorries which they furnish themselves.

The 250 Tunnelling Co. has been obtaining what limbers it requires forward direct from the M.G. Battalion. G.S. wagons required by them have been found by C.R.E. who applies to "Q" for them.

(e) SUPPLY. The quantity of stores available fluctuates from day to day. On the whole, it is very restricted compared with pre-Bosche-offensive days.

Barbed wire. This has been short on one or two occasions. The main trouble is that small coils are often out of stock. At present I can only get 440 yd. coils weighing about 1 cwt and have to recoil them.

Brushwood hurdles, & pickets. The state of supply has often held up our work.

Revetting materials generally have been very short and I have

R.E. MATERIALS (contd.)

given very little to back area work, reserving practically the whole supply for trenches. This applies to brushwood hurdles, X.P.M. hurdles, X.P.M. sheets, wirenetting, long angle iron pickets and plain wire, which latter is very scarce.

Sand is purchased at 2fr.50c. per cubic metre from M. BOULNOIS at BERGUETTE.

(f) DEMAND. The demands for materials have often been out of all proportion to the supply and as far as Field Artillery are concerned, they have been supplied by allotment to each Brigade: details will be given you verbally. Supplies for back area work have been run on similar lines.

(g) TRANSPORT. I have had 3 lorries permanently attached to me (This is essential) and an average of 4 additional lorries per day has been obtained from S.M.T.O. XI Corps. These are used almost entirely for moving stores from behind, up to the Field Co. and C.R.E's dumps.

A light railway is under construction from Corps dump to our dumps and should be complete in a few days time, when it should cut out most of the motor lorry traffic.

12/7/18.

MACHINE GUN EMPLACEMENTS.

Map. Ref.	Description.	Remarks - Complete, Under constr. or proposed.
AMUSOIRES SYSTEM.		
P.24.c.85.25.	Concrete	Complete
P.24.c.9.3.	Concrete	Complete
P.24.c.30.50.	Concrete	Complete
P.24.c.30.50.	Concrete	Complete
P.17.d.5.1.	Concrete	Complete
P.17.d.5.8.	Concrete	Complete
P.18.a.2.3.	Timber	Double emplacement complete.
P.18.a.05.65	Concrete	Complete
P.17.b.2.8.	Brick	Complete
P.11.c.9.8.	Concrete	Complete
P.11.c.95.95.	Concrete	Complete
P.5.d.30.30.	Concrete	Double emplacement complete
P.5.c.5.1.	Brick	Complete
P.5.c.5.1.	Brick	Complete
P.5.c.00.85	Concrete	Complete
J.35.c.30.20.	Concrete	Complete
J.35.c.30.20.	Concrete	Complete
CARVIN SWITCH.		
P.24.b.95.30.	Brick	Complete
P.24.b.95.35	Concrete	Complete
P.24.d.8.8.	Brick	Complete
P.24.d.75.80	Concrete	Complete
ST. FLORIS SWITCH.		
P.6.a.6.4.	Brick	Complete
P.6.a.6.5.	Brick	Complete
P.6.c.6.2.	Concrete 2 guns	Under constr^n. Double emplacement
RESERVE LINE.		
Q.19.b.15.05	Concrete	Proposed. Shelter only.
Q.19.b.1.1.	Concrete	Complete.
Q.19.a.55.50	Concrete	Under construction.
Q.13.a.6.3.	Concrete	Proposed. Shelter only.
Q.13.a.6.4.	Concrete	Proposed. Shelter only.
Q.7.c.05.10	Concrete	Proposed. Shelter only.
P.12.d.8.2.	Concrete	Under construction. Shelter only.
P.6.d.6.4.	Concrete	Under construction. Shelter only.
P.6.b.5.6.	Concrete	Complete
P.6.b.6.7.	Concrete	Complete
P.6.b.40.65	Brick	Complete
J.36.d.30.60	Concrete	Complete
J.36.d.4.5.	Concrete	Complete

N.B. "Complete" means "fightable" and not necessarily complete with Gas Curtains, etc.

LIST OF MAPS HANDED OVER.
TO
C.R.E 74th. DIVN.

Map No.	Map.	Copy Nos.	No of copies
L.M. 152.	AMUSOIRES LINE. 1/40000	17 - 28	12
L.M. 148.	CALONNE.	-	9
61.M.S.15.	TRENCH MAP - AMUSOIRES LINE. (Showing progress to date)	7	One
	RESERVE LINE 1/2500	-	two
J	BRIDGE MAP. 1/20000	-	one
F	TRAMWAYS MAP 1/40000	-	One
E	MAP Showing line of DEMARKATION.	-	One
	VIELLE CHAPELLE. 3rd. Ed. 1/20000	-	27
	VIELLE CHAPELLE. 3rd. Ed. 1/20000 (Harrassing Fire Map)	-	4
H	LINES of DEFENCE. 1/40000	-	1

Aeroplane photos   ?

DEFENCE SCHEME. 61st Div

ADMINISTRATIVE INSTRUCTIONS
issued with
61st. Divisional R.E. Order No. 104.

1. Each Field Company will collect all its tents, trench shelters and other Government property into a dump on the village green.

2. No tents or canvas trench shelters are to be taken out of the area. The Adjutant will visit Companies this morning and arrange with them which temporary structures are not to be dismantled.

3. Field Companies will take what training stores they require with them. The remainder will be listed and dumped on the green. 479 Field Co. will furnish a storeman for the dump and he will check all lists of stores handed in.

4. Each Field Company will detail a rear party of 1 N.C.O. and 7 cyclists to clean up billets and load area stores in to a lorry for delivery to the Area Commandant. 479 Field Company will detail an officer to take charge of rear parties. This officer will report to the Adjutant for instructions.

5. Each Company should send forward an officer with a few cyclists to RACQUINGHEM to act as guides to billets.

6. 476 Field Co. should send out a party to reconnoitre the route from ROQUETOIRE to RACQUINGHEM and the remaining Companies should keep touch with the leading Company during the march.

7. Supply wagons with rations for consumption 23rd.inst. are to accompany units.

8. D.A.D.O.S. will be at HANDECOURT.

9. Field Cashier is at STAPLES and is open daily from 9.30 a.m. to 12.30 p.m. and 2 p.m. to 4 p.m. (Sundays 9.30 a.m. to 12.30 p.m.)

10. All Fifth Army and XI Corps Standing and Routine Orders will be returned to this office as soon as possible.

22.7.18.

Capt. - Adjutant,
for C.R.E. 61st. Div.

SECRET.   Copy No. 9

                    61st. DIVISIONAL R.E. ORDER No.104.

Ref. Map   22.7.18.
HAZEBROUCK Sh.
1/100,000.

1.   The 61st.Division is being transferred from XI to
        XV Corps today 22nd. inst. and is moving today:

            Divl. H.Q.   to   WARDRECQUES.
            182 Bde. H.Q.   to   CHATEAU HAMBROUCK.
            183 Bde. H.Q.   to   HUBINGHEM.
            184 Bde. H.Q.   to   Factory at PONT-ASQUIN.
            1/5 D.C.L.I.   to   STAPLE

2.   Field Companies will move to RACQUINGHEM via
        MAMETZ - ECQUEDIRES.

3.   The following intervals will be maintained on the
        march:
            Dismounted personnel - 100 yds.- Section vehicles -
            25yds. - remainder of transport - 25yds. - cyclists.
            Intervals between Companies and other units -
            minimum 500yds.

4.   Each Company will picquet the narrow road leading
        Northwards from HAM Green to ensure its being kept
        clear of traffic while the Company is passing.

5.   Starting point for Field Companies - HAM Green.

        Starting times:-
            476 Field Co. - 2.15 p.m.
            478 Field Co. - 2.30 p.m.
            479 Field Co. - 2.45 p.m.

6.   Completion of moves will be reported to C.R.E.

7.   R.E.H.Q. closes at HAM at 1.45 p.m. and reopens at
        WARDRECQUES on arrival.

8.   Administrative instructions will be issued
        separately.

9.   Field Companies to acknowledge.

                                            [signature]

Issued at 9.30 a.m.   Capt. - Adjutant,
22.7.18.   for C.R.E. 61st.Div.

                        Distribution:-
    Copy No.1 to 476 Field Co.   Copy No.6 to C.E.XI Corps.
      "   2 to 478 Field Co.   "   7 to C.E.XV Corps.
      "   3 to 479 Field Co.   "   8 to War Diary.
      "   4 to 61st.Div."G".   "   9 to   "   "
      "   5 to 61st.Div."Q".   "   10 to File.

SECRET.   Copy No. 7.

R.E. ORDER NO. 104.

Ref. Sheet.
HAZEBROUCK So.
1/100000.

1. 476 Field Co and one Company 1/5 D.C.L.I.
    (Pioneers) will move to-morrow 23rd. inst to camp
    in neighbourhood of RECK ROUT CASTEEL (i.e. Cross
    Roads 1½ miles N.N.E. of SERCUS.

2. Route for 476 Field Co is Cross Roads
    SANDRINGHEM - WARDRECQUES Station - LYNDE - SERCUS

3. Advance parties of both Companies will
    meet at office of the Area Commandant, 31st. Division
    WALLON CAPPEL (1½ miles N.N.E. of SERCUS) at 10.30 a.m.
    who will give details of the accomodation.

4. Moves to be completed by 6 p.m.

5. Completion of moves to be reported to this
    office.

6. On arrival at destination the Companies
    will be employed on the EAST HAZEBROUCK Line under
    orders of C.E. XV Corps.

7. Field Co and Pioneers to ACKNOWLEDGE.

R.E.Hd.Qrs. 61st. Div
Issued at 11.15 p.m.   Capt. Adjutant.
July 22nd. 1918.   For C.R.E. 61st. Divn.

Distribution.

Copy No. 1. 476 Field Co.
        2. 1/5 D.C.L.I.
        3. 61st. Div G.
        4. C.E. XV Corps.
        5. 61st. Div Q.
        6. 61st. Signal Co.
     7 & 8 War Diary.
        9   File.

SECRET.

476 Field Co.
478 Field Co.
479 Field Co.

1. Reference warning order No. 24/2 sent you today, definite orders about the move have not yet been received, but it will not be before the evening of 31st.
In this event, the following are the probable arrangements for the move:-

(a) 476 Field Co bridging vehicles with kits etc report to 478 Field Co morning of the 31st, where they will be loaded and will move to HAM with 478 Field Co.

(b) Each Field Company to send an advance party of cyclists under an officer of 479 Field Co on the morning of the 31st.

(c) All units billet in HAM in exactly the same billets as previously.

(d) 476 Field Co not to work on the 31st, and to march in the evening, possibly taking "A" Coy 1/5 D.C.L.I. with them (busses have been applied for)

2. It is not certain whether units will be relieved by corresponding units, but Appendices of Defence Scheme and Trench Maps of this area will be got ready for handing over, these papers to be sent to this office if there is no relieving unit.

3. 476 Field Co papers referring to work in hand to be disposed of according to orders of C.E. IV Corps or his representative.

4. The usual receipt for area stores and clean billets will be required.

29.7.1918.

Capt. Adjutant.
For C.R.E. 61st. Divn.

SECRET.   Copy No......

Ref. Maps   61st. DIVISIONAL R.E. ORDER No.106.
Sheets 27 & 36a,
1/40,000.
                                                                29.7.1918.

1.   476 Field Co. will move from ECK HOUT CASTEEL to
     LES BRUNEHES tomorrow, 30th. instant.

2.   "A" Company, 1/5 D.C.L.I., is rejoining its Battalion
     tomorrow, 30th. inst., under orders of O.C. 1/5 D.C.L.I.

3.   There are no restrictions as to time and route.

4.   The usual intervals will be maintained on the march,
     viz:-
              (a) 500 yds. between Units;
              (b) 100 yds. between dismounted personnel
                  and transport;
              (c) 25 yds. between section vehicles and
                  H.Q. vehicles;
              (d) 25 yds. between transport and cyclists.

5.   All papers referring to work in hand will be handed
     over by 476 Field Co. according to instructions of C.E.
     XV Corps, or his representative; in the absence of any
     such instructions papers will be sent to this office
     without delay.

6.   478 Field Co. will arrange billets for 476 Field Co.
     at LES BRUNEHES.

7.   Receipts for Area Stores handed over will be sent to
     this office.

8.   476 Field Co. to acknowledge.

                                              Capt. - Adjutant,
Issued at 11.40 p.m.   for C.R.E. 61st.Division.
29.7.18.

                         Distribution:
                    Copy No.1 to 476 Field Co.
                       "   2 to 478 Field Co.
                       "   3 to 479 Field Co.
                       "   4 to 61st.Signals.
                       "   5 to War Diary.
                       "   6 to "   "
                       "   7 to File.

MARCH TABLE

To accompany 61st. DIVISIONAL R.E. ORDER No.10 dated 30.7.1918.

Serial No.	Date	Unit.	From:	To:	Route:	Starting point	Starting time.	Remarks
1	July 31st.	475 Field Co.	LES LOBELIES	M.H. (366/mg)	MEURCHIN-GHENT	East Junction 36n/A.24.d.7.9.	11 p.m.	
2	July 31st.	R.H.Q.	MEURCHIN-GHENT	"	"	"	11.6 p.m.	50yds. behind 475 Field Co.
3	July 31st.	476 Field Co.	LES LOBELIES	"	"	"	11.13 p.m.	
4	July 31st.	477 Field Co.	LES LOBELIES	"	"	"	11.25 p.m.	

* Matches will be subsequently to 476 Field Co. H.Q.

M.7.18.

Capt. - Adjutant,
61st Co.R.E.
61st. Div.

SECRET.   Copy No. 9...

61st. DIVISIONAL R.E. ORDER No. 187.

                                                                  30.7.18.

Ref. Sheets:
HAZEBROUCK 1/100,000.
No.27 - 1/40,000.
No.36a. - 1/40,000.

1. The 61st. Division is marching from XV Corps area to XI Corps area on the night 31st. July/1st. August, 1918.

2. Field Companies will march from LES BRUNEHES 36a/A.17. in accordance with March Table attached.

3. The following distances will be maintained on the line of march:-
   (a) 300-yds. between Field Companies and other units;
   (b) 100-yds. between dismounted personnel and transport;
   (c) 25-yds. between Section and H.Q. transport;
   (d) 25-yds. between transport and cyclists.

4. All instructions with regard to defences in the XV Corps area, including appendices to Defence Scheme and maps belonging thereto, will be returned to this office not later than 8 a.m. 31st. inst.

5. All tents, trench shelters and other area stores, will be handed over to the Area Commandant, WARDRECQUES. 476 Field Co. will detail an officer to arrange details with the Area Commandant and to take charge of rear parties from each Field Company. Receipts for area stores will be sent to this office.

6. Supply wagons, with rations for consumption August 1st., will accompany units to the new area.

7. All Second Army, XV Corps Standing Orders and Routine Orders will be returned to this office at once.

8. An Advance Party of 1 officer of 479 Field Co. and 2 cyclists per Company will assemble at 479 Field Co. H.Q. at 10 a.m. 31st. instant.

9. Attention is called to the following Routine Orders which will apply on arrival of units at HAM:-
   No. 66 - SANITATION.   No. 86 - GUARDS, &c.
   No. 67 & 100 - BUGLES.   No. 88 - ROUTINE.
   No. 97 - LIGHTS.   No. 96 - HOURS OF TRAINING.
   No. 103 - RECREATION.

   476 Field Co. will mount guard on arrival at HAM on Aug.1st.

10. R.E.H.Q. (less C.R.E. & Adjutant) will move with Field Coys. according to march table attached.
    C.R.E. and Adjutant will remain at WARDRECQUES until 10 a.m. Aug. 1st.

11. Field Companies to ACKNOWLEDGE.

Issued at 4.15 p.m.   Capt. - Adjutant,
30.7.18.   for C.R.E. 61st. Div.

Distribution:
Copy No.1 to 476 Fld.Co.   Copy No.6 to 61st.Signals.
     "   2 to 478 Fld.Co.   "   7 to C.E. XI Corps.
     "   3 to 479 Fld.Co.   "   8 to C.E. XV Corps.
     "   4 to 61st.Div.S.   "   9 & 10 to War Diary.
     "   5 to 61st.Div.Q.   "   11 to File.

WAR DIARY
ORIGINAL
JULY 1918.
C.R.E. 61ST DIVN.

APPENDIX 3

WORK ORDERS
&
INSTRUCTIONS

Notes on Conferences

476 Field Co.
478 Field Co.
479 Field Co.

NOTES ON CONFERENCE
held at Div.H.Q. 4.7.1918.

1. **Importance of Gas Discipline.**
   Officers Commanding Field Companies to ensure that all men including details wear their Box Respirator for at least one hour continuously once a week.

2. **Wearing of Equipment.**
   Companies are reminded that the permission given for men to go up to their work with rifle and 50 rounds S.A.A. instead of full fighting order was only meant to hold good during hot weather. The importance of men being able to wear their equipment for a long time without undue fatigue is very great and must not be lost sight of. During cool weather fighting order should be worn except by the two men per section detailed to carry the stretcher.

4th. July 1918.

Major,
A/C.R.E. 61st.Division.

NOTES ON CONFERENCE
held at R.E.H.Q. 8.7.1918.

Present:
C.R.E. & Adjutant;
O's.C. Field Companies.

Divisional Relief.

Relief of 61st.Division by 74th.Division commences 10th.instant; work policy not therefore discussed.

Advance parties.

C.R.E. will suggest to C.R.E. 74th.Division that the Companies coming into line should send advance parties of 2 Officers and 4 N.C.O's. each, in addition to billet parties.

Demolitions.

Bridge parties to come up 24 hours before relief. Companies of 74th.Division to hand over exploders etc. in exchange for any left behind.

Billets.

All billets to be disinfected with sprays before handing over.

Daily Fighting Strength return.

Companies returns vary. Q.M.S. & Transport Personnel should include men at Q.M.S., Drivers, Batmen, tool cart men, postman, tailor, H.Q. clerk, water duty men, 1 cook per section, and brakesmen, man in charge A.A. Lewis Gun, L.G. instructor. Extra shoemakers etc. should be brakesmen.

Corps Schools.

Division has been asked to arrange for Field Company Commanders to attend for 3 days.

Education Scheme.

All Companies want to run classes and it will probably mean Companies working independently.

8th.July 1918.

Capt.
Adjutant, 61st.Divl. R.E.

NOTES ON CONFERENCE
held at R.E.H.Q.
11 a.m. 14.7.18.

Corps HORSE SHOW - Entries:
    476 - 478 - 1 Pontoon or Trestle wagon each.
    476 - 479 - 1 Tool-cart each.

HAIR CUTS.
    Mens hair requires cutting; drivers are especially bad.

PAINTING VEHICLES.
    Bolts and plate on wheels to be black.

A.A. LEWIS GUNS.
    Each Company to mount its gun in its respective billetting area.

BILLETTING.
    Interpreter to settle all billets and get "no claim" certificates.

MUSKETRY.
    Each Company to have its own range. Positions pointed out. S.A.A. should be drawn at once.

SURPLUS KITS.
    Companies to go into this matter carefully, paying special attention to officers kits, mess kits, Q.M. stores.

WIRING. - Suggested amendments to S.S.177.
    Suggestion in G.C. 32/20 approved.
    Knee-high wire to be cut out as soon as medium pickets can be used up, as it cannot compare with high wire.
    High wire - space pickets 4yds. instead of 3 yds. and add an extra apron each side.
    Hasty wire with screw posts and French wire. Cut out trip wire.

P.U.O. CASES.
    M.O. to isolate all cases and 478 to cook for the lot.

TRAINING AND ROUTINE.

6.45 to 7.30 a.m.	Physical exercises preceded by tea and biscuits.
9 a.m.	Company parades – (Battle order unless when followed by route march.)
9 a.m. to 1 p.m.	Infantry training, schemes, &c. – (in Battle order.)
Afternoon	Musketry (in Battle order) and R.E. special training.

Following to be included in training :-
  Route marching with transport (marching order).
  Tactical schemes.
  Field defences.
  Ceremonial.
  Wearing respirators to include one continuous hour per week.

About Turn: Order to be given "two rights". (or)

Officers Drill Class:
  Company Commanders to be in charge of parades in turn.
  C.S.M. 478 Field Co. to drill the parades.
  With exception of O's.C. all Officers and C.S.M's to attend.
  Parade – 6.45 a.m.
  Dress – Fatigue.

Inspections:
  C.R.E. will inspect Companies (complete) as follows:-

  Wednesday 10 a.m. – 476 Field Co.
      "   11 a.m. – 478 Field Co.
      "   3 p.m. – 479 Field Co.
  General parade Divl. R.E. Thursday 11 a.m.

Officers dress for marching order.
  Each Company to send an Officer to R.E.H.Q. at 5.30 pm 15th. for inspection – full marching order;

  also – 1 N.C.O. or man in marching order and
  1 N.C.O. or man in "Battle order",

Programmes.
  Daily programmes to C.R.E. during previous evening.

14th. July 1918.

Capt. – Adjutant,
61st. Divisional R.E.

Minutes of Meeting of Recreation Committee held 10 a.m.
20.7.1918.

Present:-   Captain M.E.W. FITZGERALD.
             Captain B. LONG, M.C.
             Capt. H. HOLBROW.
             Capt. H.G. ROBINSON.

Mess Dinner. Captains Long and Robinson to arrange for combined officers dinner at HAM. Wednesday suggested, but the day to depend on the FROLICS. Adjutant to ask O.C. FROLICS to fix a day.

   Note:- Frolics are being asked for Wednesday, but proposed general inspection by Divisional Commander may clash with this day.

Sunday 21st. 182 Brigade band will be playing in the park from about 3 p.m. to 9 p.m. and is being entertained by 476 Field Co. Captain Holbrow is arranging for football match between 478 and 479 Field Coys at 6 p.m. During the afternoon there will be boxing competitions commencing at 3.30 p.m. and these are being arranged by C.S.M. HICKMAN who will post notices at 476 Field Co orderly room in the park and send copies to other Coys.

Allotting of football ground. This is being done by Capt. Holbrow who will publish fixtures on 476 Field Co notice board in the park.

Inter-Battalion Football Match. Adjutant to challenge D.C.L.I. to football match at 6 p.m. Tuesday. Sergt. TRUPP and one N.C.O. from 478 and 479 to select the R.E. team.

Cricket. Officers v N.C.O's. C.R.E. to be asked to Captain the officers team and each Company to send him 4 names for selection. Capt. Robinson to arrange about the N.C.O's team and gear. Each Company to send list of suggested players and list of available gear to Captain Robinson today. Fixture:- 2.30 p.m. Wednesday.

   Note:- This fixture is liable to variation in the event of general inspection by the Divisional Commander.

                                              Adjutant.
                                              61st. Div R.E.
20.7.1918.

SECRET

476 Field Co.
478 Field Co.
479 Field Co.

1. Instructions have been issued for the Division to reconnoitre the whole Corps front up to the Line of Resistance (known as the Z-Z-Z Line)

2. This line now runs as follows, and maps previously issued should be corrected accordingly:-

M K.4.c.central, E.28.a.central,- E.21.b.central- E.15.central,- E.9.central.- E.4.central.- W.29.d.central.- W.24.d.central.- X.13.central- X.8.central.- X.9.d.central.- X.10.c.central.- X.10.b.central.

3. Division sectors are as shown on map T.S.216, and are held as follows from the right

        31st. Division.
        1st. Australian Division
        9th. Division.

4. Maps should be carefully studied both from a defensive and offensive point of view.

5 Infantry Brigades are reconnoitring the in front as follows:-

	July 28 & 29	July 30 & 31.	August 1 & 2.
182 Inf. Bde.	31 Div. area	1st. Aust.Div. area	9th. Divn area
183 Inf. Bde.	1st.Aust. Div.area.	9th. Div area	31 Divn. area
184 Inf. Bde	9th. Div area	31st. Div. area	1st. Aust. Div. area

and I have asked Brigade Commanders to take Field Company commanders with them.

I will let you know their replies.

Lieut-Colonel, R.E
C.R.E. 61st. Division

27.7.1918.

478 Field Co.
Copy to 476 Field Co.

478 Field Co will arrange to collect on their own wagons, bridging equipment from 476 Field Company. This equipment will be stored at 478 Field Co transport lines.

This transaction to be completed by dusk tomorrow 28th. inst.

Capt. Adjutant.
For C.R.E. 61st. Divn.

27.7.1918.

WAR DIARY
ORIGINAL.
JULY 1918.
C.R.E. 61ST DIVN.

APPENDIX 4

NOMINAL ROLLS

NOMINAL ROLL OF UNIT.

1st. July 1918.

Officers.

Lieut-Colonel	G.E.J. DURNFORD, D.S.O.	C.R.E.
Captain	H.E.W. FITZGERALD.	Adjutant
Captain	J.K. RENNIE (R.A.M.C)	M.O.

(at present in charge of P.U.O. camp)

Other Ranks.

52959	R.S.M.	H. DEYERMOND, D.C.M.
500121	Sergt.	W.A. FEATHERSTONE.
500336	L/Cpl.	A. SKINNER
498197	L/Cpl.	F. HAYCRAFT.
99315	Sapper	G. BOLLAND
500171	Driver	L. WATTS
500303	Driver	J.A. GREGORY.
56185	Driver	A. DAVIES.
61497	Driver	G.W. PATTEN with M.O.

T4/248151 Driver E. LORTON   (A.S.C)

Attached.

476 Field Co.

498210	L/Cpl.	E.G. ANCELL
498134	L/Cpl.	L. MOTT
498223	Sapper	J. COLLINS
498276	Sapper	T.A. ELLISON
84339	Driver	G. KING.

478 Field Co.

496773	A/Cpl.	F.L. PENNY.

479 Field Co.

494375	Sapper	H. TALBOT
488601	Sapper	E.S. NEWTON.
494779	Driver	G. DOLLING.

French Mission.

Interpreter GUEUX.

Detached.

Driver F. FOXON.   to 479 Field Co. R.E

61st. (S.M) DIVISIONAL ROYAL ENGINEERS.

R.E. HEADQUARTERS.

Rank		Name	Initials	Nature of Comm.	Remarks
Substantive	Acting				
Major	Lt-Col.	BURNFORD, D.S.O.	G.E.J.	Reg.	
Lieutenant	Captain	FITZGERALD	H.E.W.	T.F.	

476 FIELD Co. R.E.

Lieutenant	Major	DAVIS, M.C.	H.S.	T.F.	
Lieutenant	Captain	HILDROT.	H.	T.F.	
Lieutenant	Lieut.	HIGHER.	G.S.	T.F.	
2nd. Lieut	2nd.Lt	KING, M.C.	M.W.	T.F.	
2nd. Lieut	2nd.Lt	DICKINSON.	A.R.	T.F.	
2nd. Lieut	2nd Lt	WOOD	D.S.	T.F.	
2nd. Lieut	2nd Lt	HUGH	R.H.	T.F.	

478 FIELD Co. R.E.

Lieutenant	Major	WHITWILL, D.S.O, M.C.	M.	T.F.	
Lieutenant	Captain	ROBINSON.	H.O.	T.F.	
Lieutenant	Lieut.	RAWLING, M.C.	J.D.	T.F.	
Lieutenant	Lieut	HOULDSWORTH.	A.F.	T.F.	
Lieutenant	Lieut	HARES.	T.M.D.	T.F.	
2nd. Lieut	2nd Lt	BRISSEN	S.	T.F.	
2ND LIEUT	2ND Lt	ASHWIN	H.M.H.		

479 FIELD Co. R.E.

Lieutenant	Major	HOLTHOUSE	R.	T.F.	
Lieutenant	Captain	IONS, M.C. & bar	B.	T.F.	
Lieutenant	Lieut.	SIMMONS, M.C.	G.H.	T.F.	
Lieutenant	Lieut.	GIBBS, M.C.	G.H.	T.F. A/GHQ, 5th. Army
Lieutenant	Lieut.	BOARD	R.F.	T.F.	
2nd. Lieut	2nd Lt	ELLISON	D.	T.F.	
2nd. Lieut	2nd Lt	HOWARD	G.B.	T.F.	
2nd. Lieut	2nd Lt	WARREN	J.F.	T.F.	

Capt. Adjutant.
For C.R.E. 61st. Divn.

WAR DIARY
ORIGINAL.
JULY 1918.
C.R.E. 61ST DIVN.

APPENDIX 5.

DEFENCE

SCHEMES

&

INSTRUCTIONS

S E C R E T. Copy No. 13.

APPX 5

DEFENCE SCHEME.

61st. DIVNL. R.E.

Paras.

1. Employment of Field Coys and Pioneer Battalion.
2. Supply of R.E. Materials.
3. Demolitions.
4. Action in Case of Hostile Attack.
5. Local Defence.

Appendices.

A. Locations.
B. Trench and Area Stores (Tools).
C. Demolitions (Bridges etc).
D. Local Defence (Map).
E. Gas Defence.
F. Action in Case of Hostile Attack.

Distribution.

Copy No.	To.	Appendices.
1.	476 Field Co.	A. B. C. D. E. F.
2.	478 Field Co.	A. B. C. D. E. F.
3.	479 Field Co.	A. B. C. D. E. F.
4.	1/5 D.C.L.I.	B. D.
5.	61st. Div. G.	A. B. C. D. E. F.
6.	61st. Div. Q.	A. B. C. D. E. F.
7.	61st. Div Art.	C.
8.	182 Inf. Bde.	B. C. D.
9.	183 Inf. Bde.	B. C. D.
10.	184 Inf. Bde.	B. C. D.
11.	C.E. XI Corps.	A. B. C. D. E. F.
12.	War Diary.	A. B. C. D. E. F.
13.	War Diary.	A. B. C. D. E. F.
14.		
15.		

(Page 1. - 6.7.1918.)

Defence Scheme. 61st. Div R.E.

Para.

1.   (a) The Field Companies are under the executive command of and are employed on Engineer work under the C.R.E.

    (b) When employed in the line, each Company works normally on a "Section" of the forward area, the boundaries coinciding with Infantry Brigade "Sections".

    (c) The Pioneer Battalion works under instructions which are issued by the C.R.E.

    (d) Field Company Commanders are the technical advisers on Engineering matters of the Infantry Brigade Commanders in whose "Sections" they are working. They keep the Infantry advised as to the situation with regard to supply of R.E. defence materials and arrange supplies. They arrange direct with Brigades for Infantry working parties.

    (e) Similarly, Field Company Commanders are responsible for giving technical advice and necessary supervision and assistance to Field Artillery covering their respective Infantry Brigade "Sections" and also to Machine Gunners in their areas. Field Companies supply defence materials to Machine Gunners, but not to Field Artillery (see para 2.b)

    (f) Present distribution of Field Companies is shown in Appendix A.

Defence Scheme. 61 Div R.E.

Para.

2. (a) The C.R.E. is responsible for the supply and disposal of such R.E. materials and tools as the Corps issues to the Division. This may be augmented to a small extent by local purchase either through his own Imprest Account or by sanctioning purchase by other units.

(b) Materials for use by all troops in the trench system - except Divisional Artillery - are supplied through the Field Companies.

(c) Materials for Divisional Artillery and back areas are supplied by the C.R.E. through Headquarters of formation concerned.

(d) Tools supplied from R.E. sources are distinct from those supplied to units by A.O.D. to form their mobile equipment. The former are trench stores which must be handed over on relief. During mobile operations the supply from R.E. sources becomes uncertain and may fail entirely. It is to meet such a situation that units carry a mobile reserve. The distinction between a pick supplied by the C.R.E. and a pick supplied by the D.A.D.O.S. is the same as the difference between a dugout and a rifle. The former is always handed over on relief, and the latter moves with the troops. The former cannot be supplied during moving warfare, but the latter must never be left behind.

(e) Establishment of tools held as trench or area stores by units is shown in Appendix B.

(f) R.E. dumps vary from "NIL" (during moving warfare) to a definite system (during stationary warfare) on the following lines:-

(i) C.R.E's dump fed from the Corps dump by motor **lorry** and light railway and located where all work can proceed during daylight.

(Page 3. - 6.7.1918.)

Defence Scheme.   61st. Div R.E.

Para   (f) (contd)

2. (contd)

    (ii)   Field Company dumps located where they can be fed by lorry during daylight either from the C.R.E's or direct from Corps dumps. Certain stores which the Company has to work up must be near the Company billet, and others, such as wiring stores, must be placed so as to be convenient for day loading into horse transport going forward to the trench system. This may necessitate each Company having two or more dumps.

    (iii)   Forward dumps (usually temporary) which are fed by horse transport or trench tramways and are within carrying distance of the work in hand. These may be either Field Company or Infantry dumps.
          Locations of dumps are shown in Appendix A.

    (iv)   Explosives for Field Company use are carried in the unit transport and are mobilization stores. The S.A.A. Section of the D.A.C. carries a mobile reserve, (vide G.R.O. 4315 dated 20.6.1918) which can be drawn on by Field Companies.

(g)   The size of dumps depends very largely upon the tactical situation. When stationary warfare is assured the policy is to carry a reasonable stock at all dumps; when an advance is contemplated reserves of stores are pushed well forward.

    During the present phase, the policy is to bring forward only those stores which are required for immediate use and to keep the stock of surplus stores down to a minimum.

(h)   <u>Transport of Stores</u>.

    (i)   The C.R.E. is responsible for transporting such stores as are available for the Division to his dump, the Corps assisting with such means of transport as may be available; such as Light Railway, Lorries, and occasionally horsed transport. As the C.R.E. has no transport, except that of Field Companies, any requirements in addition to facilities supplied by Corps must be provided by the Division.

Defence Scheme. 61st. Div R.E.

Para.
2.
(Contd)

(h) contd.

(ii) In order to save transport and double handling -

(a) as much material as possible is delivered from Corps dump direct to Field Coy. dumps.

(b) Stores allotted to R.A are, whenever possible, drawn direct from Corps dump under R.A. arrangements.

(c) Units in back areas requiring stores, are required whenever possible, to draw direct from Corps dump.

(iii) Stores are transported from Field Company dumps to the line by -

(a) Field Company transport.
(b) Brigade transport.
(c) Pioneer Battalion transport.

Should the above be insufficient, further transport is obtained from the Division.

(iv) Additional transport has often to be obtained from Division when units such as Tunnelling Coys, Labour Companies, etc. are placed at the C.R.E's disposal for work.

(v) The general principle is to make use of the R.E, Pioneer and Brigade transport available, with due regard to condition of animals and vehicles. Should these sources prove insufficient, the Division supplies the balance of requirements.

Defence Scheme. 61st. Div R.E.

Para.

3. **DEMOLITIONS.**

    (a) The C.R.E. is responsible for certain demolitions in the event of the enemy advancing over the area now occupied by his Division.

    (b) Field Companies are responsible for the destruction of their respective dumps and for this purpose, tar and other materials suitable for starting a fire are kept at the principal dumps. Failing receipt of orders to the contrary, it is the duty of Field Companies to do all that is reasonably possible to prevent R.E. materials from falling into the hands of the enemy.

    (c) The chief duty of the Divisional R.E. is the destruction of communications which would be of assistance to the enemy during an advance by him. Destruction by explosives is to be carried out by the Field Companies. Destruction by fire is to be carried out by the fighting troops on the spot, but preparations for the demolition are made by the Field Companies.

    (d) The responsibility for ordering the demolition of communications lies with the Infantry Brigade Commanders but all ranks must clearly understand that if no orders have been received the senior soldier <u>on the spot at the time</u> is responsible for seeing that the demolition is carried out before it is too late. Recent experiences have shown that there is a grave tendency to delay the demolition until all our troops are clear. Cases occurred where this policy enabled the enemy to capture bridges before they were demolished.

    (e) The preparations for demolitions of communications are carried out by the Field Companies under orders issued by the C.R.E.
        Preparations already made are shown in Appendix C.

Defence Scheme. 61 Div R.E

Para. 4.

(a) In the event of Hostile Attack (or Heavy Bombardment or order to MAN BATTLE STATIONS) all R.E. parties, no matter where working, will at once return to billets in formed parties under proper control. (This does not apply to demolition parties and the like who are already standing by at Battle Stations)

(b) In case of Hostile attack the Field Companies are in Divisional Reserve and are held in readiness to do engineer work or do duty with the rifle and bayonet.

(c) Special action to be taken by R.E. and men working with them is shown in Appendix F.

Para 5.

Field Companies are reminded that they are always responsible for the local defence of their commands.

A combined scheme for the Divisional R.E. to act upon in the event of an unexpected break through, and in the absence of orders to the contrary is shown on Map Appendix D.

W.E. FitzGerald
Captain. Adjutant.
61st. Divisional R. E.

APPENDIX A.

Defence Scheme. 61st. Div R.E.

LOCATIONS.
(Map Sheet 36a.).

Headquarters.

R.E.H.Qrs.		O.6.b.8.4.
476 Field Co.		O.13.a.7.9.
478 Field Co.	(Left "Section")	P.1.a.3.4.
479 Field Co.	(Right Section.)	P.8.b.3.8.
1/5 D.C.L.I. (Pioneers)		P.1.d.5.0.
250 Tunnelling Co. R.E.		H.29.c.9.4.
No.1.Section. 250 T Co	(Left "Section")	P.8.b.8.8
No.4.Section. 250 T Co	(Right Section.)	P.27.b.1.3.

Transport.

R.E.H.Qrs.	O.6.b.8.4.
476 Field Co.	O.13.b.7.1.
478 Field Co.	O.6.b.5.2.
479 Field Co.	O.6.b.7.2.

Dumps.

No. 11. R.E. Park (Late No.4. R.E.Park)	M.28.a.8.8.
XI Corps.	I.32.a.5.3
C.R.E.	O.6.b.8.3.
476 Field Co.	
478 Field Co.	O.6.b.5.2. & P.8.b.7.8
479 Field Co.	P.8.b.8.8

(6.7.1918)

Defence Scheme. 61st. Div. R.E.

APPENDIX B.

	RIGHT BRIGADE				LEFT BRIGADE				RESERVE BRIGADE	PIONEER BATTALION.
	Right Battn	Left Battn	Res. Battn	Total	Right Battn	Left Battn	Res Batt	Total		
Shovels.	500	500	500	1500	500	500	500	1500	500@	600@
Picks.	120	120	120	360	120	120	120	360	120@	300@
Mauls	40	40	–	80	40	40	–	80	–	–
Saws, hand.	6	6	–	12	6	6	–	12	–	–
Hooks, bill	20	20	–	40	20	20	–	40	–	–
Axes, hand	6	6	–	12	6	6	–	12	–	–
Axes, felling	4	4	–	8	4	4	–	8	–	–
Hooks, reaping	10	10	–	20	20	20	20	60	–	–

@These numbers have not yet been made up.

(7.7.1918)

Defence Scheme. 61st. Div. R.E.

APPENDIX C.

PREPARED DEMOLITIONS.

(1) BY EXPLOSIVES. Guards include one sapper. On Manning Battle Stations, two Sappers are stationed at each "demolition". Field Company is responsible for patrolling, testing, and keeping structure and explosives in order.

Serial No.	Map Ref.	Structure	Bde. Sect.	Field Co.	Remarks.
45	P.4.b.1.1.	Brick Arch.	Left	Left)	1 N.C.O &
46	do	Pont Levis.	Left	Left)	2 sappers on M.B.S.
45a.	do	Girder Bdge.	Not to be blown.		
91.	P.29.d.3.1.	SYPHON & footbridge	Right	Right	
44.	P.29.c.7.2.	Pont Levis.	Right	Right	
49	P.27.b.9.1.	Field Art.	Right	Right)	
51	P.27.b.3.5.	Pont Levis.	Right	Right)	1 guard with one sapper until M.B.S.
52) 92)	P.27.b.1.7.	Tank Bridge & SYPHON.	Right	Right)	
55	P.20.b.15.25	Pont Levis	Right	Right	
56	P.20.a.6.6.	Iron footbr.	Right	Right	
59	O.12.c.25.90	Pont Levis.	Left	Left	
60	I.33.d.3.3.	Pont Levis	Left	Left	

(7.7.1918)

Defence Scheme. 61st. Div. R.E

APPENDIX C. (Contd)

2. BY FIRE.   Field Company is responsible for patrolling and keeping the structure and combustibles in order.

Serial No	Map. Ref.	Structure	Bde. Sect.	Field Co.	Remarks.
41.	P.5.b.2.7.	Footbridge	Left	Left	
43	P.5.a.7.3.	Footbridge	Left	Left	
43a.	P.5.a.2.1.	Footbridge	Left	Left	
48	P.4.a.5.4.	Field Arty	Left	Left	
50	P.3.b.90.70	Footbridge	Left	Left	
50a.	J.33.d.1.7.	Footbridge	Left	Left	
53	J.33.a.9.1.	Field Arty	Left	Left	
	P.29.c.0.4.	Field Arty	Right	Right	Made by 4th. Division.
47	P.28.d.3.6.	Pack Bridge	Right	Right	
54	P.20.d.8.5.	Pack Bridge	Right	Right	
57	P.20.a.05.95	Pack Bridge	Right	Right	
61	P.13.d.15.70	Field Arty	Left	Left.	
58a	O.18.b.95.70	Pack Bridge	Left	Left.	
58	O.12.c.9.4.	Field Arty	Left	Left.	
62	O.11.b.5.4.	Field Arty	Left	Left.	
59b	O.5.c.50.15	Pack Bridge	Left	Left	
59c	O.4.b.5.0.	Field Arty	Left	Left	
63	O.4.a.4.7.	Field Arty	Left	Left.	

(7.7.1918)

Defence Scheme. 61st. Div.R.E.

APPENDIX C. (Cont'd).

3. Other demolitions for which the DIVISION is responsible, but with which Field Companies are not concerned.

Serial No.	Map. Ref.	Structure and Remarks.
77) 77a)	P.13.a.3.3.	Railway bridge with pack bridge under it.
75	I.33.d.7.3.	High level railway bridge
76	I.33.d.6.2.	Low level railway bridge.
78	O.16.d.8.4.	Railway Bridge.
79	O.21.d.8.1.	Railway Bridge.

(7.7.1918).

APPENDIX D.

HAUTE VENT.

479

SCALE 1:5000

Defence Scheme. 61st. Div R.E.

GAS DEFENCE. APPENDIX E.

1. It is the duty of Field Company guards and horse pickets to warn all officers and men when gas shelling occurs and to clang a gong when the presence of gas is detected.

2. Strombos Horns are fixed at the following points and will be sounded in the event of cloud gas.

    478 Field Co guard room   P.1.c.3.4.
    479 Field Co guard room   P.8.b.3.8.

3. Supplies of Chloride of Lime will be kept at Headquarters and Transport lines of 478 and 479 Field Companies.

4. The limits of the ALERT, READY and PRECAUTIONARY Zones will be as follows:-

    ALERT ZONE. East of a line drawn through BUSNETTES - O.31.b.5.2. - cross roads LA PIERRIERE (P.19.a.3.3) - P.1.d.O.C. - B in BAS HAMEL (J.31.d.4.8).

    READY ZONE. East of LILLERS - THIENNES Railway.

    PRECAUTIONARY ZONE. East of and including the villages AMES - LINGHEM - WITTERNESSE - GLOMENGHEM - ROQUETOIRE.

(7.7.1918)

APPENDIX F.   Defence Scheme. 61st. Div R.E.

                          HOSTILE ATTACK
ACTION IN CASE OF   HEAVY ENEMY BOMBARDMENT, or
                          ORDERS TO MAN BATTLE STATIONS.

(1) 1/5 D.C.L.I. have orders to proceed to their Battle Stations.

(2) Infantry parties have orders to man the nearest defences, if they are in the forward system. If in the AMUSOIRES system they are to stand fast and report to the nearest Battalion Commander in that system.

(3) Reinforcements for demolition parties will proceed to their posts as ordered. (See Appendix C).

(4) Transport of 478 and 479 Field Companies will be loaded and ready to move to about C.2. or C.3. (Sheet 36a) on receipt of orders from this office. On arrival, a report centre will be established at ISBERGUES Church and the senior R.E. Officer present will assume command of transport. This officer will keep touch with
   (a) "Q" Branch, 61st. Division.
   (b) R.E. Headquarters, and
   (c) Field Company Commanders.

(5) The following will report at R.E.H.Qrs.

   478 Field Co. - 2 runners.

   479 Field Co. - 1 officer.
                   2 runners.

(6) 476 Field Co will detail an officer to report at Div. H.Q. ("G" Branch) for orders, and the Company will be in readiness to move at 30 minutes notice.

(7) 478 and 479 Field Companies will be held in readiness to move at 15 minutes notice.

(6.7.1918.)

S E C R E T.

476 Field Co.
478 Field Co.
479 Field Co.

Reference 61st. Div. R.E. Defence Scheme dated 6.7.18.

1. Appendices A. B. C. D. & F. are in abeyance and will remain so whilst they are inapplicable.   Appendix E. (Gas Defence) para. 4 is still applicable.

2. Should the formation of Infantry Brigade Groups become necessary, the Divisional R.E. will join groups as follows :-
    R.E.H.Q. to D.H.Q.
    476 Field Co. to 182 Bde. Group.
    478 Field Co. to 183 Bde. Group.
    479 Field Co. to 184 Bde. Group.

3. Infantry Brigades are referred to as follows :-

    ST.HILAIRE Bde.   .. .. .. Bde. billetted at ST.HILAIRE -
    (at present 184)   BOURECQ.
                                    Bde.H.Q. - ST.HILAIRE.

    MAZINGHEM Bde.   .. .. .. Bde. billetted at FONTES -
    (at present 182)   LAMBRES - GUERNES.
                                    Bde.H.Q. - ST.ANDRE Fm.N.2.d.

    LINGHEM Bde.   .. .. .. Bde. billetted at LINGHEM -
    (at present 183)   LEITTRES.
                                    Bde.H.Q. - FONTES.

4. The Division (less 184 Bde. Group) is at 24 hours notice.   184 Bde. Group is at 8 hours notice.

5. G.Os.C.Brigades have been instructed to make provisional arrangements for the concentration of their respective Groups.
    Field Companies will inform this office what arrangements are made in this respect for them.

6. Should it be necessary to form Brigade Groups suddenly, D.H.Q. will send out the order "FORM BRIGADE GROUPS" and Field Companies will at once march to the rendezvous arranged by their respective Brigade group Commanders.

18th.July 1918.   Capt. - Adjutant,
                                        for C.R.E. 61st.Divn.

Defence Scheme, 61st. Div R.E

APPENDIX B.

GAS DEFENCE.

1. It is the duty of Field Company guards and horse pickets to warn all officers and men when gas shelling occurs and to clang a gong when the presence of gas is detected.

2. Supplies of Chloride of Lime will be kept at Headquarters and Transport Lines of Field Companies billeted in localities likely to be gas shelled.

3. The limits of the "ALERT" and "PRECAUTIONARY" Zones will be as follows:-

    ALERT ZONE.   The country East of the following line-

    MORBECQUE - HAZEBROUCK - CAESTRE Railway within the Corps area.

    PRECAUTIONARY ZONE. The country between the Western limits of the "ALERT" Zone and the following line:-

    MONT DUPIL, B.26.b. (exclusive) - BLARINGHEM - ESQUELBECQ - CASSEL (all inclusive)

Distribution.

476 Field Co.
478 Field Co
479 Field Co.
61st. Div G.
War Diary.

(25.7.1918)

476 Field Co.
478 Field Co.
479 Field Co.
61st. Division, "G".
61st. Division, "Q".
C.E. XV Corps.

Herewith Appendix F (part 1) to 61st. Divl. R.E. Defence Scheme dated 6.7.18.

Appendix F dated 6.7.18 should be destroyed.

Copy of Defence Scheme referred to is enclosed herewith to C.E. XV Corps.

24th. July 1918.

Capt. - Adjutant,
for C.R.E. 61st.Div.

S E C R E T.

Ref. Maps 27 and 28a.

61st.Div.R.E. Defence Scheme.

APPENDIX F. (Part 1).

(1) In the event of an enemy attack on the IV Corps front the following action is to be taken by the 61st.Division.

(2) On receipt of the words "MAN BATTLE STATIONS":-

    (a) Advanced Div.H.Q. (including R.E.H.Q.) is to be established at EBBLINGHEM Chateau, U.19.c.5.7.

    (b) Div.Arty. is to move to assembly areas "D" or "F" or both as ordered, via Route "C".

    (c) 182 Inf.Bde. is to move to Area E - via LYNDE & Route C.
        183 Inf.Bde. is to move to Area B - via Route "A".
        184 Inf. Bde. is to move to Area A - via cross-roads
        T.22.b.9.4 & Route A.)

    (d) The M.G. Battn. moves to WALLON-CAPPEL via Route B and then splits up (see 3 (b) below), one Company remaining in Divisional Reserve.

    (e) All other troops of the Division are to remain in their present positions ready to move at half-an-hours notice.

(3) On receipt of the words "OCCUPY POSITIONS":

    (a) The Divisional Artillery is to move to positions from which it can cover the Army line.

    (b) Infantry Brigades (with M.G. Coys. attached) are to march and occupy the Army Line as follows :-

    184 Inf.Bde. From LA KREULE V.16.b.5.0 (LA KREULE and road both incl.) to bend in road at W.1.c.8.7.(excl.)
        2 Battalions in Front,
        1 Battalion in Support.

        Headquarters: Brigade   P.34.c.5.6.
                        Right Bn. V.10.d.central.
                        Left Bn. V.6.a.central.
                        Support Bn. V.5.d.2.6.

    183 Inf.Bde. From bend in road at W.1.c.8.7 (incl.) to the CAESTRE - FLETRE road (excl.)
        2 Battalions in Front.
        1 Battalion in Support.

        Headquarters: Brigade   P.35.c.8.6.
                        Right Bn. W.1.c.
                        Left Bn. W.3.c.
                        Support Bn. Q.32.c.

Defence Scheme 61st.Div. R.E.

APPENDIX F. (Part 1 contd.)

183 Inf.Bde. from CAESTRE - FLETRE Road (incl.) to
Corps Boundary at R.31.c.0.0.
    2 Battalions in Front.
    1 Battalion in Support.

Headquarters: Brigade Q.25.d.0.0 or Q.27.a.2.7.
                    Right Bn. Q.34.c.5.4.
                    Left Bn. Q.34.b.4.5.
                    Support Bn. Q.33.b.central (about)

    (c) The remaining troops of the Division are to stand fast.

(4) On receipt of different instructions than those contained in paras. 2 & 3 above, the Division may have to operate on any portion of the Corps front, particularly in the Battle Zone.

(5) Maps T.S.223 and T.S.218 already issued to Field Coys. show:

    Assembly areas marked "A", "B", etc.,
    Routes to assembly areas "AAA", "BBB" etc.,
    Corps and Divisional boundaries,
    Defensive systems.

(6) Field Companies will not move without specific orders from this office.

(7) As soon as it is known that an enemy attack has commenced or on receipt of the words "MAN BATTLE STATIONS":

    (a) Field Companies will prepare to move at half-an-hours notice;

    (b) Each Field Company will send one mounted officer and 2 cyclist orderlies to R.E.H.Q. for orders.

Distribution:
476 Field Coy.
478 Field Coy.
479 Field Coy.
61st.Div."G".
61st.Div."Q".
C.E. XV Corps.
War Diary (2).

476 Field Co.
478 Field Co.
479 Field Co.
61 Div G.
61 Div Q.
C.E. XV Corps.

1.   Herewith Appendix F (Part 1) dated 27.7.1918 to 61st. Divisional R.E. Defence Scheme, which cancels Part 1 dated 24.7.1918.

2.   Combined special map T.S.206 will be sent to Field Companies later.

3.   Following amendments should be made to Appendix F (Part II) dated 24.7.1918.

Cancel paras 1, 2 and 3.

27.7.1918.

Capt. Adjutant,
For C.R.E. 61st. Divn.

SECRET.   Defence Scheme, 61st. Div H.Q.

Ref Maps 36a & 27.- T.S. 823   APPENDIX F. (Part 1)
D.22.7.18 . T.S. 818 D.23.6.18.
Combined special T.S. 206.

1. The XV Corps holds the HAZEBROUCK front with three Divisions
   in line. Each Division has two Brigades in line and one
   Brigade in Corps Reserve. Each Brigade in line has one
   Battalion in Reserve for counter attack.

2. Divisional sectors are held as follows:-

       LA MOTTE SECTOR.   61st. Division.
       STRAZEELE SECTOR.   1st. Australian Division.
       METEREN SECTOR.   9th. (Scottish) Division.

3. Defended localities are as follows:-

       LA MOTTE - R.26, PETIT SEC BOIS - R.9,- STRAZEELE -
       R.29, CROUTE OBIER - V.16, - MERRISDOEM - X.6, - LA BRARDE
       X.9, LES QUATRE FILS AYMON - X.4, FONTAINE HOUCK - X.2.

4. Defensive lines run as follows, and Divisional boundaries
   are shown on special combined map T.S. 206.
       The HHH Line is the Line of Resistance.
       The Forward Zone comprises all defences East of the HHH
         Line exclusive.
       The Second Zone comprises all Defences West of the HHH
         Line inclusive.

5. The 61st. Division forms part of XV Corps, Second Army,
   and is temporarily held in G.H.Q. Reserve.

6. In the event of attack on XV Corps Front the 61st. Division
   is prepared to
       (a) Assemble in the area STAPLE U.9 - RONDEGHEM V.2.-
           WALLON CAPPEL U.26. (Assembly positions are shown in
           map T.S. 823)
       (b) Occupy the Army Line from LA KREULE (inclusive) V.16.b
           to about R.31.c.8.8. (40th. Division now in Reserve
           is prepared to occupy the Army line on our right.
       (c) Operate on any portion of the XV Corps Front

7. The Division is to be prepared to move at 2 4 hours notice
   by night (7 p.m. to 4 a.m.) and 6 hours by day (4 a.m. to
   7 p.m.). Zero for this move is calculated from the time the
   code word "PERCY" is sent out from D.H.Q.   Non-fighting
   transport East of the CANAL DE HAUT PONTE is to move West
   of the canal, - the move commencing at ZERO plus 4 hours.

8. The fighting portion of each Field Company consists of
   Company H.Q., sappers, cyclists, and section transport.
       The non-fighting portion of each Field Company comprises

Defence Scheme. 61st. Div R.E
APPENDIX F (part 1)
Contd.

the second in command, bridging vehicles, (unless special orders are issued to the contrary). - remainder of H.Q. transport, C.Q.M.S. and runners.

9. The Field Company at HIGH BOUT CASTER O.8.d.7.7. (at present 476 Field Co) with its fighting transport will be prepared to move at 2 hours notice by night (7 p.m. to 4 a.m.) and 4 hours notice by day (4 a.m. to 7 p.m.)   The fighting portion will move as soon as possible, (irrespective of ZERO hour) after receipt of orders, to the vicinity of STAPLE (not in the village) by the nearest route and get into touch with the 1/5 D.C.L.I. now at camp at U.3.b.7.7. and await further orders from C.R.E.
    The non-fighting portion will move at ZERO plus 4 hours to BARDRINGHEM and join the other Field Companies. Completion of moves will be reported to C.R.E. (If by wire, the code "MOVE COMPLETE" will be used). Routes will be reconnoitred at once.

10. Field Companies at BARDRINGHEM will be prepared to move at 4 hours notice by night (7 p.m. to 4 a.m.) and 6 hours by day (4 a.m. to 7 p.m.) and once this notice expires they will be ready to move at short notice on receipt of orders.

11. All non-fighting transport which has been separated from its Company Headquarters will be grouped together and will come under the command of the senior R.E. officer present. It will be this officer's duty to keep in close touch with "Q" branch at Rear D.H.Q.

12. At ZERO, R.E. Headquarters will move to Advance D.H.Q. at U.10.c.8.7.- EBBLINGHEM Chateau.

13. Rear R.E. Headquarters will be i/c Sergt. PEATHERSTONE. The Medical Officer will remain at rear R.E.H.Q until further orders.

14. Road spaces for Field Companies on the march are as follows:-

Complete Company (transport grouped)

    500 yards - Dismounted portion - 100 yards - Section transport - 25 yards - Headquarter transport - 25 yards cyclists - 500 yards.

Page 2.   (27.9.1918)

Defence Scheme. 61st. Div R.?

APPENDIX F (Part 1)
contd.

Fighting portion only. (Transport grouped)

500 yards - Dismounted portion - 100 yards - section transport - 25 yards - cyclists - 500 yards.

Fighting portion only (Transport with sections)

500 yards - Headquarters & No.1. section - 25 yards - No. 2. Section - 25 yards - No. 3. Section - 25 yards - No. 4. Section - 500 yards.

Non Fighting portions grouped.

500 yards in front and behind and 25 yards between each group of 6 vehicles or equivalent.

13. A.S.C. will deliver rations at C.Q.M.S. stores where bulk will be broken,- the supply wagons will then take rations forward for fighting portions under Field Company guides.

Distribution.

476 Field Co.
478 Field Co.
479 Field Co.
61 Div G.
61 Div Q.
C.E. XV Corps.
War Diary.

(page 3)   (27.7.1918)

SECRET.   Defence Scheme 61st.Div.R.E.

Ref. maps 27 & 36a.   APPENDIX F (Part II).

(1) All transport (unless orders to the contrary are received) will move with Field Companies.

(2) Any transport ordered to be kept back in rear will be accompanied by an officer from each Field Co. concerned.

(3) All "rear" R.E. transport will be grouped together and the senior officer present will assume command and will keep in close touch with "Q" branch at rear D.H.Q.

(4) The XV Corps main ammunition dump is at U.20.central (sht.27) EBBLINGHEM.

(5) Railhead is at WARDRECQUES where it is to remain.

(6) R.E. dumps are located as follows :-
    XV Corps R.E. Park .. .. FORT ROUGE, T.20.a.2.7.
    R.E. Stores Officer XV Corps.. FORT ROUGE.
    H.A. R.E. dump .. .. T.21.c.8.9.
    Right Division R.E. dump .. .. V.21.b.5.5.
    Centre Division R.E. dump.. .. D.8.d.5.6.
    Left Division R.E. dump. .. .. V.10.b.central.
    Camouflage Officer. .. .. FORT ROUGE, T.20.a.2.7.

(7) Water points in XV Corps area are located as follows :-
    HEURINGHEM   -   LYNDE   B.6.d.5.8.
    WARDRECQUES   A.12.a.4.5.   BLARINGHEM   B.23.b.1.4.
    RACQUINGHEM   B.13.a.9.3.   BORRE BSQUE W. U.17.a.2.3.
    PONT ASQUIN   B.8.a.8.8.   WALLON CAPPEL   U.28.b.8.8.
    RENESCURE   T.30.d.8.8.   Serous   C.11.a.7.5.
    EBBLINGHEM   U.19.c.4.9.   BORRE BSQUE Cent. V.12.b.5.9.
    GUDEWELL   D.2.a.1.1.   BORRE BSQUE E. V.4.c.3.0.
    GASTRE MILL   Q.33.d.4.0.

(8) It is the duty of every officer to prevent traffic blocks on roads and keep traffic moving. He should turn any broken down vehicle off the road. O.s.i/c.of troops or transport are authorised to turn civilian transport off any road if it is interfering with military movement. The civilian vehicles may be turned into the nearest field.

(9) In the event of evacuation of the civilian population, the following main routes are to be kept clear of civilian traffic :
    (a) BLARINGHEM - SEROUS - ECK HOUT CASTRE -
        LA CUNEMELLE - HAZEBROUCK.

Defence Scheme 61st.Div.R.E.

APPENDIX F. (Part II ctd.)

    (b) REMESCURE - EBBLINGHEM - HAZEBROUCK.

    (c) EBBLINGHEM - U.7.central - LONGUE CROIX - LA BREARD - LE PEUPLIER.

    (d) WALLON CAPPELL - BOIS DES NUIT HUNS - MORBECQUE.

Civilians are to be evacuated by rail from PONT ASQUIN B.8.b. (Sheet 36a.)

(10) In the event of active operations on XV Corps front, the following medical arrangements come into force:-

    Sick and wounded will be evacuated through the A.D.S. & M.D.S. of their Divisions, which are situated as follows :-

	A.D.S.	M.D.S.	Position of remaining Fd.Ambce
1st.Aust.Div.	BORRE.	V.9.b.1.5.	U.5.a.9.5.
9th. Division	CAESTRE V.2.b.3.6.	V.4.c.8.6.	STAPLE.
31st.Division	D.16.a.4.2. D.9.d.0.6.	C.5.a.5.9.	T.18.c.9.9.
40th.Div.N.Sector	V.1.d.9.5.	T.16.d.2.7.	T.22.a.3.4.
" C.Sector	V.20.b.9.4.	B.18.c.0.0.	
" S.Sector	C.14.a.1.0.		

Corps walking wounded collecting Station - U.19.a.5.0.

Motor Amb. Convoy B.14.c.9.2. HACQUINGHEM.

Adv. Post of M.A.C. T.22.a.3.4.

(11) It is important that tents and shelters should be salved if possible. Any in the forward camps should be struck and collected in good time and placed on a lorry route where they can be picked up.

Distribution:
475 Field Co.
476 Field Co.
479 Field Co.
61st.Div. "G".
61st.Div. "Q".
C.E. XV Corps.
War Diary (2).

Vol 28

Confidential

WAR DIARY

OF

H.Q. 61st Divn. RE

FOR THE MONTH OF

AUGUST 1918.

Vol XXVIII

Army Form C. 2118.

WAR DIARY
or
INTELLIGENCE SUMMARY

Headquarters 61st. Divn. Royal Engineers.

Vol. XXVIII.   Page 1.

Place	Date	Hour	Summary of Events and Information	Remarks and references to Appendices
HAM. M.5.c.7.3	AUGUST 1918. FRANCE. Sht. 36a. 1/40000.			
	1st		R.E. Headquarters moved from WARDRECQUES to HAMM transferring from XV to XI Corps. Nominal Roll of Unit. Received 61st. Division Defence Instructions.	Appx 4
			Issued Notes on Conference held today.	Appx 3
			Issued Appendix F to 61 Div R.E. Defence Scheme	Appx 5
	2nd		Issued Routine Orders 110 - 114 re Training and Parades C.R.E. attended conference at XI Corps Headquarters.	Appx 1
	3rd.		Issued Routine Order 115 re Church Parade Divisional R.E. Parade cancelled owing to rain.	Appx 1
	4th.	2.25am	Received 61 Div. Order 182 re relief of 5th. Division by 61st. Division.	
		9.15am	Issued Warning Order to Field Companies re relief of 5th. Division by 61st. Division on 6th/7th. August.	Appx 2
		6.15pm	Issued R.E. Order 108 re move of 479 Field Company from HAM to billets of 491 Field Company (5th. Division) in THIENNES	Appx 2
			Issued Notes re relief of 5th. Divisional R.E.	Appx 2
		7.10pm	Received 61st. Divisional Order 183 giving details of relief of 5th. Division by troops of 61st. Division.	
			Received A.D.M.S. Order 65 re relief of Division. Box car reported to us from 61st. M.T. Co for attachment. C.R.E. and Adjutant visited C.R.E. 5th. Division, taking over an advance party from 478 Field Company.	

WAR DIARY
INTELLIGENCE SUMMARY

(Erase heading not required.)

Army Form C. 2118.

HEADQUARTERS
61st. DIVN. ROYAL ENGINEERS.

Vol XXVIII   Page 2

AUGUST. 1918.

Place	Date	Hour	Summary of Events and Information	Remarks and references to Appendices
HAM. M.5.c.7.3.	5th		Issued R.E. Order 109 re relief of 5th. Divisional R.E. Received 184 Brigade Order 200 re relief by 61st. Division. Received 5th. Divisional R.E. Order 29 re relief Received 183 Brigade Order 229 re relief C.R.E. went round line with C.R.E. 5th. Division. Adjutant went round dumps in 5th. Division area. Lieut. SIMMONS commenced taking over duties from Roads Officer 5th. Division.	Appx 2
	6th.		Issued Routine Order 116 re Acting Rank of Major HUMPHREYS & CAPT ROBINSON. Issued Routine Order 117 re Losses of Animals Issued Order for move of R.E. Headquarters tomorrow C.R.E. attended conference at 5th. D.H.Q re proposed offensive to take place on the 12th.	Appx 1 Appx 1 Appx 2
I.20.a.5.7.	7th.	10am. 11am.	Relieved R.E. Headquarters 5th. Division. Received 61 Div Order 184:- 183 Brigade will relieve 182 Brigade on 8/9th. but this was subsequently cancelled.	
		2.30pm	Received 61 Div Order 185:- Enemy withdrawing.- Brigade to keep touch.	
		6.50pm	Issued R.E. Order 110:- Re probability of enemy withdrawal on our front and two sections of 478 Field Co to move forward for reconnaissance work. During the day reports were received that the enemy was withdrawing in front of the 74th. Division on our right and conference was held at 61 D.H.Q at 2 p.m. where Brigades were instructed to push patrols forward at 7 p.m.- 2 sections 478 Field Co to be attached to 183 Brigade, who would act as Advance Guard.	Appx 2

Army Form C. 2118.

WAR DIARY
or
INTELLIGENCE SUMMARY.

HEADQUARTERS.
61st. DIVN. ROYAL ENGINEERS
Vol. XXVIII.
Page 3.

AUGUST. 1918.

Place	Date	Hour	Summary of Events and Information	Remarks and references to Appendices
I.20.a.5.7.			FRANCE. Sht. 36a. 1/40000.	
	7th.	11.45 a.m.	Received 61 Div Situation Report:- 9.40 a.m. Line held CANAL BANK due N. to FLAGON Farm - K.27.d.9.9. - LOXTON House.	
	8th	12.40 p.m.	Received 61 Div G.311. 183 Bde to cross enemy front line at 4 a.m. tomorrow.	
		1.10.	Received 61 Div G.321. 183 Bde to gain touch with 74 Div on right and petrols to form bridgehead N. of River BOURRE	
		1.15	Major WHITWILL (478 Field Co) advised that reconnoitring parties for roads had been sent out and pontoons may possibly be required tonight to bridge the LYS CANAL. Advised Capt. Robinson at 478 Field Co transport lines re this.	
		5 pm	Major WHITWILL sent report of reconnaissance of Roads CORBIE-LE SART, GLOSTER Road - INFANTRY Rd from VIA ROMA to LE SART - latter road very poor. Advised all concerned.	
		5.30pm	Major WHITWILL reports CORBIE - LE SART Road cut by trench in two places, and that steel girder bridge at K.33.b.5.2. has been demolished. Advised all concerned.	
			G.R.E. attended conference at D.H.Q.	
			C.R.E. visited G.O.C. 183 Brigade and discussed the situation. Brigade has been unable to make much progress East of the BOURRE RIVER and PLATE BECQUE.	
		9.30pm	Major WHITWILL reports that footbridges exist on PLATE BECQUE at K.16.d.2.9. and K.16.b.2.2. Road bridge at K.16.d.05.80 is partly submerged, Footbridge exists on BOURRE RIVER at K.16.c.9.5. Footbridges being erected over PLATE BECQUE at K.11c.1.3. to assist infantry to attack at dusk. River BOURRE is about 15' to 28' wide, water 4' to 5' deep and banks are 6' above water level. Advised all concerned.	
	9th.	8.40 am	Major WHITWILL reports that road K.8.c.5.2. to Road bridge K.16.b.5.5. is good, debris requires clearing near ARREWAGE, - available for horse transport. Road under observation S. of ARREWAGE. No sign of any road mines. Reported to all concerned.	
		9.55	Received 61 Div G.337. Situation of Corps front unchanged. 184 Brigade to be prepared to move across PLATE BECQUE.	
		9.55	Received 184 Brigade Order 202 re inter-Battn relief.	
		2.35	Received 61 Div Order 186 re 183 Bde withdrawing into Div. Reserve.	
		5 pm	Issued R.E. Order 111 re 183 Brigade withdrawing into Div. Reserve.	
		5.15	Major WHITWILL reports he is moving back to THIENNES and Major HUMPHREYS (478) knows all about the work.	
			24' bridges being made at C.R.E's dump and a number of these were sent forward to MEREDITH Dump during the evening for Companies to get into assembly positions tonight.	Appx 2.

Army Form C. 2118.

WAR DIARY
or
INTELLIGENCE SUMMARY

(Erase heading not required.)

HEADQUARTERS.
61st. DIVN. ROYAL ENGINEERS.
Vol. XXVIII.   Page 4.

Instructions regarding War Diaries and Intelligence Summaries are contained in F.S. Regs., Part II. and the Staff Manual respectively. Title pages will be prepared in manuscript.

Place	Date	Hour	Summary of Events and Information	Remarks and references to Appendices
FRANCE. Sht. 36a. 1/40000.	AUGUST 1918.			
I.20.a.5.7	9th	9am.	Received C.E. XI Corps 14/78 - C.R.E. XI Corps Troops to put in bridge for lorries at J.36.c.9.5.	
		12.1pm	Received 61 Div Order 187 re operation by 182 and 184 Inf. Brigades	
	10th	7.15pm	Issued R.E. Order 112 re operation by 184 and 182 Brigades - 476 and 479 Field Co to construct and strengthen bridges over the BOURRE and PLATE BECQUE.	Appx 2
		7.35pm	Received 184 Brigade Order 204 re operation.	
		10pm	Received A.D.M.S. Order 66. re medical arrangements in connection with operation. C.R.E. and Adjutant visited HARSTONE Dump, 182 Bde. H.Q, 476 Field Co, 479 Field Co and CHAPEL BOOM - C.R.E. and O.C. 479 also explored CAUDESCURE and ARREWAGE reconnoitring roads.	
	11th.		This morning's attack made little progress and during the day we were pushed back to our original line. There was considerable difficulty in getting bridges across the River in front of us. On the left the infantry with Sapper assistance got three bridges over. On the right the infantry failed to get their bridges across and sappers of 479 Field Co went forward to assist, two being killed and one wounded. Informed by Division that the above operation is to be repeated. This was cancelled later.	
	12th	pm 6.10	Received 61st. Div. Order 188 re relief of 184 by 183 Brigade. Issued instructions to Field Coys re delay in train service and provision to be made to avoid it. Issued to Field Co Extracts from C.E. Conference held 8th. August. C.R.E. reconnoitred the old front line which is also the line of retention on the right, then up to present front line near our right boundary, then back via 184 Brigade, 479 Field Co. and 1/5 D.C.L.I. arranging to resume work on the Line of Retention.	Appx 3
	13th		C.R.E. reconnoitred the left half of our Line of Retention with G.S.O.1. OC DCLI & OC.479. Adjutant visited No.11. R.E. Park ESTREE BLANCHE and collected Lce.Cpl. E.G. ANGELL from XI Corps Rest Station.	

Army Form C. 2118.

WAR DIARY
or
INTELLIGENCE SUMMARY.

HEADQUARTERS. 61st. DIVN. ROYAL ENGINEERS. Vol. XXVIII.

Page 5.

(Erase heading not required.)

AUGUST. 1918.

Place	Date	Hour	Summary of Events and Information	Remarks and references to Appendices
I.20.a.5.7 FRANCE. Sht. 36a. 1/40000.	14th	a.m. 8.45 5.30	Received 183 Brigade Order 232 re relief of 184 Brigade Conference at 479 Field Co Headquarters. C.R.E. & G.S.O.1. reconnoitred right portion of Line of Retention. Capt. RENNIE rejoined R.E. HD. Qrs from 478 Field Co.	Appx 3
	15th		C.R.E. with O.C. M.G.Battn and O.C. 257 (T) Co R.E. reconnoitred for Machine Gun positions on the right of the Line of Retention.	
	16th.		Various proposals for building hutted camps in the Forest for winter accomodation discussed with D.H.Q.	
	17th.		C.R.E with officers of 478 Field Co reconnoitred the Forest in connection with proposed hutting scheme. Indications of further enemy withdrawal. Interpreter GUEUX went on leave.	
	18th.	6pm	Received advice from Division that enemy appears retiring on our front - 182 and 183 Bdes to establish close touch with 74th. Division on our right C.R.E. with D.A.Q.M.G and O.C. 478 Field Co visited proposed sites of camps in Forest. During the day some German posts were occupied and prisoners taken. At 10 p.m. it was reported that 183 Brigade crossed the PLATE BECQUE. During the evening a special train of foot bridges was sent up to MEREDITH Dump, the load includes some cork floats foot bridges which were recently salved near AIRE Bridging School.	
	19th.		Issued instructions for employment of D.C.L.I. (Pioneers) During the day progress was made on our front which reached the general line COBHAM - LOXTON House - Junct. of PLATE BECQUE - BRIDGE HOUSE - RENNET FARM. C.R.E. visited 479 Field Co & 182 Brigade and reconnoitred crossings of BOURRE & PLATE BECQUE and arranged bridging programme for tonight. 476 Field Co to get bridging material for these bridges into the River BOURRE tonight ready for floating into position	Appx 3

Army Form C. 2118.

WAR DIARY
or
INTELLIGENCE SUMMARY.

(Erase heading not required.)

HEADQUARTERS.
61st. DIVN. ROYAL ENGINEERS
Vol. XXVIII
Page 6

Place	Date	Hour	Summary of Events and Information	Remarks and references to Appendices
I.20.a.5.7	AUGUST 1918. FRANCE. Sht. 36a. 1/40000.			
	20	11.5am	Issued R.E.Order 116 instructing 478 Field Co to place two sections at disposal of 476 Field Co from 2 p.m. today.	Appx 2
		4.5pm	Issued R.E. Order No. 114 instructing 478 Field Co to attach two sections to 183 Brigade who are acting as Advance Guard to the Division, and two sections at disposal of 476 Field Co to revert to command of 478 Field Co.	Appx 2
		6 pm.	Received 61 Div. Div. Order 189. Advance Guard (183 Brigade) to push forward maintaining touch with 74 Division on the right.	Appx A
		9.30pm	Received 184 Brigade Order re operation of Advance Guard During the day further progress was made on our front, 182 Brigade reaching the outskirts of MERVILLE and in touch with 74th. Division on the right. Field Companies and Pioneers engaged principally on bridges and roads. - C.R.E. reconnoitred roads towards MERVILLE and forward area generally. MERVILLE fell into our hands during the day. Reconnaissance of bridges over the River BOURRE.	Appx 3
	21st	7.50pm	Received 61 Div Order 190 - 184 Brigade to take over and be responsible for Main Line of Retention. Transport Line of 476 and 478 Field Companies to move forward. Advised all concerned that footbridges have been completed at K.29.c.7.0 - K.29.c.7.1.- K.29.c.6.2. Sent A.D.M.S. and 61 Div Q. Reconnaissance of Wells. Advised G, Q, Brigades & Field Coys of cellar accomodation still remaining in MERVILLE. C.R.E. reconnoitred forward area and arranged work for tomorrow. Ordered to return Box Car to its unit as a result of a G.R.O. stating that these box cars are not to be permanently detailed. C.E. reports bridge capable of taking 3 ton lirries has been constructed by Corps R.E at J.36.c.9.5.	Appx 2. Appx 3

Army Form C. 2118.

WAR DIARY
or
INTELLIGENCE SUMMARY. HEADQUARTERS 61st. DIVN. ROYAL ENGINEERS.

Vol. XXVIII.

(Erase heading not required.)

Page 7.

Instructions regarding War Diaries and Intelligence Summaries are contained in F.S. Regs., Part II. and the Staff Manual respectively. Title pages will be prepared in manuscript.

Place	Date	Hour	Summary of Events and Information	Remarks and references to Appendices
FRANCE. Sht. 36a. 1/40000. I.20.a.5.7.	22nd		Sent all concerned reconnaissance report of LYS CANAL, E. of MERVILLE. Width of Canal at water level 12'. Height of banks above water level 10'. Width between banks 75'. Towing path along S. bank impassable owing to fallen trees and damage by shell fire. Sent A.D.M.S. and 61 Div Q Report on reconnaissance of wells in working order C.R.E. and G.O.C. Division visited MERVILLE and reconnoitred the BOURRE River to decide whether a new Line of Retention could be sited here with advantage. Field Companies to use any spare labour on erecting shelters on the Eastern edge of the Forest. We took NEUF BERQUIN this morning, but the 31st. Division on our left has not yet come up to the line.	Appx 3
	23rd.	10.15am.	Received 61 Div. Order 191 re operation by 40 Division (who relieved 31 Div) on our left,- Our Advance Guard to co-operate. Sent A.D.M.S. and 61 Div Q. reconnaissance of well out of repair in forward area	Appx 3
		7.10pm	Received 61 Div Order 192 re relief of 183 Brigade by 184 Brigade.	
		7.25pm	Received instructions from Division to move Field Coys and Pioneer Battalion	
		11 pm	Issued R.E. Order 116.- 479 Field Co to relieve the two sections of 478 Field Co with the Advance Guard.	Appx 2
		11.30pm	Issued R.E. Order 117 - Re moves of Field Coys and Pioneers. Asked by Corps to improve the MEREDITH - MERVILLE Road so that heavy artillery can be got forward. Adjutant visited the road during the day and, with the exception of two shell holes which motor lorries can get past the road is open for two way traffic. Q. states that the Corps wishes us to repair the damage done to houses in HAVERSKERQUE and LE PARC, but pointed out that we had no men available for this sort of work, but were prepared to give troops sufficient material to make billets temporarily habitable.	Appx 2

Army Form C. 2118.

WAR DIARY
or
INTELLIGENCE SUMMARY
(Erase heading not required.)

HEADQUARTERS
61st. DIVN. ROYAL ENGINEERS.

Instructions regarding War Diaries and Intelligence Summaries are contained in F. S. Regs., Part II. and the Staff Manual respectively. Title pages will be prepared in manuscript.

AUGUST. 1918.

Page 8.

Place	Date	Hour	Summary of Events and Information	Remarks and references to Appendices
FRANCE. Sht. 36a. 1/40000.				
I.20.a.5.7.	24th	7.15pm	Received 183 Bde. Order 238 re relief by 184 Brigade. Received 184 Bde. Order 209 re relief of 183 Brigade C.R.E. visited forward area going over roads with O.C. 479 Field Co and arranging for bridges to be built across the BOURRE and PLATE BECQUE which will be built tomorrow for artillery in preparation of expected advance.	Appx 3
	25th	9 pm.	Issued instructions re work of D.C.L.I. (Pioneers) Received 61st. Div Order 193 re relief of Artillery covering Division front C.R.E. and Adjutant visited Portuguese Brigade, part of which is to be employed by 478 Field Co on the Line of Resistance - arranged for construction of bridge across river at N.W. end of MERVILLE, then to D.C.L.I. to arrange for repair of roads.	Appx 1
	26th	6.50pm	Received 61 Div Order 194 re operation tomorrow by our Advance Guard in conjunction with 40th. Division on our left. Issued Routine Order 118 and 119 re award of M.M. to 2nd. Cpl. NODDER, 479 Field Co. C.R.E. visited PURESBECQUE, MERVILLE College and all Field Companies, arranging all details for work. Adjutant went to CROIX MARRAISSE and arranged for repair of buildings for Advance D.H.Q.	
	27th.		C.R.E. and Adjutant visited Line of Resistance and forward area C.R.E. attended Q Conference on "Winter accomodation".	
	28th.		Wrote Div Q deprecating the use of canal as means of conveying R.E. stores, pointing out that it was of more value as a drain for forward area. Received letter of congratulation from Divisional Commander on work of R.E. C.R.E. inspected roads in forward area and visited Field Companies and D.C.L.I. (Pioneers)	Appx 3 Appx 6

Army Form C. 2118.

Page 9

WAR DIARY
or
INTELLIGENCE SUMMARY.   HEADQUARTERS. 61st. DIVN. ROYAL ENGINEERS.

(Erase heading not required.)   Vol. XXVIII.

Instructions regarding War Diaries and Intelligence Summaries are contained in F.S. Regs., Part II. and the Staff Manual respectively. Title pages will be prepared in manuscript.

Place	Date	Hour	Summary of Events and Information	Remarks and references to Appendices
I.20.a.5.7.	AUGUST 1918 FRANCE. Sht. 36a. 1/40000.			
	29th.	6.50pm	Received 61 Div Div Order 196 re extension of front.	
		11.40pm	Received 184 Bde. Order 214 re extension of front C.R.E. visited Field Companies working on billet repairs then on to Line of Resistance to arrange for 257 Tunnelling Co to re-commence concrete construction.	
	30th		Advised all concerned of move of R.E.H.Q tomorrow to CROIX MARRAISSE Issued H.Q. Routine Order 35- all ranks to be properly dressed when outside billet.	Appx 2 Appx 1
		12.20pm	Received 61 Div Div Order 195 - 182 Bde to relieve 183 Bde 1/2nd. Sept.	
		6.20pm	Received 61 Div Div Order 197 amending Divisional Order 195	
		11.59pm	Instructed 479 Field Co to erect bridges across LYS CANAL commencing on daylight tomorrow C.R.E and O.C. 1/5 D.C.L.I. reconnoitred forward roads as far as our front line at Rue MONTIGNY then visited Companies and arranged that O.C. Field Company would be attached to Advance Guard and would have one Pioneer Company under his orders for work on forward roads.	Appx 3
CROIX MARRAISSE. J.21.c.5.3.	31st	1 am	Received 61 Div Div Order 198. Advance Guard Brigade to push forward with utmost vigour	
		6.30am	Received 184 Bde. Order 215 - patrols to push forward Issued Instructions to Field Coys and Pioneers re organization of and opening up of communications.	Appx 3 Appx 3
			advised G, O.E XI Corps, that bridges have been erected over LYS CANAL.	
		11 am	Received 183 Bde. Order re relief 182 Bde on 1st. Sept.	
		10 a.m.	R.E. Headquarters moved with G. to CROIX MARRAISSE. C.R.E. and adjutant visited MERVILLE and forward area - 59th. Div. R.E constructing a foot bridge across the canal at BEAUPRE. Visited Companies on return. Out patrols reached LA GORGUE during the day. S.O.R.E. XI Corps called and explained the Corps roads policy	

Signature

Capt. Adjutant.
For C.R.E. 61st. Divn.

August 31st. 1918.

War Diary
ORIGINAL.
AUG T. 1918.
C.R.E. 61ST DIVN.

APPENDIX 1

ROUTINE ORDERS BY C.R.E.

ROUTINE ORDERS

Issued by:- Lieut-Colonel G.E.J. BURNFORD, D.S.O.
Commanding:- 61st. (South Midland) Divisional Royal Engineers

R.E.H.Q. 2nd. August 1918

---

110. **SALUTING.** A.O. 211 of 1918 is repeated for information and compliance.

    A.O. 211. SALUTING. The left hand salute by warrant officers, non-commissioned officers and men is abolished.
    The salute will be given by all ranks with the right hand. When saluting to the side, the head will be turned towards the person saluted.
    In cases where from physical incapacity a right-hand salute is impossible, the salute will be given with the left hand.
    The necessary amendments to the various Regulations and Training Manuals will be issued shortly.

111. **SANITATION.** Sanitary Areas in HAM are now as follows:-

    479 Field Co from Village Green (inclusive) westwards.
    478 Field Co from Village Green (exclusive) eastwards.

    R.E.R.O. 85 will be amended accordingly.

GUARDS.

    The guard at HAM is now being found by

    479 Field Co on August 2nd, 4th, 6th, and so on
    478 Field Co on August 3rd, 5th, 7th, and so on.

    R.E.R.O. 86 will be amended accordingly.

112. **HOURS OF TRAINING.**

    (a) R.E.R.O 96 is cancelled.

    (b) **Mondays, Tuesdays, Thursdays, Fridays**

        5.45 - 6.15 a.m.   Physical (after tea & biscuit)
        7.45 am to 1 p.m.   Company parade & training with half an hour break.

    (c) **Wednesdays & Saturdays.**

        7 - 7.30 a.m.   Physical (after tea and biscuit)
        9 a.m. to 1 p.m.   Company parade & training with half an hour break.

    (d) **Sundays.**

    Check parade and Company conservancy during the morning Church parade when ordered.

113. **HAM PARK.** The Northern entrance is to be used as little as possible by vehicles. Bridging vehicles will always use the BLESSY entrance.

(Cont'd)

114. PARADE.

(a) The Divisional R.E. will parade in HAM PARK at 10.30 a.m tomorrow the 3rd. inst. The parade will be followed by a practice General Inspection and March Past in Column of Route.

(b) DRESS.
Marching Order as for inspection
Steel helmets worn.
Breech covers off.
Officers valises not packed.

(c) STRENGTH.- as strong as possible.

(d) PARADE STATES.- as usual.

(e) One officer and one right hand marker per Company will meet the Adjutant on the parade ground at 10 a.m.

(b) Companies will march on to their markers at 10.15 a.m.

Notes. Companies will be dressed with ranks "open".
viz:-
Rear rank 3 paces behind front rank, supers 2 paces behind rear rank. Cyclists (not cycles) 1 pace behind supers.
Bayonets will not be fixed before the C.R.E takes the parade.

Supernumerary officers will parade with their Captains in rear of Companies.

On the Command "Take posts in review order" the Second in Command will trot out to one horses length in front of the right hand man of his Company., the supernumerary officer (if there is none there, the commander of No.4. Section) will take post at one horses length in front of the left hand man of his Company. - All officers, less the Company Commander will adjust their positions so as to be equally spaced along their Company front.

Saluting on the march is explained in diagram issued separately.

(Sd) M.E. FITZGERALD.
Capt. Adjutant.

FIELD COY. R.E. SALUTING
(to the right)
ON THE MARCH.

Command			Given by
NIL.		CQMS - Sergt. Capt. Super^y officer	Salute independently.
"___ Field Coy will eyes right".		O.C.	O.C. as warning order only.
"No. 1. Dismounted Section Eyes Right"		No.1.Sect. cyclists. No.1.Sect sappers	Dismounted N.C.O. of No. 1. Section.
"No. 1. Mounted Section Eyes Right".		No.1. Sect Transport.	Mounted N.C.O. of No.1. Section. (The section officer salutes independently.
Nos. 2, 3 and 4 sections - same as No. 1.			
"Headquarter details - Eyes Right"		H.Q. Dismtd C.S.M. Spare drivers & horses	C.S.M.
"No.1. Wagon Section - Eyes Right"		Water cart Cooks cart	Lead driver of water cart.
"No 2. Wagon section - Eyes right"		No.1 Pontoon No.2.Pontoon	Lead driver of No.1. Pontoon.
"No.3. Wagon section - Eyes right".		Trestle wgn' G.S.	Lead driver of trestle wagon
"No.4. Wagon section - Eyes right"		Surplus Transport.	Lead driver of leading vehicle.
NIL.		CQMS - Sergt., Capt. Super^y officer	Salute independently.

Notes. The Command "Eyes Right" is given when the leading man of the party or section concerned is 10 yards short of the officer taking the salute.

The command "Eyes Front" is given when the rear of the party or section is 10 yards past the officer taking the salute. The same N.C.O or man gives the order as in Col. 3. The command is the same as in col. 1. but substituting "Eyes front" for "Eyes Right"

All officers, C.S.M. and Mounted Sergeant salute independently commencing at 10 yards from the officer taking the salute and finishing at 10 yards beyond him.

A Field Company marching "Transport Brigaded" is sub-divided in the same way for saluting purposes, the only changes to be noted are as follows:-

(a) The C.S.M is with the dismounted portion of H.Q in rear of the 4 dismounted sections and gives the order "Headquarters - Eyes Right" etc.

(b) The leading man of H.Q. transport gives the order "Head quarter details - Eyes Right" and this is obeyed by 4 pack animal leaders in front of him.

ROUTINE ORDERS,
issued by
Lieut.-Colonel G.E.J.BURNFORD, D.S.O., R.E.
Commanding:- 61st. Divisional ROYAL ENGINEERS.

R.E.H.Q. 3rd.Aug.1918.

---

115. CHURCH SERVICE.

A Special "Anniversary of the War" Service is being held in the Church at BLESSY at 11 a.m. tomorrow, SUNDAY, 4th. inst. to which all British Troops are invited and for whom special seats are being reserved. The service will be in French and Latin, as usual.

Facilities will be given by Os.C. Companies to all Roman Catholics to attend.

(Signed) M.E.FITZGERALD,
Capt.,
Adjutant.

Lieut.-Colonel G.E.J. DURNFORD, D.S.O., R.E.
Commanding:- 61st.(South Midland) Divisional ROYAL ENGINEERS.

R.E.H.Q. 6th. August 1918.

116. ACTING RANK.
The following extracts from List No.198 dated 28.7.18, Appointments, Commissions, etc. approved by the Field Marshal Commanding-in-Chief, are published for information:-

To be Acting Major whilst Commanding a Field Co.:
Lieut.(A/Capt.)H. HUMPHREYS, 479 Field Co. 2nd. July 1918.

To be Acting Capt. whilst employed as 2nd.-in-Command Field Co.
Lieut. E.C. ROBINSON, 479 Field Co. 2nd. July 1918.

(Auth: 61st. Div. No.A.26 dated 5.8.18).

- -

(Signed) M.E. FITZGERALD,
Capt.,
Adjutant.

ROUTINE ORDERS,
by
Lieut.-Colonel G.E.J.DURNFORD, D.S.O., R.E.
Commanding:- 61st.(South Midland)Divisional ROYAL ENGINEERS.

R.E.H.Q. 6th.August 1918.

117. LOSSES OF ANIMALS.

The following Extract from Fifth Army Routine Order No.3098 "Remounts" is re-published for information.

"All losses of animals are to be reported immediately by Os.C. Units concerned to the Headquarters of the Formations in which they are serving, who will ensure that the loss is published in Divisional, Corps, or Army Routine Orders, and that the A.P.M. is informed of the loss.

A full description and particulars of the loss will be given by the O.C. Unit when reporting it.

Should the animal not be recovered within 24 hours, a Court of Enquiry must be held in accordance with King's Regulations, para. 668, and proceedings forwarded to Army Headquarters.

The following information must always be given:-
 1. The date the loss was published in Routine Orders.
 2. When the A.P.M. was informed of the loss.
 3. Full description of the lost animal, and state whether Rdg., L.D., H.D., mule or pack.
 4. The approximate value of the animal.

With reference to 4. the following copy of a recent price list, received from the War Office, shows the average cost of each class of animal landed in France, and is published for guidance:-

Horses	£		Mules	£
Heavy Draught	96	Heavy Draught	87
Artillery	90	Light Draught	79
Cavalry	85	Pack	69
Cobs	81		

(Signed) M.E.FITZGERALD,
Capt.,
Adjutant.

ROUTINE ORDERS
by
Lieut.-Colonel G.E.J. DURNFORD, D.S.O., R.E.
Commanding:- 61st.(South Midland)Divisional ROYAL ENGINEERS.

R.E.H.Q. 26th.Aug.1918.

118. HONOURS AND AWARDS.
The following award for gallantry and devotion to duty has been made:-

THE MILITARY MEDAL.
494967 2nd.Cpl. H. HODDER, 479 (S.M.)Field Co.R.E.

119. PHOTOGRAPHY.
G.H.Q. No.4775 dated 15.8.18 is re-published for information.

"No Officer, soldier or other person subject to Military Law is permitted to be in possession of a camera or to take photographs unless he has been issued with the necessary permit signed by the Adjutant General. Such permits are only granted in very exceptional cases.

"This order will be promulgated to all troops arriving in this country, and will be republished periodically in the orders of Units.

"Any officer or soldier or other person subject to Military Law who disobeys this order will be placed in arrest and the case will be reported to the Headquarters of the Army or Lines of Communication Area.

"G.H.Q. 3065 is cancelled."

(Sd.) M.E.FITZGERALD, Capt.
Adjutant.

ROUTINE ORDERS.

HEADQUARTERS, 61st. DIVISIONAL R.E.

30th. Aug. 1918.

35. DISCIPLINE.
All ranks, when outside their billet, in villages or walking on the roads, must be properly dressed and wear belts.

(Signed) M.E. FITZGERALD,
Capt.,
Adjutant.

War Diary
ORIGINAL.
AUGT 1918.
C.R.E. 61ST DIVN.

APPENDIX 2

MOVE & RELIEF ORDERS BY C.R.E.

"A" Form
MESSAGES AND SIGNALS.

Army Form C. 2121
(In pads of 100)

No. of Message..............

Prefix...... Code......m	Words.	Charge.	This message is on a/c of:	Recd. at.........m
Office of Origin and Service Instructions	Sent			Date............
Secret	At.........m		............Service.	From............
	To..........			
	By........		(Signature of "Franking Officer.")	By..........

TO

476			
478			
479			

Sender's Number.	Day of Month.	In reply to Number.	AAA
* Two	4		
The	61	Divn	as
thing	5	Divn	on
left	sector	of	XI
Corps	are	Infantry	ants
now	today	are	Relief
will	be	on	6th
not	night	of	6/7th
are	Field	Cos power	will
probably	move	on	6th

From: CRE
Place:
Time: 9.15 am

The above may be forwarded as now corrected. (Z)

............Censor............ Signature of Addressee or person authorised to telegraph in his name.
* This line should be erased if not required.

(4715) Wt. W3253/P511 1,113,336 Shts. 2/18 C. & Co. (.864)

SECRET.   Copy No. 9.

Ref. Map
FRANCE.   R.E. Order 159.
sht. 36a.

1.   479 (S.M) Field Co will march from HAM (M.S)
     to present billets of 491 (Home Counties) Field Co
     tomorrow the 5th. inst.

          Company H.Q.   in the Square   THIENNES
          Transport Lines   I.22.c.9.4.

2.   Starting time:-   6.30 a.m.

3.   Route:-   AIRE - NEUFPRE - PECQUEUR.

4.   Intervals on the march:-

     300 yards between Units.
     100 yards between dismounted and transport.
     25 yards between section vehicles & H.Q. transport.
     25 yards between Transport and cyclists.

5.   476 Field Coy is moving into the above accomodation
     on the 6th. inst. and has already sent advance parties.
     479 Field Coy moves forward on the 6th. inst.

6.   Further orders will be issued for moves which are
     to take place on the 6th. inst.

7.   476 Field Co will detail an officer with a fatigue
     party to take over area stores at HAM from 479 Field Co.

8.   479 Field Co to ACKNOWLEDGE.

61st. R.E.H.Q.
Issued at 6.15 p.m.   Capt. Adjutant.
August 4th. 1918.   For C.R.E. 61st. Divn.

     Distribution.

     Copy No. 1.   476 Field Co.
             2.   476 Field Co.
             3.   479 Field Co.
             4.   61st. Div G.
             5.   61st. Div Q.
             6.   61st. Signal Co.
             7.   C.E. XI Corps
             8.   C.R.E. 5th. Div.
          9 & 10   War Diary.
            11.   File.

SECRET.   Copy No. 17

Ref. Map
FRANCE,
Sheet 36a.
1/40,000.

61st. DIVISIONAL R.E. ORDER No.109.

1. The 61st. Division is relieving the 5th.Division in the left Sector of the XI Corps front.

2. Moves of Field Companies will be carried out according to Table "A" (attached).

3. Completion of relief will be reported to both C.R.E. 5th.Division and C.R.E. 61st.Division.

4. R.E. Headquarters closes at HAM at 9 a.m. on the 7th.instant and opens at 1.20.a.d.5 at 10 a.m. the same day.

5. All Field Companies and detachments of the 61st. Divisional R.E. come under the orders of C.R.E. 5th. Division on arrival in the 5th.Divisional area and remain under his orders until 10 a.m. on the 7th.inst.

6. Field Companies to ACKNOWLEDGE.

61st.R.E.H.Q.
Issued at 9 p.m.   Capt. - Adjutant,
6th.August 1918.   for C.R.E. 61st.Div.

Distribution:

Copy No.1 - C.R.E.
" 2 - Adjutant.
" 3 - R.S.M.
" 4 - 475 Field Co.
" 5 - 478 Field Co.
" 6 - 479 Field Co.
" 7 - 61 Div. G.
" 8 - 61 Div. Q.
" 9 - 61st.Signal Co.
" 10 - 182 Inf. Bde.
" 11 - 183 Inf. Bde.
" 12 - 184 Inf. Bde.
" 13 - 1/5 D.C.L.I.
" 14 - C.E. XI Corps.
" 15 - C.R.E. 5th.Div.
" 16 - 257 (T) Co. R.E.
" 17 - War Diary.
" 18 - War Diary.
" 19 - File.

Copy No. 17

TABLE "A"
issued with
61st. DIVISONAL R.E. ORDER No. 109.

Serial No.	Date	Unit	From	To	Route	Relieving	Remarks
1.	Aug. 6th.	479 Field Co.	TRIENNES	H.Q. B.26.d.8.9. Transport Lines 1.4.b.2.5.	-	54? Field Co. R.E.	Affiliated to 184 Bde. in line LEFT Section. Route and time of march to be arranged between Field Co. Commanders concerned.
2.	Aug. 6th.	476 Field Co.	MARTRES	H.Q. J.16.c.3.6. Transport Lines J.25.c.9.5.	AIRE - RUFFEC - PROCHON - TRIENNES - SABLY.	59 Field Co. R.E.	Affiliated to 182 Bde. in Line Right Section. To pass Road Junction H.27.d.3.9 at 12 noon.
3.	Aug. 6th.	475 Field Co.	HAM	H.Q. TRIENNES. Transport Lines I.21.a.9.4.	AIRE - RUFFEC - PROCHON.	491 Field Co. (In Reserve).	To pass road Junction H.27.d.3.9 at 12.15 P.m.

Note: Usual intervals to be maintained on the march.

Capt. - Adjutant,
for O.R.E. 61st.Div.

S E C R E T.

476 Field Co.
478 Field Co.
479 Field Co.
1/5 D.C.L.I.

Ref. RELIEF of 5th. Div. by 61st. Div.
NOTES.

1. Right Bde. area. 59th. Field Co., H.Q. at J.16.c.3.6,
   Transport Lines at J.25.a.9.5 (relief 6th.inst. by 476)

   Left. Bde. area. 527th.(Durham) Field Co., H.Q. at D.26.d.2.9
   Transport Lines at I.4.b.2.5 (relief 6th.inst. by 479).

   Reserve R.E. Company. 491st. (Home Counties) Field Co., H.Q.
   at THIENNES SQUARE, Transport Lines at I.22.c.9.4 (relief
   by 478 - 491 moves out 5th., 478 moves in 6th., 479 uses
   billets night 5th./6th.)

2. 1/5 D.C.L.I. H.Q. and 2 Coys. at VISUADELLO Camp J.7.d.2.3.
   N.B. "Q" Company employed on Line of Resistance with 479th.
   Field Co. and 1 Company employed with 257 (T) Coy. R.E.
   and Foreways; one Company in Reserve at THIENNES.

3. No.3 Foreways Coy. I.23.d.3.2 operates the 20lb. lines.
   Field Companies in line will take over push lines serving their
   respective Brigade areas.

4. 257 Tunnelling Co. (H.Q. at H.28.c.7.3) - 2 Sections
   employed on Divisional front.

5. C.R.E. at D.H.Q. I.20.a.4.5.

6. 5th. Division has a traffic officer at "Q" Branch who
   arranges all Light Railway trains (not push trams).

7. C.R.E's dump is at HARTSTONE Station I.29.a.0.6. An
   advance party of R.S.M. and 6 Pioneers will commence taking
   over tomorrow 5th.

8. 5th. Division has a Roads Officer (from Pioneer Battalion)
   living at D.H.Q. He employs 75 men of 194 Labour Coy.
   living at I.6.a.2.3. Lieut. SIMMONS, M.C., R.E. will take
   over on the 5th. and 6th. pending the appointment of a Roads
   Officer for 61st. Division.

9. HAVERSKERQUE - LAMOTTE LINE. The Reserve Battn. of each
   Brigade in line provides a working party of two Companies to
   work on posts in this line; Field Companies in line provide
   for supervision.

10. ST.VENANT - BORRE Line. 200 men from 194 Labour Coy. are
    employed on this line in the left Section. The Field Co. in
    the left Section provides superintendence - at present done by
    C.S.M. of 527 Field Co.

11. **Advance parties.**

    (a) 476 Advance parties went forward today.

    (b) Box car leaving R.E.H.Q. at 9.30 a.m. 5th. to take C.R.E. and adjutant, O.C. & Second i/c. 1/5 D.C.L.I., O.C. 476 and O.C. 479 Field Coys.

    (c) Lorry at R.E.H.Q. at 8 a.m. 5th. to take :
            2 Officers & 8 o.r. of 476 Field Co.
            2 Officers & 8 o.r. of 479 Field Co.
            1 Officer & 2 N.C.Os. "C" Coy. D.C.L.I.

    Route for lorry AIRE - NIEUPPRE - PECQUEUR - THIENNES - TANNAY - CROIX MARRAISE - L'EPPINETTE-(change here for 476) - H.25.d.7.7 (change here for 479 accompanies by D.C.L.I. party).

    (d) Lorry at 1/5 D.C.L.I. H.Q. at 8 a.m. 5th. to take R.S.M. R.E., with 2 o.r. R.E., and 6 o.r. 1/5 D.C.L.I. (dump party) to THIENNES. Remaining accommodation at disposal of 1/5 D.C.L.I.

4th.Aug.1918.   Capt. - Adjutant,
                                            for C.R.E 61st.Divn.

SECRET.

ORDERS FOR MOVE OF
61st. Divl. R.E. HEADQUARTERS.

Ref. Map
Sheet FRANCE,
56a 1/40,000.

1. R.E.H.Q. will move from HAM (M.5) to the neighbourhood of PEQUEUR (I.20) tomorrow, 7th. instant.

2. On arrival, R.E.H.Q. will be located as follows :-

   (a) Office and clerks in Hut at I.20.a.4.4 at present occupied by C.R.E. 5th.Division.

   (b) Officers quarters in camp to be constructed in field at I.20.a.4.7.

   (c) Transport in quarters at present occupied by transport of C.R.E. 5th.Division about I.20.d.7.7.

   (d) Attached M.E. on canal bank at I.21.a.8.3.

3. Transport (including all horses) will move off at 7 a.m. and march via ST. QUENTIN - AIRE - BRUFFE - PEQUEUR and take over the billets and horselines at present occupied by transport of R.E.H.Q. 5th.Division. The Interpreter will meet transport on arrival at PEQUEUR.
   Horse lines at HAM will be cleaned up, and the tent, shed and all other stores not carried by transport will be moved to R.E.H.Q. by 6.30 a.m.
   Driver WATTS is in charge of transport.
   The medical cart with M.O's. horse and personnel will join 478 Field Co. at SHIRNESS during the day under the orders of the medical officer.

4. Interpreter CUEUX will join 478 Field Co. during the day.

5. The box car will leave HAM at 9 a.m. with C.R.E., Adjutant, M.O., L/Cpls. Skinner, Haycraft, and Mott.

Distn.
C.R.E
Adjt.
Lt. SIMMONS.
Sgt. F.
Dr. Watts
(para.3)

6. A lorry loaded under the instructions of Lieut. SIMMONS will leave HAM at 7.30 a.m. with Lieut. SIMMONS, Interpreter CUEUX, Sapper Bolland, 1 N.C.O. and 8 cyclists of 478 Field Co. and its load will include 2 armstrong huts, R.E. materials and all mess kit not required for breakfast. (Cycles which cannot be loaded will be ridden.

7. Sergt. FEATHERSTONE will be in charge of all details and loading of the lorry for the second journey.

8. All breakfasts to be finished by 8 a.m.

6.6.18.

Capt.,
Adjutant R.E.

SECRET.

23/2

478 Field Co.
Copy to 476 Field Co.
479 Field Co.

Reference R.E. Order 110.

Your parties carrying out Engineer Reconnaissance should endeavour to send back information on the following points.

CANALS & RIVERS.

LYS CANAL. Water level, position and type of any bridges, ferries, etc, East of MERVILLE.

River BOURRE. Position and type of any bridges E. of the swing bridge K.15.d.4.8. Width of stream and water level both East and West of its junction with the PLATE BECQUE.

River PLATE BECQUE. Position and type of any bridges from junction with River BOURRE to VIEUXBERQUIN. Width of stream and water level.

WATER SUPPLY. Position of any wells and type and state of lifting gear

ROADS. (including Road bridges)

(a) CORBIE - LE SART from "Bridge of Sighs" K.25.b.0.5. Eastwards.

(b) GLOSTER ROAD from "Via ROMA" to LE SART.

(c) LA MOTTE AU BOIS - MERVILLE from "Les LAURIERS" K.14.d.6.2. Eastwards.

(d) LES LAURIERS (K.15.c.5.1) - ITCHEN FARM - L'EPINETTE - VIEUXBERQUIN.

(e) CAUDESCURE - ARREWAGE - LES PUREBECQUES.

N.B. A sharp look out should be kept for any signs of mining.

Lieut-Colonel, R.E.
C.R.E. 61st Division.

August 7th. 1918.

SECRET   Copy No. 5

Ref. Map
Sht. 36a.
1/40000.   R.E. ORDER No. 110.

                                has withdrawn
1.   The enemy ~~is withdrawing~~ from his line
    in front of the Right of the XI Corps and it is
    probable that he will withdraw on the front of this
    Division.

2.   The Brigades in line have been instructed
    to keep in close touch with the enemy.

3.   In the event of Brigades in line establishing
    themselves on a general line about two or three hundred
    yards east of the present enemy front line and the
    PLATE BEEQUE, it is the intention to push forward the
    183 Brigade to act as advance guard to the Division.

4.   Two sections of 476 Field Co will move at
    once to SHETLAND Camp J.14.b.9.1. These sections
    will come under the orders of G.O.C. 183 Inf. Bde on
    arrival. O.C. 476 Field Co will personally keep
    in close touch with G.O.C. 183 Inf. Bde at STATION
    HOUSE about K.8.c.2.2.

5.   All information, which would affect
    Engineer work, should be sent to this office as quickly
    as possible.

6.   One section 476 Field Co will remain in
    reserve at Company Headquarters at J.16.c.3.6. and
    is at the disposal of O.C. 476 Field Co to be used
    by him only in case of emergency.

7.   476 Field Co to ACKNOWLEDGE.

                                        [signature]
Issued at 6.50 p.m.   Capt. Adjutant
61st. R.E.H.Q.   for C.R.E. 61st. Div
August 7th. 1918.

Distribution.

Copy No. 1.   476 Field Co.
        2.   476 Field Co.
        3.   479 Field Co.
        4.   War Diary
        5.   War Diary.

SECRET.   Copy No. 5.

R.E. ORDER No. 111.

Ref Map
Sht 36a
1/40000

1. 183 Inf. Brigade is withdrawing into Divisional Reserve tonight.

2. On completion of the relief Brigade boundaries are to be as follows:-

   182 Inf. Brigade   Right section
   184 Inf. Brigade   Left section.

   Inter-Brigade boundary,- BOURNE River ~~inclusive~~ (inclusive to 182nd Brigade) from present front posts to a point about K.15.a.3.2. thence to the present boundary at K.14.b.1.5.

3. Relief to be complete by daylight tomorrow 10th.

4. The two sections of 478 Field Co now employed in the forward area will withdraw to Company Headquarters tonight, all work in hand being handed over to 476 and 479 Field Companies.
   O.C. 476 Field Co will meet Major WHITWILL at STATION HOUSE at 6 p.m. tonight

5. ACKNOWLEDGE.

Issued at 61 R.E.H.Q
August 9th. 1916.
5. p.m.
                                                Capt. Adjutant.
                                             For C.R.E. 61st. Divn.

Distribution.

Copy No. 1.   476 Field Co.
        2.   476 Field Co.
        3.   479 Field Co.
        4.   War Diary
        5.   War Diary
        6.   File.

SECRET.

SECRET.   Copy No. 8

R.E. ORDER NO. 112.

Ref. Map
Sht 36a N.E.
1/20000

1. 184 Infantry Brigade has been ordered to cross
    the PLATE BECQUE and establish a bridgehead on the
    general line K.22.b.7.7. (LES PUREBECQUES inclus) -
    houses at K.17.a.6.6. (inclusive) - PLATE BECQUE
    at approx. K.11.c.7.8.

2. 182 Infantry Brigade is to conform to this advance
    and establish itself on the general line K.22.c.0.5. -
    K.22.b.7.7.

3. The operation is to take place tomorrow the 11th.
    inst.
    Zero hour:- 4.15 a.m.

4. Infantry will be using red flares in connection
    with contact planes.

5. 479 Field Co will strengthen the assault bridges
    placed across the PLATE BECQUE.

6. 476 Field Co will construct two foot bridges
    over the BOURRE south of the junction of BOURRE and
    PLATE BECQUE in order to provide lateral communication.

7. Field Company Commanders will not send bridging
    parties forward until they have obtained information
    from their respective Brigades that the situation
    permits.

8. During the above operation 184 Brigade Headquarters
    is to be at STATION INN at K.14.a.5.9.
    182 Brigade Headquarters remains in their present
    position.

9. 479 Field Company will issue from MEREDITH
    Dump, materials required by 476 Field Co.

10. 476 and 479 Field Cos to ACKNOWLEDGE.

Issued at 7.15 p.m.
61st. R.E. HQ. Qrs.   Capt. Adjutant.
August 10th. 1918.   For C.R.E. 61st. Div.

Distribution.

Copy No. 1.   476 Field Co.
        2.   479 Field Co.
        3.   61st. Div G.
        4.   182 Inf. Bde.
        5.   184 Inf. Bde.
        6.   C.E. XI Corps
      7 & 8 War Diary.
        9.   File.

SECRET.   Copy No. 7

R.E. ORDER No. 115.

Ref. Sht.
55a.
1/40000.

1. 478 Field Co will place two sections at the disposal of 476 Field Co.

2. One officer of 478 Field Co will report at Headquarters 476 Field Co at 1 p.m. today.

3. The two sections 478 Field Co with tool carts will report at LE CORBIE at 2 p.m. today.

4. 476 Field Co will arrange accomodation for these two sections from tonight onwards.

5. 478 Field Co to ACKNOWLEDGE.

Issued at 61 R.E.H.Q.
   11.5 a.m.
August 20th, 1918.

                                            Capt. Adjutant.
                                        For C.R.E. 61st. Divn.

Distribution.

Copy No. 1. 476 Field Co.
        2. 478 Field Co.
        3. 479 Field Co.
        4. 61 Div G.
        5. 61 Div Q.
       6&7 War Diary
        8   File.

SECRET.   Copy No. 9.

Ref. Map.
Sht. 36a N.E.   R.E. ORDER No. 114.
1/20000.

1.   The Division is about to advance with
103 Inf. Brigade leading.   The first objective
being a north and south line approximately L.32
L.26. L.14.

2.   476 Field Co will attach two sections to 183
Brigade.   These two sections should be got ready at
once for moving and O.C. 476 Field Company will get
into touch with O.C. 183 Brigade at once to arrange
details.

3.   The two sections of 478 Field Co at present
attached to 476 Field Co for work will revert to the
command of O.C. 478 Field Co forthwith and every effort
will be made by O.C. 478 Field Co to get the road
bridge reconstructed at K.29.a.3.0. (Note:- There are
30 to 40 pieces of 14" x 14" timber from 10 to 20 feet
long at the Saw Mill K.29.a.1.6)

4.   It is reported today that the road from
MEREDITH to K.28.b.7.9. and the road from LE CORNET
to PLUM FARM are clear for first line transport.
O.C. 1/5 D.C.L.I. will keep these roads clear and
press forward a loop road from PLUM FARM to K.28.b.7.9
thence eastwards towards MEREDITH.

5.   478 Field Co to ACKNOWLEDGE.

Issued at 61 R.E.H.Q.   Capt.   Adjutant.
         4.5 p.m.
August 26th. 1918.   for C.R.E. 61st. Division.

Distribution.

Copy No. 1.   476 Field Co.
         2.   478 Field Co.
         3.   479 Field Co.
         4.   1/5 D.C.L.I.
         5.   61st. Div G.
         6.   61 Div Q.
         7.   C.E. XI Corps.
       8 & 9   War Diary
        10.   File.

SECRET.   Copy No. 8

Ref. Sht.
50m. N.E.
1/40,000.

D.S. ORDER No. 135.

1.   (a) 183 Inf. Brigade is still acting as
Advance Guard to the Division.

     (b) 184 Inf. Brigade has been detailed
to hold the line of Nebuslano, with two Battalions
in line and one Battalion in Reserve at NEBUSIANO
Camp. Brigade Headquarters at J.4.c.V.4.

     (c) 182 Inf. Brigade is to be withdrawn into
Reserve with Brigade Headquarters and one Battalion
at STRADELLA, one Battalion at WIJSHIA Camp
and one Battalion at LAZADRE.

          The above moves are to be completed
by dawn tomorrow 22nd.

2.   Transport lines and Q.M.Stores of
476 Field Co will move to J.29.c. (LA MOTTE BASSE)
with Q.M. stores at farm J.29.c.0.5.   Present
accommodation at LA FORET will be handed over to 478
Field Company.

3.   478 Field Co Transport lines and Q.M.
Stores will move from present accommodation near
HERB. THISANGE to accommodation at J.29.c.9.5.
(LA FORET) which is being vacated by 476 Field Co.

4.   The above moves will be completed by dawn
tomorrow 22nd. inst.   Completion of moves will
be reported to this office and to Area Commandants
concerned.

5.   Remainder of Divisional R.E is now
located as below and will not move until further
orders from this office.

     476 Field Co.   H.Q & 4 sections   J.16.c.5.6.
     478 Field Co. (H.Q & 2 sections   J.16.c.5.6.
                    (2 sections   Attached Adv.Guard.
     479 Field Co.   H.Q & 4 sections)
                    Transport & (QM)   D.26.d.8.9.

6.   The Three Field Companies (less two sections
of 478 Field Co with the Advance Guard) are now being
employed direct under C.R.E's orders.

                                     [signature]
Issued at 61 R.E.H.Q.   Capt. Adjutant.
          5 p.m.   For C.R.E. 61st. Div.
August 21st. 1918.

                   Distribution.

          Copy No. 1.   476 Field Co.
               "   2.   478 Field Co.
               "   3.   479 Field Co.
               "   4.   61 Div G.
               "   5.   61 Div Q.
               "   6.   D.A.D. 61 Div.
               "   7.   C.E. XI Corps.
               8 & 9.   War Diary.
               "   10.   File.

SECRET.   Copy No. 12

61st. Divisional R.E. ORDER No. 117.

Ref. Map: FRANCE   23.8.18.
Sheet 36a. 1/40,000.

1. Accommodation for Field Companies and 1/5 D.C.L.I. has been arranged as follows :-

    (a) 476 Field Co. - H.Q. and 4 Sections in shelters at K.14.c.

    (b) 478 Field Co. - H.Q. and 3 Sections in shelters at K.14.a. & c.
        1 Section (employed on back area work) at 476 Field Co. Transport Lines - E.25.a.9.5.

    (c) 479 Field Co. - H.Q. and 4 Sections in shelters in K.7.d

    (d) 1/5 D.C.L.I. - LE GROS CHENE, J.11.

2. Units (less 2 Sections with Advanced Guard) will move into the above locations before 6 p.m. tomorrow the 24th. instant.

3. On arrival in their new positions Field Companies will maintain runner communication with the Advanced Signal Office at STATION HOUSE until telephone communication has been established.

4. Completion of moves and exact locations to be reported to this office.

5. Transport lines of Field Companies will not move.

6. Field Companies and 1/5 D.C.L.I. to acknowledge.

Issued at 11.30 p.m.   Capt. - Adjutant,
23.8.18.   for C.R.E. 61st. Div.

Distribution:-
Copy No. 1 to 476 Field Co.
       2 to 478 Field Co.
       3 to 479 Field Co.
       4 to 1/5 D.C.L.I.
       5 to 61st. Div. "G".
       6 to 61st. Div. "Q".
       7 to 61st. Signals.
       8 to C.E. XI Corps.
       9 to 183 Inf. Bde.
      10 to 184 Inf. Bde.
      11 to War Diary.
      12 to War Diary.
      13 to File.

SECRET.   Copy No. 9

61st. DIVISIONAL R.E. ORDER No. 116.

1. 184 Inf. Bde. is relieving 183 Inf. Bde. in the Advance
    Guard on the nights 24th./25th. and 25th./26th. O.C. 184
    Inf. Bde. taking over command on completion of relief.

2. On completion of above relief, 183 Inf. Bde. becomes
    responsible for the defence of the Main Line of Resistance.

3. (a) 2 Sections 479 Field Co. will relieve 2 Sections 476
        Field Co. with the Advance Guard on the night 24th./
        25th. August.

    (b) An advance party consisting of 1 N.C.O. and 2 Sappers
        per section will go forward tomorrow to take over
        details of work in progress.

    (c) Other details of relief will be arranged between
        O's.C. Field Companies concerned.

4. 476 and 479 Field Companies to acknowledge.

Issued at 11 p.m.   Capt. - Adjutant.
23rd. August 1918.   for C.R.E. 61st. Div.

Distribution:-

Copy No. 1 to 476 Field Co.
  "   " 2 to 478 Field Co.
  "   " 3 to 479 Field Co.
  "   " 4 to 61st.Div."G".
  "   " 5 to 61st.Div."Q".
  "   " 6 to 183 Inf.Bde.
  "   " 7 to 184 Inf.Bde.
  "   " 8 to War Diary.
  "   " 9 to   do.
  "   " 10 to File.

476 Field Co.
478 Field Co.
479 Field Co.
C. E. XI Corps.
Divl. Signals.
L/C McLeod.

C.R.E. Headquarters will close at 1.30 p.m. on 10 a.m. tomorrow 31st. inst. and reopen at 4.30 p.m. on arrival.

30.8.18.

Capt. - Adjutant,
for C.R.E. 61st. Div.

War Diary
ORIGINAL.
AUGT. 1918.
C.R.E. 61ST. DIVN.

APPENDIX 3

Work Orders & Instructions

Notes on Conferences. Reconnaissance

NOTES ON CONFERENCE held at R.E.H.Q. 1st. August 1918.

Present: C.R.E. & Adjutant;
O's.C. Field Companies.

1. Divisional R.E. parade to be at 10.30 a.m. 3rd.inst. G.O.C. Inspection will probably be any day after Sunday.

2. Hours of Training:
    Physical - 6.45 - 6.15 a.m. after tea & biscuits.
    Company parade - 7.45 a.m.
    Break off - 1 p.m.
    ½ hours break between 7.30 a.m. and 1 p.m.
    Wednesdays and Saturdays starting times 1½ hrs. later.
    Sundays as before.

3. Combined dinner for R.E. Officers to be 6 p.m. Saturday. C.R.E. to ask for FROLICS 6 p.m. Saturday.

4. Sanitary areas:
    479 Field Co. from Village green (incl.) westwards;
    476 Field Co. from Village green (excl.) eastwards.

5. Divisional Defence Instructions were read and explained by C.R.E.

6. All Companies report arrival of 4 Lewis Guns. These should be included in schemes.

1.8.18.
Capt.,
Adjutant, 61st. Divl. R.E.

SECRET.

476 Field Co.
478 Field Co.   1/5 D.C.L.I.
479 Field Co.

Extracts from proceedings of a Conference
held by the Chief Engineer, XI Corps at Corps H.Q
on the 8th. August 1918.

ADVANCED CORPS R.E. DUMP.   An advanced Corps R.E.
dump will be formed at the broad guage siding at ST VENANT
about P.16.b.   This dump will be fed by broad gauge from
LA LACQUE.   For this purpose A.D.G. Tn. Fifth Army
has agreed to place 20 trucks at the Corps disposal at
LA LACQUE, and move them forward when asked to do so.

ROADS and BRIDGES.

Organisation of Labour.   The Corps has agreed that
two A.T. Companies R.E and two Tunnelling Companies R.E
together with a proportion of the unskilled labour at
present employed on the Corps Defence Line (see distribution
of labour attached) be organised in such way as to follow
up Divisions to make good roads and bridges.

Divisions have been told that all that is expected
of them is to get their roads through and bridges repaired
for wheeled Transport.   It is their work - with Field
Companies R.E and Pioneers - to make Roads and Bridges
possible for first Line Transport.   Divisions have also
been told that they are not to expect supplies of road
making material, but they are to use all the local produce
they can find.

Behind Divisions will come the Corps organisation of
Corps R.E and Labour and their work will be to get roads
through and bridges repaired for Lorry traffic, and perhaps
heavy guns -- ultimately if necessary putting in permanent
bridges.

Behind the Corps R.E. organisation will come the Corps
Roads Officer.

Application.   It will be necessary to wait until
Divisions have driven the enemy up to or East of the HINGES -
MERVILLE Road before the above organisation can be started.

Lines of Demarkation   Assuming the enemy is either
driven back or goes back to line NEUF BERQUIN - LESTREM -
LAWE RIVER:-

The Corps R.E. organisation
and Labour responsibility for work will be from our old
Front Line (shown on attached map in dotted red) up to the
HINGES - MERVILLE Road; that of the Corps Roads Officer up
to our old Front Line.

Priority of Roads. 1.   From HAVERSKERQUE through LA
CORNIE - LE SART - then North East through K.28.a. central -
then moving round North of the sawmill on to the LA MOTTE
- MERVILLE Road.   This road is marked in green on attached
map.

2.   From ROBECQ through CALONNE
through Q.4.c.central to LE GRAND PACAUT on the MERVILLE -
HINGES Road.   This road is marked in blue on attached
map.

3.   From/

-2-

3. From ST VENANT through ST FLORIS - CORNET MALO to CALONNE. This road is marked in brown on attached map.

4. The cross communication from CALONNE Q.3.d.4.4. then due North through FERRY to LE SART. This road is marked in violet on attached map.

Method of Repair of Roads. In order that all roads are repaired in the same way the attached instructions for filling in shell holes, and making plank roads will be carried out.

In certain cases it may be necessary to make diversions, but as far as possible shell holes should be filled in, and the road or roads made the same as they were in the first instance.

BRIDGES:- The 552 A.T. Co R.E (with a proportion of 125TH Labour Company) will primarily undertake this work.

The C.R.E's of Divisions have been asked to keep me informed of conditions of bridges as they go forward. If they want help they must let me know at once, and if possible a party of the 552 A.T. Co R.E. will be detailed to assist.

Bridges requiring re-erection are as under

Bridge over the BOURRE River near sawmill at K.29.a.4.5.
Bridge at K.23.b.3.1.

FOREWAYS.

No. 3. Forways Co. R.E.
194 Labour Company.

The linking up of
ST VENANT - CALONNE line with a siding into the Corps Advanced R.E. Dump.
LES LAURIERS - FURNESECQUES.
A cross link from CALONNE station to proposed 20 lb line at K.20.b.2.5.
For this purpose the whole of the 194 Labour Company will be put at the disposal of O.C. No. 3. Forways Co R.E.

ADDITIONAL WORK FOR TUNNELLING COYS. R.E.

O's C. of Tunnelling Companies will get in touch with C.R.E's of Divisions in whose area they are working and see if they can help them by detailing personnel of their Companies to search for road mines, etc.

11.8.1918.

Lieut-Colonel, R.E.
C.R.E. 61st. Division.

	TASK	UNIT	LABOUR COMPANIES	
			Company	Working Strength.
1.	GREEN ROAD	257 Tunnelling Co R.E.	130th.	363
2.	BLUE ROAD	250 Tunnelling Co R.E.	36th.	390
3.	BROWN ROAD	284 Army Troops Co R.E.	185th.	314
4.(a)	VIOLET ROAD	552 Army Troops Coy. R.E.	proportion 123rd.	390
(b)	Bridges			
5.	Advanced Corps R.E. Dump	239 Army Troops Coy. R.E.	proportion 123rd.	
6.	NURLNA IS	No. 3. Foresrs Coy. R.E.	194th.	388

METHOD OF REPAIR.

Shell holes and craters.
The first thing to do is to make a deviation round the shell holes or craters.

Loose debris thrown up by the mine should be carefully stacked for filling in the holes.

Cut out the hole as follows:-

FIRST stage

Sludge or water to be removed.

Second stage

Earth from sides to be kept well rammed.

Third Stage.

Half fascines or other suitable material.

Broken brick or other hard material not required when slab road is laid.

Note:- Dont use all the hard material at the bottom (except in the cases where slabs are going to be laid) and finish up with soft filling near the top.

SLAB OR HALF PITPROP ROADS.

These roads or diversions will be laid (where absolutely necessary only) to a width of 9' to 10' single way to start with, provision being made to enable the road to be widened to 18 to 20 feet (double way) if ultimately required.

The following is the section of single way slab road so designed for widening to double way road if required.

Corduroy or Slabs

Berm — 9" to 10" — Picket — 9" to 10" — Riband 4'.0"

Runners at 3' 0" centres.

476 Field Co.
478 Field Co.
479 Field Co.
R.S.M.
    Copy to No.3 Foreways Co.

1. Considerable difficulty is being experienced in working the light railways satisfactorily.

   (a) Tractor drivers cannot always find the exact destinations for their trains.

   (b) Sufficient loading and off-loading parties are not on the spot when they are required.

2. The result has been that trains which were destined to make a double journey have not been able to do so.

3. (a) 479 Field Co. will erect a notice board, as soon as possible, so that it will catch the eye of tractor drivers, thus:-

       MEREDITH R.E. DUMP.
       STOREMAN

   (b) 476 Field Co. will erect a similar notice board at CANADA.

4. Field Coys. will arrange to have not less than 6 men at each dump during the hours of 10 a.m. and 6 p.m., and when trains are expected this number should be increased to at least 10.

5. Storemen must be told of the importance of clearing trains at once and that all available labour must be got on to the job without delay.

6. All R.E. trains pass through HARTSTONE and it has been arranged that each R.E. train, whether going to LA LACQUE empty, or going forward loaded, will stop at HARTSTONE to pick up guides. Trains going forward may be kept for 5 minutes to enable loads to be checked.

7. The R.S.M. will put a guide on each train, whether going to LA LACQUE for stores or going forward with stores. The guides' duty will be to :

   (a) See that the train gets to its destination;
   (b) Find the storemen and off-loading parties; and
   (c) Report to the R.S.M. the times of arrival and departure, as well as any difficulties he had with the train.

8. Tomorrow, the 13th. inst., 476 and 479 Field Companies, will each send one train guide to the R.S.M. at 9.30 a.m. and the R.S.M. will send 2 men on each train so that they can act as guides afterwards.

12th. August 1918.

    Capt. - Adjutant,
    for C.R.E. 61st. Div.

NOTES ON CONFERENCE
at
H.Q. 479 Field Co. R.E.
5.30 p.m., 14th.Aug.18.

1. Present: C.R.E., Adjutant, & Lt. Simmons.
O's.C. 476 & 479 Field Companies.
O's.C. "B" & "C" Coys., 1/5 D.C.L.I.

2. No definite work policy yet laid down by Corps. R.E. policy at the present is to improve present line of retention so that if we are attacked soon Brigades will have a decent line to fight on.
Present line is pretty well sited.
Wiring is of first importance up to three belts; as much any work as possible is to be done.
Each ½ Brigade front to have normally:
1 Section R.E.
2 platoons Pioneers.
1 Company Infantry.
Posts in the Line of Resistance to be developed.
Liaison at flanks is essential to ensure good junctions.
Gaps in wire to be spaced 150yds. and marked with cross thus :- ✗

3. 476 re-nim stores dumped at various points between CANADA and MERETIEL.
479 would like revetting materials, wiring stores and 40 concrete blocks at BOOM siding.

4. In developing the Line of Resistance the ultimate forming of strong localities should be born in mind.

5. Shelters in traverses are good but any put in must have the equivalent of a normal traverse each side of the shelter.

6. Action in case of hostile attack was discussed. 5th. Divl. Scheme still holds good, pending 61st.Division getting out fresh orders.

7. Working dress: Battle order in front of Company H.Q.

8. Field Co. progress reports to include work on Line of Retention by Pioneers.

14.8.18.

Capt.,
Adjutant, 61st.Divl. R.E.

Distribution:
476 Field Co.
478 Field Co.
479 Field Co.
1/5 D.C.L.I.
"B" Coy., 1/5 D.C.L.I.
"C" Coy., 1/5 D.C.L.I.

WD

1/5 D.C.L.I.
476 Field Co.
478 Field Co.
Copies to 61 Div G.
61 Div Q.

Employment of 1/5 D.C.L.I. (Pioneers) from 20. 8. 1918 inclusive.

One Company (strength 166) with No. 3. Foreways Co for Light Railways extension.

One platoon in Reserve finding parties for C.R.E. dump as at present.

One platoon on repair of back roads as at present.

One platoon on repair of forward roads in Left Brigade area (less LA MOTTE - MERVILLE Road) under orders of O.C. 479 Field Company.

Two platoons on repair of LA MOTTE - MERVILLE Road from MERVILLE forward under orders of C.O. 1/5 D.C.L.I.

One platoon on repair of Road CORBIE - LE SART - K.28.c.4.3. - K.27.b.9.0 - K.26.b.7.9. - MERVILLE under orders of C.O. 1/5 D. C. L. I.

Two Platoons in Reserve at Battalion Headquarters.

[signature]

Lieut-Colonel, R.E.
C.R.E. 61st. Division.

19.8.1918.

RECONNAISSANCE OF BRIDGES
over RIVER BOURRE,
on 28th. August, 1918.

18.	K.16.d.1.4.	Footbridge infantry single file on 5 cork piers.
19.	K.16.d.5.1.	Barge in stream; river passable infantry single file.
B.1.	K.22.b.3.9.	Light railway bridge destroyed; 2 shore trestles on each side standing, 2 centre trestles in stream demolished.
20.	K.22.b.7.7.	Trestle footbridge infantry single file. (Barge under bridge under left bank). Bosch first line transport bridge destroyed 20yds. down stream, timber and girder construction.
21.	K.22.b.9.3.	Trestle footbridge for infantry in single file.
B.2.	K.23.a.05.20.	Destroyed German first line transport bridge, small amount of material in the stream.
22.	K.23.a.3.1.	Floating footbridge, single file.
C.	K.23.a.3.0.	Destroyed Bosch first line transport bridge, timber and girders.
23.	K.23.c.20.75.	Footbridge infantry single file (old Bosch bridge repaired).
D.	K.23.c.2.5.	Bosch first line transport bridge destroyed; good deal of timber in the stream.
24.	K.23.c.45.40.	Footbridge infantry single file (old Bosch).
E.	K.23.c.40.25.	Old Bosch footbridge destroyed; 4 trestles standing; could be easily repaired.
F.	K.29.a.40.85.	Road swing bridge destroyed and approaches on both banks demolished. Bridge for first line transport is being put in hand.
25.	K.29.a.4.7.	Bosch footbridge, single file; damaged but passable.
26.	K.29.a.35.50.)	
27.	K.29.a.45.50.)	Bosch footbridges; passable.
28.	K.29.a.55.50.)	
29.	K.29.a.70.45.	Road bridge damaged; passable for limbers.
G.	K.29.a.3.3.	Bosch footbridge destroyed; 2 trestles standing.
30.	K.29.a.4.2.	Floating footbridge of timber; passable for infantry in single file.
31.	K.29.a.45.15.	do. do. do. but in bad condition.
32.	K.29.c.50.95.	Bosch trestle footbridges; passable.
33.	K.29.c.50.85.	do. do.
34.	K.29.c.6.4.	Footbridge for infantry in single file under construction.

The following are also reported:-

K.29.c.9.5.   Bosch footbridge; passable.

K.29.d.0.4.   Footbridge damaged; but passable.

K.29.d.1.5.   Footbridge; passable.

K.29.d.4.6.   do.

K.29.d.7.5.   do.

K.30.c.25.30. Transport bridge; bays 12ft. wide, several bays damaged. Infantry can get across. Width of Canal 80ft.

Canal from K.29.c.9.1 to K.35.a.5.7 has no crossings and the lock at K.29.d.5.0 has been blown in.

From road bridge K.29.a.7.5 to bend in Canal K.29.b.7.5 there are no crossings.

MATERIAL.

There is a timber yard at the saw mill K.29.a.1.0 with a good supply of baulk, ½", 1", and 1½" boarding.

There are about 1,000 shovels and 800 Bosch picks in house on north side of road in K.29.b.6.9.

20th August 1918.

Lieut.-Colonel, R.E.
C.R.E. 61st. Division.

A.D.M.S. 61st. Divn.
61st. Div Q.

The following reconnaissance is reported

WELLS.

K.3.d.5.3.   Pump is in good condition and is fixed to
             front wall of house.

K.4.c.3.3.   Two pumps in school yard, both in working
             order.
             One pump also in school building but out
             of order and water probably not good.

K.10.a.3.9. Pump in farm yard has been put out of
             action apparently by a Medical Officer
             who considered the water unfit.

21.8.1918.

                                     Capt.   Adjutant.
                                 For C.R.E. 61st. Divn.

A.D.M.S.

61 Divn.

Copy to 61 Div Q

23/2/2

Report on Reconnaissance of wells herewith includes all wells that are in working order in Squares K. 15, 16, 17, 21, 22, 23, and 29.

No of Well.	Map Ref.	Location of well.	Means of getting water to surface.	Remarks.
1.	K.15.c.6.1.	Cottage No. 54 N. side of Road.	Lift Pump	All wells were covered over making it impossible to ascertain
2.	K.21.b.4.6.	Cottage No. 41. S. side of Road	Lift Pump	
3 & 4	K.22.d.5.1.	In Cottage South side of Road.	Lift pump	(1) Diameter
5 & 6	K.22.d.7.0.	House North side of Road	Lift Pump	(2) Depth of water level (3) Depth of water.
7.	K.29.a.2.9.	North of Road	Lift Pump	
8.	Sachet Fm.	North of Road	Lift Pump.	
9.	K.23.d.3.8. College	South of Road	Lift Pump	

Lieut-Colonel, R.E
C.R.E.   61st. Division.

22.8.1918.

SECRET.

1/5 D.C.L.I.
    Copies to 475 Field Co.
                 478 Field Co.
                 479 Field Co.

1. For the present the battalion will be employed on opening up and maintaining communications, as under:-

   (a) Two Companies (B. & C.) maintaining and improving the roads already opened up, except the LE SART - MERVILLE Road via road junction K.30.b.7.9, on which Corps troops are now working.

   (b) One Company (A) repairing road from K.16.b.5.2, through Les TURCHEDIEUX, SACHET Fm. to road junction K.22.a.5.6; and opening up road from K.22.a.1.2 - APPLE Fm. - GALT Fm. and extending it by a fascine road from SALT Fm. to Les TURESBROQUES via first line transport bridge at K.22.b.7.6.

2. The line of demarkation for maintenance between the two Companies referred to in 1 (a) above will be as follows:-

LYS Canal - K.33.central - LE SART Cross roads (inclusive to C. Coy.) - road junction K.28.a.00.95 (inclusive to C.Coy.) - Cross roads K.29.d.7.5 (inclusive to B.Coy.) - Factory K.23.c.4.8 (Road inclusive to B.Coy.) - road junction K.23.b.6.2 (inclusive to B.Coy.) - road thence Road Junction L.7.c.2.0 (inclusive to B.Coy.) - road junction L.14.c.95.50 (main road inclusive to C.Coy.) - DIRK Cottages L.15.d.8.6 - COBALT Cottages L.16.c.9.7 - road junction L.17.d.2.5.

3. As the front line progresses Eastwards, B. & C.Companies will open up the roads in their respective areas by first making good a 9ft. road and subsequently, if time permits, repairing the more important roads to their full width.

4. In the event of a rapid advance:

   (a) The first requirement will be to open up communication eastwards. B. & C. Companies may therefore have to concentrate all their labour on the following two roads; whilst A. Coy. is kept in Reserve for employment where most urgently needed.

      B. Coy. - Main ESTAIRES Road via CHAPELLE DUVELLE.
      C. Coy. - COGNEE CORNER - road junction L.14.c.95.50 PEM MONTIGNY - SELSEY Fm. L.11.c.1.5 - Road junction L.11.c.2.0 - Cross roads - NEWBET Cross L.11.d.5.1.

   (b) B. & C. Companies will also reconnoitre and report as soon as possible on roads generally in the areas allotted them. In addition to the two roads mentioned above, they will open up lateral communication forthwith if men are available to do so. The O's.C. B. & C. Companies must therefore keep in touch with each other.

<u>Continued</u>

-2-

5. The result of all reconnaissances, and reports stating what work is in hand, should be sent to this office with the least possible delay so that the Div. Art., Infantry Brigades, etc. can be informed of what communications are open or being worked on.

6. The areas allotted to Companies and the main arteries to be opened up in case of advance are shown on attached map.

7. 1/5 D.C.L.I. to acknowledge.

25.8.18.

Lieut.-Colonel, R.E.
C.R.E. 61st.Division.

WATER SUPPLY REPORT - WELLS OUT OF ORDER.

No.	Map refce.	Location of well.	Means of getting water to surface.	Condition of well.	Repairs, if required.	Time & No. of men required.	Remarks.
10.	K.15.c.7.6	In cottage south of road.	Lift pump.	Pump broken.	New pump.	6 hrs. 4 men.	
11.	K.15.c.6.0	Cottage N. of road.	do.	do.	Suction pipe of plunger damaged.	8 hours. 2 men.	All wells are covered over making it impossible to ascertain: (1) Diameter. (2) Depth of water level. (3) Depth of water.
12.		In billet No.48 N. of road.	do.	do.	do.	do.	
13.	OYSTER Fm.	South of road.	do.	Damaged leather.	New leather & plunger.	2 men. 8 hours.	
14.	K.20.c.8.9.	At LES LAURIERS.	do.	Pump out of condition.	New pump.	4 men. 6 hours.	
15.	K.21.a.2.9.	South of road.	do.	Broken.	New leather.	2 men, 6 hrs.	
16.	BEDFORD Fm.	North of road.	do.	do.	New pump.	4 do.	
17.	Cottage 200 yds. from BEDFORD Fm.	North of road.	do.	do.	do.	4 do.	
18.	K.21.cent.	North of road.	do.	do.	do.	4 do.	
19.	BOSHAM Fm.	South of road.	do.	do.	do.	4 do.	
20.	COURTEROIE Fm.	South of road.	do.	do.	New leathers.	2 men, 8 hrs.	2 ponds, 90' x 15' x 6' deep, suitable for horses.
21.	BLANC Fm.	North of road.	do.	do.	New pump.	4 men, 6 hrs.	
22.	LOXTON Ho.	South of road.	do.	do.	do.	do.	
23.	LOBSTER Fm.	South of road.	do.	do.	do.	do.	

- 2 -

No.	Map refce.	Location of well.	Means of getting water to surface.	Condition of well.	Repairs, if required.	Time and No. of men reqd.	Remarks.
24.	K.22.central.	North of road.	Lift pump.	Pump broken.	New pump.	4 men, 6hrs.	
25.	K.23.c.6.8.	Factory.	Steam pump.				Not worth repairing.
26.	Opposite Factory.	North of Rd.	Lift pump.	Perished leathers.	New leathers.	2 men, 8hrs.	
27.	do.	do.	do.	do.	do.	do.	
28.	APPLE Fm.	South of Rd.	do.	Pump broken.	New pump.	4 men, 6hrs.	
29.	K.15.c.9.4.	do.	do.	do.	do.	do.	

23.8.18.

Capt. - Adjutant,
for C.R.E. 61st.Div.

61st. Division, "Q".

Minute 1 is too indefinite to base an estimate on. My further reasons however for considering the Canal practically useless for R.E. material are as follows :-

(a) Canals generally are not suitable for handling R.E. Stores ahead of Corps dumps (where all stores arriving have to be off-loaded and dumped).

(b) In the case of a C.R.E's. dump, only a small portion of the stores drawn are actually dumped there, the remainder being consigned straight through from Corps to Field Co. dumps.
 (N.B. I drew 168 tons of stores yesterday; only 20 tons were off-loaded at C.R.E's dump, the remainder going straight through to nine different points in the forward area).

(c) Hence, it is essential for the C.R.E. and Field Coy. dumps to be on the Light Railway. Of course, if the C.R.E's. dump were on both Light Railway and Canal, some use might be made of the latter, but always in a comparatively small way.

(d) From the above it appears that there is no immediate prospect of the LYS Canal helping us at all.

(e) On the general question of opening the Canal up to MERVILLE I hold very strong views against the proposal for the following reasons:-

 No great use could be made of the waterway at present, and the advantage gained, from the point of view of transportation, cannot be held to compare with the disadvantages of increasing the amount of water in forward sections of the Canal. If the water level be raised, say between ST. VENANT and MERVILLE -

 (i) Bridges will have to be reconstructed.

 (ii) The tremendous value of the Canal as a drain will be discounted.

 (iii) The water level of the Rivers BOURRE and PLATE BECQUE will be raised and entirely out of our control.

 (iv) This will prevent any effective drainage of the area in which we shall probably have to construct our defences and in which troops will have to live during the winter.

To sum up: Whilst we are operating in the vicinity of MERVILLE, the Canal is of much greater importance to the Division as a means of lowering the water level in the area of the trenches, than as a means of transport. I therefore hope that every obstacle will be put in the way of opening

contd.

(2)

it up for the latter purpose, between ST. VENANT and MERVILLE.

As an illustration of the above principle, I would quote the case of the drainage of the area around GIVENCHY and the LA BASSEE Canal. During 1916 this was a complete failure owing to it being impossible at the time to obtain consent to the lowering of the water level in the LAWE Canal. I understand that the necessary consent was eventually given, with the result that the area was successfully drained during the winter 1916-17.

28.8.18.

Lieut.-Colonel, R.E.
C.R.E. 61st.Division.

SECRET.

O.C. 479 Field Co.

1. Footbridges will be constructed over the LYS CANAL in connection with an operation to take place tomorrow 31st. inst. (Zero hour not yet notified) as follows:-

(a) From MERVILLE to BEAUPRE (L.32) inclusive by 61 Div.

(b) East of BEAUPRE by 59th. Division.

2. You will undertake construction of the footbridges required in 1 (a) above as follows:-

(i) K.36.a.8.6. Infantry in file. (if possible)

(ii) K.36.b.95.50. Infantry in single file.

(iii) L.31.b.30.70 Infantry in single file.

(iv) L.32.a.90.20. Infantry in file (if possible)

3. The work should be commenced at daylight and completed as soon as possible.

4. The two sections at present employed on the M.L.R. are available for this work.

5. Reconnaissance of this section of the LYS CANAL is attached for information.

6. ACKNOWLEDGE.

11.59 p.m.
August 30th. 1918.

Lieut-Colonel, R.E.
C.R.E. 61st. Division.

O.C. 479 Field Co.
   1/5 D.C.L.I.
   Copies to 478 Field Co.
              476 Field Co.

8/6

1. The organization for opening up and maintaining communications laid down in C.R.E. 8/6 dated 25.8.1918 will be amended as follows:-

     One Company Pioneers will work under the orders of O.C. Field Co attached to the Advance Guard on forward roads.

     The remainder of the Pioneer Battalion,(less one platoon at C.R.E's dump) will be at the disposal of the O.C. 1/5 D.C.L.I. for the improvement of communications already opened up by the forward Pioneer Company.

2. The above will come into effect from 1.9.1918 inclusive.

3. The Company detailed for work under O.C. 479 Field Co will move to forward billets in vicinity of LES FOREDEQUES today under Battalion arrangements.

4. The O.C. 479 Field Co will report daily to this office (Copy to O.C. 1/5 D.C.L.I) the roads on which the Forward Pioneer Company are working. The report should state which roads in rear of his parties require further work, to be furnished from Companies in rear.

5. The Policy laid down in para 4 of C.R.E 8/6 dated 25.8.1918 still holds good, except that these duties now devolve on the forward Pioneer Company.

6. 1/5 D.C.L.I. and 479x Field Co to ACKNOWLEDGE.

31. 8. 1918.

                              Lieut-Colonel, R.E.
                              C.R.E. 61st. Divn.

61st. Division, "G".
Copy to C.E. XIth. Corps.

Reference Divl. Order No. 198; the following Bridges have been erected over the LYS CANAL:-

K.36.a.8.6 - Infantry in single file - Floating Bridge.

K.36.b.7.5 -   do.   do.   - Trestle Bridge.

L.31.b.3.7 -   do.   do.   - Floating Bridge,
                                        (under construction, will be
                                        completed tonight).

L.32.a.9.2 - Footbridge under construction by 59th.
             Div. R.E.

31st. August 1918.

Lieut.-Colonel, R.E.
C.R.E. 61st. Division.

War Diary
ORIGINAL.
Aug I. 1918.
C.R.E. 61st Divn.

APPENDIX 4

NOMINAL ROLLS

NOMINAL ROLL OF UNIT.

1st. August 1918

Officers.

    Lieut-Colonel G.E.J. DURNFORD D.S.O.   C.R.E.
    Captain   M.E.W. FITZGERALD   Adjutant
    Captain   J.K. RENNIE M.C. (RAMC) M.O.
                            (At present on leave)

Other Ranks.

52959	R.S.M.	H. DEYERMOND. D.C.M.
500121	Sergt.	W.A. FEATHERSTONE.
500336	L/Cpl.	A. SKINNER
498197	L/Cpl.	F. HAYCRAFT
99315	Sapper	G. BOLLAND
500171	Driver	L. WATTS
500303	Driver	J.A. GREGORY
56185	Driver	A. DAVIES
61497	Driver	G.W PATTEN.
T4/248151	Driver	E. LORTON. (A.S.C.)

Attached.

476 Field Co.

498154	L/Cpl.	L. MOTT.
498276	Sapper	T.A. ELLISON
84339	Driver	G. KING

478 Field Co.

496773	Corpl.	F.L. PENNY

479 Field Co.

494375	Sapper	H. TALBOT
488601	Sapper	E.S. NEWTON
494779	Driver	G. DOLLING.

Officers.

    Captain W.O. TOBIAS. (R.A.M.C)

French Mission.

    Interpreter F.A. GUEUX

Detached.

    Driver F. FOXON.   to 479 Field Co. R.E

WAR DIARY
ORIGINAL.
AUGT. 1918.
C.R.E. 61ST DIVN.

APPENDIX 5

DEFENCE SCHEMES & INSTRUCTIONS

Defence Scheme, 61st.Div. R.E.

Ref. Map Sheet 36a,
1/40,000.

APPENDIX X.

1.   The 61st.Division is in G.H.Q. Reserve at 24 hours notice.

2.   In the event of it being necessary to move the Division by Brigade groups and should these groups include Field Companies, Field Companies will be attached as follows :-
        475 Field Co. to 182 Brigade Group;
        476 Field Co. to 183 Brigade Group;
        479 Field Co. to 184 Brigade Group.
        G.Os.C. Brigades have been instructed to arrange Field Co. rendezvous for the purpose.

3.   Infantry Brigades are referred to as follows :-

ST.HILAIRE Bde. -   Bde. billeted at ST.HILAIRE - BOURECQ.
                    Bde. H.Q. at ST.HILAIRE.
                    (now 184 Inf. Bde.)

HAZEBROUCK Bde. -   Bde. billeted at LAMBRES - QUERNES - WITTES.
                    Bde. H.Q. at ST.ANDRE Fm., N.2.d.
                    (now 182 Inf. Bde.)

LIERES Bde.   -   Bde. billeted at LIERES - FONTES.
                    Bde. H.Q. at FONTES.
                    (now 183 Inf. Bde.)

4.   In the event of the XI Corps being attacked, the Division may be required to :-

(a) <u>In the event of attack on the Corps on the immediate right of XI Corps</u>:
    (i)   To extend the right flank of XI Corps along the NAVE R.
    (ii) To extend the right flank of XI Corps along the BUSNES - STEENBECQUE line and hold the L'ECKERN locality (V.5).
    (iii) To counter-attack towards MT. BERNENCHON and HINGES.

(b) <u>In the event of attack against the centre of XI Corps</u>:
    To reinforce the junction between the right and left Divisions, either on the AMUSOIRES - HAVERSKERQUE line or the BUSNES - STEENBECQUE line.

(c) <u>In the event of attack on the Corps on the immediate left of XI Corps</u>:
    (i)   To extend the left flank of XI Corps from Hre.Gd.DAM (K.2.a.4.0) along the BOURRE R. and the BRAS-DE-LA-BOURRE (K.2.a. - R.25.d. - D.24).
    (ii) To extend the left flank of XI Corps from LA-MOTTE-AU-BOIS along the canal running through D.10 and D.11.
    (iii) To counter-attack North East to drive the enemy back across the canal in D.10 and D.11.

Page 1 (1.3.1918)

Defence Scheme, 61st. Div. R.E.

APPENDIX F. (contd.)

5. In order to be in a position to deal with any one or more of the situations as set forth in para. 4 which may arise, the following three Brigade Concentration Areas have been selected:-
   Area "X" - MIQUELRNIX - JUNCT HAMEAUT - COMBAT BOURGOIS.
   Area "Y" - ISBERGUES - LA ROUPIN - THRUINNES.
   Area "Z" - STEENBECQUE - ECHENGHEM - THRINNES.

6. On receipt of the order "MAN BATTLE STATIONS", the Divl. R.E. will stand fast, unless they are specially referred to in the order.

Distribution:

476 Field Co.
478 Field Co.
479 Field Co.
61st. Div. "G".
61st. Div. "Q".
C.E. XI Corps.
War Diary.

(Copy)

476 Field Co.
478 Field Co.
479 Field Co.

APP 6

I have much pleasure in publishing the following letter from the Divisional Commander, and my reply thereto, the contents of which are to be communicated to all Officers, N.C.O's. and men.

I wish to add my congratulations to all ranks on their receiving such an appreciation of their work and to take this opportunity of thanking all Officers, N.C.O's, and men under my Command for their unfailing co-operation and support in carrying out our many duties in the Field.

(Sd.) G. DURNFORD,
Lieut.-Colonel, R.E.
C.R.E. 61st. Division.

28.8.18.

(Copy)

61st.Div.No. A.76/1.

C.R.E. 61st.Division.

The work of the R.E. is sometimes overlooked for it goes on generally unseen. Will you please let your Officers and men know that I do not forget them, and that I fully understand and appreciate all they do.

The work they have been doing lately is particularly worthy of recognition. The way in which they have put up bridges, repaired roads, and consolidated ground has been first class. I should be very glad if you would let all ranks know that I have watched their work with great interest, and I hope they will accept my best congratulations on the excellent results of their conscientious efforts carried out in so keen and cheerful a spirit.

Div.H.Q.
27th.August 1918.

(Sd.) F.J.DUNCAN,
Major-General,
Commanding, 61st.Division.

C.R.E 61st.Div. No.19/4.

G.O.C. 61st.Division.

I have to acknowledge the receipt of your letter (A.76/1 dated 27th.August, 1918), the contents of which have been communicated to all ranks under my Command.

May I be permitted, on behalf of myself, my Officers, N.C.O's. and men, to thank you for your appreciation of the work which has recently been carried out.

The knowledge that our work has been so fully appreciated by our Divisional Commander will, I know, act as a great incentive to further efforts.

May I also add that a large measure of our success is attributable to the zeal and efforts of our comrades in the 1/5 D.C.L.I. (Pioneer) Battalion.

28th.August 1918.

(Sd.) G.DURNFORD,
Lieut.-Colonel, R.E.,
C.R.E. 61st.Division.

Confidential
ORIGINAL

WAR DIARY
of
H.Q.ʳˢ 61ˢᵗ Div R.E.
For month of
SEPTEMBER 1918

WA 29

Vol XXIX

Army Form C. 2118.

WAR DIARY
or
INTELLIGENCE SUMMARY.
(Erase heading not required.)

HEADQUARTERS
61st. DIV. ROYAL ENGINEERS.
Vol. XXIX.

SEPTEMBER 1918.

Page 1

Instructions regarding War Diaries and Intelligence Summaries are contained in F. S. Regs., Part II. and the Staff Manual respectively. Title pages will be prepared in manuscript.

Place	Date	Hour	Summary of Events and Information	Remarks and references to Appendices
CROIX MARRAISSE. J.21.c.5.3.	1st		FRANCE. Sht. 36a. 1/40000. Nominal Roll of Unit. Advised all concerned that CHAPELLE DU VELLE Road is fit for field guns as far East as L.28.c.0.7. Advised Field Companies to be always prepared to carry out bridging operations at moments notice and warned them of necessity of bridging LYS East of ESTAIRES. Issued instructions to Field Companies and Pioneers re work orders & moves for tomorrow.	Appx 4. Appx 3 Appx 3
		12.25pm	Received 61 Div Order 199 re moves and reliefs of Brigades. C.R.E. visited Advance Guard and Forward Battalion with Divisional Commander. Our advanced troops got East of Estaires today. Suggested to Corps that the roads should be cleared through MERVILLE in preference to present policy of constructing avoiding roads" and Corps agreed to put the matter to Army	
	2nd	8.45am	Received 61 Div Order re relief of 184 Brigade by 182 Brigade.	
		11.50am	Received 184 Brigade Order re relief by 182 Brigade. Issued letter 13/4 to Field Coys and Pioneers re move of C.R.E's dump from HARTSTONE to MEREDITH. Issued instructions to Field Coys and Pioneers re work and moves for tomorrow. Sent reconnaissance report to Div G., 182 Bde and C.E. Corps re roads, bridges, railways and dumps. Five large bombs dropped near R.E.H.Qrs. C.R.E. visited Advance Guard Brigade H.Qrs and right Battalion H.Q at FAGGOT FARM then on to ESTAIRES and back via the Canal.	Appx 5 Appx 3 Appx 3
	3rd	12.50pm	Issued instructions to Field Companies and Pioneers re work orders and moves for tomorrow. Issued R.E. Order 118 increasing Advance Guard Brigade Engineers from two sections to one Company.	Appx 3
		11.15pm	Issued orders to Field Companies re moves forward of Field Companies tomorrow C.R.E. and Adjutant visited CHAPELLE DU VELLE, 479 Field Co and Brigade H.Q at CHAPELLE DU VELLE.	Appx 2 Appx 2

Army Form C. 2118.

WAR DIARY
or
INTELLIGENCE SUMMARY

(Erase heading not required.)

HEADQUARTERS 61st. DIV. ROYAL ENGINEERS.

Vol. XXI k.

Page 2

SEPTEMBER 1918.

Place	Date	Hour	Summary of Events and Information	Remarks and references to Appendices
CROIX MARRAISSE. J.21.c.5,3.			Issued 13/4/1 to Field Companies re establishing C.R.E. dump at CHAPELLE DUVELLE. Sent Reconnaissance Report to Field Companies on Dumps and bridges in recaptured area.	Appx 5 Appx 3
	4th	6.30 pm	Received 61 Div Order 2 01 re move of 183 Bde to CHAPELLE DUVELLE and 184 Bde to TROU BAYARD area	
		6.30 pm	Received 183 Bde Order re move to CHAPELLE DUVELLE Area. C.R.E. with G.O.C. visited CHAPELLE DUVELLE and LA GORGUE. C.R.E. then reconnoitred the LYS CANAL up to 1000 yds of SAILLY sur la LYS. Later, G.O.C. gave verbal instructions to 479 Field Co officer to order up all Field Co pontoon equipment and place pontoon bridges across the LYS CANAL near ROUGE MAISON and PONT TOURNANT. C.R.E. remained out until 7 p.m. supervising the construction of bridges.	
	5th	9.50 am	Advised all concerned that two pontoon and 2 trestle, and 1 pack animal bridge completed. Issued instructions to Coys re priority of work	Appx 3
		6 pm	Received 61 Div Order 2 02 re re-adjustment of front.	
		11.5pm	Instructed 478 Field Co to construct pontoon bridge at G.21.d.6.2. as the two pontoon bridges already in position have been destroyed. Advised all concerned pontoon bridge G.21.d.8.8. completed Recd. 61 Div Art Instructions No. 12. C.R.E. and Adjutant visited RILL WORKS, where Advance Division intends moving tomorrow. 479 Field Co – LYS Bridge under construction by 479 Field Co – ESTAIRES Bridge now completed for Field guns and being strengthened for 60 pdrs – pontoon bridges ROUGE MAISON and SAILLY – 182 Brigade – 476 Field Co – returning via Rue MONTIGNY. During the evening it was reported that both pontoon bridges were destroyed by shell fire and C.E. XI Corps was asked to arrange for 5 bridging sets to be sent up to ESTAIRES at once, & being to replace destroyed bridges and the other three to re-equip Field Coys with	Appx 3
	6th	10.30 am	Received 183 Brigade Order re relief of 182 Bde.	
		12.25am	Advised 478 Field Co that only one pontoon bridge has been destroyed viz at SAILLY. Advised all concerned that pontoon bridge has been completed at G.21.d.6.5.20 Received 183 Bde. Order 241 re forward moves of Battalions Issued instructions to Field Coys re duties of Advance Guard Engineers Sent Coys copy 61 Div instructions No. 1. – O.C. 478 Field Co to give technical advice to Infantry Brigades in siting the Corps battle line.	Appx 3 Appx 3

Army Form C. 2118.

WAR DIARY
or
INTELLIGENCE SUMMARY.

(Erase heading not required)

HEADQUARTERS 61st. DIV. ROYAL ENGINEERS

Vol XXIX   Page 3

Instructions regarding War Diaries and Intelligence Summaries are contained in F.S. Regs., Part II. and the Staff Manual respectively. Title pages will be prepared in manuscript.

Place	Date	Hour	Summary of Events and Information	Remarks and references to Appendices
CROIX MARRAISSE J.21.c.5.3.	6th cont'd		FRANCE. Sht. 36a. 1/40000. Wrote Companies drawing attention to various points in connection with recent operations. Major wOOLCOMBE from Engineer-in-Chiefs office called. C.R.E. visited C.E. XI Corps during the afternoon - 5th. Army has not yet agreed to send the pontoon equipment up to us.	Appx 3
	7th.		Received message of congratulation from Div Commander on work of R.E Advised all concerned that Jack mile bridges have been constructed at G.21.b.9.6. & G.16.b.3.4. C.R.E. visited 479 Field Co and bridges with O.C. 478 Field Co. Move of Advance D.H.Q is still postponed, but G.O.C. agrees to R.E.H.Q moving to RILL WORKS tomorrow. Adjutant visited D.H.Q and LA GORGUE Two sets of pontoon equipment arrived at our dump from Pontoon Park	Appx 1
	8th.	10 am	Advised all concerned that Jack bridge has been constructed at G.18.a.4.45.45. R.E.Headquarters moved to RILL WORKS. C.R.E. visited all Field Companies and bridges as far East as SAILLY.	
L.27.d.8.4.	9th		Received 183 Bde Defence Instructions No. 1. Wrote 257 Tunnelling Co asking them to repair Rue MONTIGNY. Issued instructions to Field Companies re Bridging Programme over LYS CANAL. Advance D.H.Q moved to RILL WORKS. C.R.E. and Adjutant visited NOUVEAU MONDE.	Appx 3 Appx 3
	10 th	11.55 am 9 pm	Received 61 Div Order 203:- 184 Bde to relieve 183 Bde. Recd. 184 Bde Order 223 re relief of 183 Bds. Advised all concerned that bridge at G.27.c.4.5. is open for 8 ton axle loads. C.R.E. inspected all work on the canal from LA GORGUE to FORT ROMPU. Arranged for attachment of two tunnellers to each Infantry Bde and one N.C.O. to R.E.H.Q for searching for mines and booby traps.	

WAR DIARY

HEADQUARTERS
61st. Div. ROYAL ENGINEERS
Vol. XXIX

Army Form C. 2118.
Page 4

Place	Date	Hour	Summary of Events and Information	Remarks and references to Appendices
FRANCE Sht 36a. 1/40000	SEPTEMBER 1918			
L27.d.8.4	11th	10am.	Issued R.E. Order No 119 re Brigade Relief	Appx 2
		12.5pm	Issued Warning Order re relief of 476 by 478 Field Co	Appx 2
		5 p.m	Issued R.E. Order 120 re relief of 476 by 478 Field Co - former to do back area work under 61st. Division Q.	Appx 2
			Issued Amendment to Bridging programme sent Companies 9th. inst.	Appx 3
			Advised Companies of two selected sites for pontoon bridges in case of emergency & gave details.	Appx 3
			Advised all concerned that pack bridge at G.17.b.50.65 is completed	
			Advised G, Q, and C.E. that mine exploded at 12.30 p.m today at L.29.b.8.0	
			Advised all concerned that First Line Transport bridge open for traffic at G.16.b.90-75	
	12th		Advised all concerned that pack bridge at L.30.c.5.5 is completed.	
			Advised all concerned that medium trestle bridge G.21.d.75.95 is completed.	
			C.R.E. with O.C. 479 Field Co visited CROIX DU BAC, FORT ROMPU returning via work on the canal.	
			Adjutant visited old dumps at NIEPPE FOREST which we are still salving by motor lorry.	
	13th	6.15pm	Received Div. Order 204: 184 Bde to relieve 182 Inf. Bde	Appx 2
		9 pm	Issued R.E. Order 121 re Brigade Relief	Appx 3
			Instructed 479 Field Co to carry out reconnaissance of forward area re defences which can be put into use by us	
			C.R.E. Adjutant and O.C. 479 Field Co visited CALONNE to inspect the water sterilizing plant which we are instructed to copy. Corps have laid dowb that it is the duty of the Divisional R.E to erect this plant. Whilst at CALONNE the Fifth Army Water Supply Officer arrived and stated that it was his duty to erect these plants and he promised to put one in hand for us at LA GORGUE forthwith.	
			Canal has risen considerably and is interfering with our bridges - Asked Corps to see if I.W.T. cannot relieve us of some of the water.	

Army Form C. 2118.

WAR DIARY
or
INTELLIGENCE SUMMARY

HEADQUARTERS 61st, DIV. ROYAL ENGINEERS

(Erase heading not required.)

Vol XXIX

Page 5

Place	Date	Hour	Summary of Events and Information	Remarks and references to Appendices
FRANCE. Sht 36a 1/40000	SEPTEMBER 1918			
L.27.d.3.4	14th		Received 184 Brigade Order 226 re relief by 182 Inf Bde	
			Received 61st Div Art Instructions No 16	
			Received 183 Brigade Instructions No 4	
			Received 184 Bde Order 226 re relief by 182 Inf Bde	
			C.R.E. reconnoitred bye roads W of Canal. We are having considerable difficulty with these roads owing to our having repaired them for first line transport and their being used very largely by motor lorries.	
			Adjutant made preliminary arrangements for opening dump in LA GORGUE which has already got Light Railway leading into it.	
	15th		Wrote Engineer in Chief in reply to his request giving particulars of anti-tank minefields laid by us in front of ST QUENTIN.	
			Advised Companies of further site for pontoon bridge	Appx 3
			Asked Brigades and Div Art to report roads essential for their use.	Appx 3
			Issued Instructions Defence Against Gas	Appx 3
			Issued extracts from Divisional Instructions No 4 (Operations)	Appx 3
			C.R.E. and Adjutant with O.C. 479 Field Co visited LYS Bridge, ESTAIRES Bridge, NOUVEAU MONDE, SAILLY, CROIX DU BAC and FORT ROMPU	
	16th		Instructed Companies that in view of delayed action mines in houses etc. none are to be occupied until further orders	Appx 3
			C.R.E. visited LYS Bridge, road crater S.E. from SAILLY, CROIX DU BAC, SAILLY.	
			Lieut-Colonel MAURICE R.E. from G.H.Q called re ST QUENTIN Minefields	
			C.R.E. visited 476 Field Co and "Q"	

WAR DIARY

or INTELLIGENCE SUMMARY.
(Erase heading not required.)

HEADQUARTERS 61st. Div, ROYAL ENGINEERS Vol XXIX

Army Form C. 2118.
Page 6

SEPTEMBER 1918

Instructions regarding War Diaries and Intelligence Summaries are contained in F. S. Regs., Part II. and the Staff Manual respectively. Title pages will be prepared in manuscript.

Place	Date	Hour	Summary of Events and Information	Remarks and references to Appendices
FRANCE, Sht 36a. 1/40000				
L.27.d.8.4.	17th	7.10pm	Recd. 61 Div Order 205 re relief of 182 Brigade by 183 Brigade C.E. XI Corps called. C.R.E. with OC 479 Field Co reconnoitred defences near LAVENTIE, then on to NOUVEAU MONDE and SAILLY Map showing reconnaissance of trenches etc in the forward area was handed to 61 Div G.	
	18th	11 am	Issued R.O. 120 re return of R.A.M.C. personnel to their Units Issued R.E. Order 122 re relief of 182 Infantry Brigade Received 183 Bde Order 247 re relief of 182 Inf. Bde C.R.E. and Adjutant went round roads and our old dumps which are still being salved.	Appx 1 Appx 2 pp
	19th		Issued Routine Order 121 re March Discipline Issued Instructions re Maintenance of Bridges Wrote Div Q making suggestions re development of Light Railway S.O.R.E. XI Corps called – XI Corps does not seem to be very clear as to the situation about provision of sterilizing lorries – is it Q or R.E. matter? Major H.S. DAVIS, M.C. O.C. 476 Field Co joined R.E.H.Qrs preparatory to relieving Lt-Col. G.E.J. DURNFORD, D.S.O. R.E. when he goes on leave.	Appx 1 Appx 3 Appx 5
	20th.	12.15pm	Issued R.E. Order 123 – 479 Field Co to take over work in the Right Brigade area from 476 Field Co tomorrow 21st. C.R.E. with Major H.S. DAVIS visited 182 Inf Bde and 478 Field Co then on to CROIX DU BAC, FORT ROMPU and and back along Canal to NOUVEAU MONDE Arranged for 478 Field Co to place one section at disposal of R.A. Adjutant visited LYS Dump where men are getting dump in readiness for our move there when the Light Railway is operating.	Appx 2

Army Form C. 2118.

WAR DIARY
or
~~INTELLIGENCE~~ SUMMARY

(Erase heading not required.)

HEADQUARTERS
61st. DIV. R.&ENGINEERS.
Vol XXIX

Page 7

Instructions regarding War Diaries and Intelligence Summaries are contained in F.S. Regs., Part II. and the Staff Manual respectively. Title pages will be prepared in manuscript.

Place	Date	Hour	Summary of Events and Information	Remarks and references to Appendices
	SEPTEMBER 1918			
	FRANCE Sht 36a 1/40000			
L.27.d.8.4	21st		Major H.S. DAVIS, M.C. 476 Field Co took over from Lt Col DURNFORD, D.S.O. R.E. who is proceeding on Leave of Absence	
	22nd		Issued 8/7 to Field Companies amending instructions for maintenance of Bridges W.R.E. visited all bridges N. of SAILLY with O.C. 478 Field Co also river new baths under construction at NEUF BERQUIN. Arranged with O.C. 479 Field Co for him to rest two sections on 23rd and two on 24th. Lieut-Colonel G.E.J. DURNFORD, D.S.O, R.E. proceeded on leave	Appx 3
	23rd	10 am	Issued Routine Order 122-124 re leave and Major DAVIS assuming command Div R.E. A/C.R.E visited 184 Inf Bde and arranged for programme of work on billeting. Reconnoitred roads with C.O. 1/5 D.C.L.I. (Pioneers) and arranged priority of work.	Appx 1
	24th		Advised all concerned that bridges at G.16.b.8.7 and G.16.b.9.4 are now open for 5½ ton axle loads. A/C.R.E. reconnoitred forward drains with C.O. 1/5 D.C.L.I. and arranged for a start to be made on ROUGE Drain tomorrow then visited work in hand with O.C. 478 Field Co.	
		7 p.m	A/C.R.E. saw G.S.O. 1 and discussed question of forward billet repairs and at his request instructed 478 Field Co to reconnoitre area in squares G.29 and 28 for suitable accomodation for two Infantry and two Artillery Brigades, and to commence work as soon as possible.	
	25th	7.10pm	Received 61 Div Order 205- 184 to relieve 182 Bde as Advance Guard Brigade A/C.R.E. visited all billet repairs in hand in Div Area.	
		3pm	A/C.R.E attended Divisional Conference. Nothing arises on immediate interest to R.E's	

Army Form C. 2118.

WAR DIARY
INTELLIGENCE SUMMARY
(Erase heading not required.)

HEADQUARTERS
61st Div. ROYAL ENGINEERS

Vol XXIX

Page 8

SEPTEMBER 1918

Place	Date	Hour	Summary of Events and Information	Remarks and references to Appendices
L.27.d.8.4			FRANCE Sht 36a 1/40000	
	26th	11 am	A/C.R.E. attended lecture at ST VENANT	
		6.30pm	C.R.E. saw G.S.O. 1 and obtained his approval for draft of R.E. Orders	
	27th	10am	Recd 183 Bde Instr. No 6 (Operations)	
		10am	Recd 183 Bde Order No 251 re relief	
		10am	Recd 184 Bde Order 229 re relief of 183 Bde.	
			Recd 61 Div Art Instructions No 20 (Operations)	
		11.55am	Issued XXX R.E. Order No 124 re work of Field Coys and Pioneers in event of advance	Appx 2
		11 pm	Recd 61 Div Order 207 cancelling Div Order 206 and organizing Div front into a two Bde front Reconnoitred forward roads with C.O. 1/5 D.C.L.I. Medium Bridge at BAC ST.MAUR damaged by shell fire yesterday. Repaired by 478 Field Co and now open for traffic.	
	28th	9.15am	Recd 184 Bde Order 230 re attack by 2/5 Glosters	
		12.1pm	Recd 184 Bde Instructions in event of enemy withdrawal	
		1.30pm	Issued R.E. Order 125. adjusting Field Coys to conform to two Bde front.	Appx 2
		4.45pm	Received 184 Bde Order 231 re adjustment of front to two Brigades	
			Recd 61 Div Art Order 157 re adjustment of artillery to conform to two Bde front	
		9 p.m	Recd 183 Bde Order re inter Battalion moves	
		10.10pm	Recd 61 Div Order 208 re Operations - 184 Bde to carry out minor operation	
			A/C.R.E. visited all O's C Companies and discussed R.E. Order 124 - questions in connection with possible advance	
		2.30pm	Major DOYLE from G.H.Q. (A.G. R.E) called. Wrote C.E. Corps re responsibility for administration of sterilizing lorries, tanks lorries etc in case of advance and ask if any scheme exists.	
		7 p.m	Saw A/C.R.E. saw G.S.O.1 and drew attention to 184 Bde Order which places sections under orders of Battalion Commanders. Early retirement expected on this front owing to BELGIAN success at YPRES.	

Army Form C. 2118.

WAR DIARY

HEADQUARTERS 61 DIV ROYAL ENGINEERS.

INTELLIGENCE SUMMARY

VOL XXIX

Page 9

(Erase heading not required).

Instructions regarding War Diaries and Intelligence Summaries are contained in F.S. Regs., Part II. and the Staff Manual respectively. Title pages will be prepared in manuscript.

Place	Date	Hour	Summary of Events and Information	Remarks and references to Appendices
FRANCE			Sht 36a 1/40000	
L.27.d.8.4	29th	2.30 am	Recd @ 199/A/1 from 184 Bde re raid by 2/4th Oxford and Bucks	
		2.30am	Recd 184 Bde Order 232 re attack by 2/5 Glosters (Amending Order 230)	
			Issued R.E. Routine Order 125 re Award of Military Medal to	Appx 1
			Sergt T. TUTTON 476 Field Co	
			Corpl W. WATTS do	
			L/Cpl M. PUDNEY do	
			Issued R.E. Routine Order 126 re adoption of Continental time	Appx 1
		10 am	A/C.R.E saw G.B.O. 1 :- no further developments. Visited work in progress and arranged Programme of work on billets with 476 Field Co and "Q". Two Brigade front adopted last night.	
	30th	10am	A/C.R.E visited sites of proposed forward Bde HdQrs with O.C. 479 Field Co then saw O.O. 1/5 D.C.L.I. and arranged for further work on drains East of Corps area.	
			O.C. 257 Tunnelling Co called.	
		5 pm	Arranged to withdraw personnel from Brigades and attach 6 tunnellers to forward R.E. sections as soon as an advance commences.	
			Maps and drawings during the month	Appx 6

Capt Adjutant
For C.R.E. 61 Division

War Diary.
(ORIGINAL.)
for SEPTEMBER 1918.
C.R.E. 61ˢᵗ DIVⁿ.

APPENDIX 1

ROUTINE ORDERS

BY

C.R.E.

War Diary.
(ORIGINAL.)
for SEPTEMBER 1918.
C.R.E. 61ST DIVN.

APPENDIX 1

Routine Orders by C.R.E

SPECIAL ORDER OF THE DAY.
-:-:-:-:-:-:-:-:-

Issued by:- Lieut-Colonel G.E.J. TURNBULL, D.S.O., R.E.

Commanding:- 61st. (South Midland) Divisional Royal Engineers. T.F.

In the Field. Sept. 7th. 1916.

The following message has been received by C.R.E. 61st. Division from Major-General F.J. DUNCAN, C.M.G., D.S.O. Commanding 61st. Division:-

Please accept yourself and convey to your officers N.C.O's and men my thanks for the splendid work you have done during the past few days ... You have fully acted up to the Royal Engineers motto "Quo fas et gloria ducunt".

(Sd) General DUNCAN.

ROUTINE ORDERS
-by-
Lieut.-Colonel G.E.J. BURNFORD, D.S.O., R.E.
Commanding:- 61st.(South Midland)DIVISIONAL ROYAL ENGINEERS.

R.E.H.Q. 18th.9.1918.

120. POSTINGS.

The undermentioned R.A.M.C. personnel will be despatched, before noon 20th.inst., to the 2/1st. South Midland Field Ambulance for duty.

No.427231 Pte. HOLYOAK, J.H. - attached 478 Field Co.
No.437362 Pte. CULL, W.H.   - attached 479 Field Co.
No.437295 Pte. BAYLEY, A.   - attached 479 Field Co.

(Signed) M.B.FITZGERALD,
Capt.,
Adjutant.

ROUTINE ORDERS
-by-
Lieut.-Colonel G.E.J. BURNFORD, D.S.O., R.E.
Commanding:- 61st. (South Midland) Divisional ROYAL ENGINEERS.

R.E.H.Q.   19.9.18.

---

121. **MARCH DISCIPLINE.**

    (a) The slovenly and unsoldierly demeanour of small parties on the march is very noticeable, particularly in the case of bathing parades and small working parties.

    (b) In future all bathing parties will parade with equipment (less packs) and rifles.

    (c) Any bathing parade of 20 and over will be commanded by an Officer.

- -

(Signed) M.E. FITZGERALD,
Capt.,
Adjutant.

ROUTINE ORDERS
--by--
Major H. G. DAVIS, M.C.
Commanding:- 61st. (S.W.) Divisional Royal Engineers.

N.E.H.Q. 29.9.1918.

125. **IMMEDIATE HONOURS AND AWARDS.**

The following awards for gallantry and devotion to duty have been made:-

THE MILITARY MEDAL.

493321 Sergt.	NIXON, J.	475 Field Co.
491197 Corpl.	YATES, V.	do.
493345 L.Cpl.	PUDNEY, H.	do.

(Signed) M.F. FITZGERALD,
Capt.,
Adjutant.

ROUTINE ORDERS
-by-
Major H. S. DAVIS, M.C.
Commanding:- 61st.Divisional ROYAL ENGINEERS.

R.E.H.Q. 29.9.18.

126. **CONTINENTAL SYSTEM OF TIME, ADOPTION OF, THROUGHOUT THE BRITISH ARMY**
G.R.O. 5104 dated 26.9.18 is re-published for information.
"The Continental system of time - i.e., the 24 hour clock - will be brought into use throughout the British Army from midnight, 30th Sept./1st.October, 1918.

"The "time of origin" that is, the time at which a message or despatch is signed by the originator, will always be represented by four figures, the first two figures, 01 to 23, representing the hours from midnight to midnight, and the second two figures, 01 to 59 representing the minutes of the hour.   For example:-

    12.10 a.m. will be written 0010.
    3.25 a.m.   "   "   0325.
    11.00 a.m.   "   "   1100.
    Noon.   "   "   1200.
    3.25 p.m.   "   "   1525.
    11.40 p.m.   "   "   2340.

"0000 and 2400 will not be used, but the message or despatch will be timed 2359 or 0001.

(Signed) M.E.FITZGERALD,
Capt.,
Adjutant.

War Diary.
(ORIGINAL.)
for SEPTEMBER 1918.
C.R.E. 61st DIVN.

APPENDIX 2

MOVE & RELIEF
ORDERS
BY
CRE

"A" Form.
MESSAGES AND SIGNALS.

Army Form C. 2121.
(In pads of 100.)

No. of Message..............

Prefix........Code........m	Words.	Charge.	*This message is on a/c of :*	Recd. at........m.
Office of Origin and Service Instructions.				
	Sent		...................Service.	Date..............
....	At..........m.			From............
	To..........			
	By..........	(Signature of "Franking Officer.")		By................

TO
476 Field Co.	61 Div G.	257 Tunnelling
478 Field Co.	61 Div Q	Co.
479 Field Co.	61 Sig Co	

Sender's Number.	Day of Month.	In reply to Number.	A A A
* T.581	3		

Two sections and transport of 479 Field Co
will move forward tomorrow 4th handing over xxxx
accomodation atthe college to 478 Field Co
aaa 478 Field Co including transport will move
tomorrow afternoon 4th. to the college K.23.d.
aaa O.C. 478 Field Co will meet O.C. 257 T.
Co at bridge K.29.a.3.8. at 10.30 a.m.
tomorrow 4th. and arrange to hand over Portugues
working parties which will come under the orders
of O.C. 257 T. Co from the 5th. inst. inclusive
aaa 478 Field Co will not continue billet
repairs taken over from 476 Field Co today but
will attach four carpenters to R.E.H.Qrs and
these men will report here tomorrow morning aaa
addressed 478 and 479 Field Cos repeated 476
Field Co, 61st. Div G, 61st. Div Q, 61st.
Signal Co and 257 Tunnelling Co R.E.

From C.R.E.
Place
Time 11.15 pm

The above may be forwarded as now corrected. (Z)

.... Censor.   Signature of Addressor or person authorised to telegraph in his name.

* This line should be erased if not required.
(3796.) Wt. W 492/M1647. 650,000 Pads. 5/17. H.W.& V., Ld. (E. 1187.)

SECRET.

Copy No. 10

Ref maps
36 & 36a
1/40,000

R.E. ORDER NO. 118.

1. The Advance Guard Engineers are being increased from two sections to one Field Company.

2. 476 Field Co will move forward today the 3rd inst to the neighbourhood of CHAPELLE D'YVRAI and be attached to the Advance Guard, relieving 479 Field Co (less 2 sections).

3. On relief, 479 Field Co will come under the orders of the C.R.E. and will complete any work in hand up to and including the road bridge over the LYS at L.26.c.0.4.

4. 478 Field Co will take over the following from 476 Field Co tomorrow.

Billet improvements at LA PAME.
RUE des MEES.
D.H.Q.
HAVERSKERQUE.

R.E. Dumps at PRUCAS and CALIX MARLAISET

The Company will remain concentrated at its present billets and parties working in back areas will have to go to work daily by train.

5. 478 Field Co will continue to employ the PORTUGUESE working party under orders issued by C.R.E.

6. One Company 1/5 D.C.L.I. at present under orders of 479 Field Co will come under the orders of O.C. 476 Field Co.

7. All other details of relief will be arranged between Company Commanders concerned.

8. Field Companies to ACKNOWLEDGE.

Issued at C.R.E. &c.
10.30 p.m.
September 3rd. 1918.

Capt. Adjutant.
for C.R.E. 61st. Divn.

Distribution.

Copy No. 1. 476 Field Co.
2. 478 Field Co.
3. 479 Field Co.
4. 1/5 D.C.L.I.
5. 61 Div G.
6. 61 Div
7. 61 Signal Co.
8. 183 Inf. Brigade
9. C.E. XI Corps.
10 & 11 War Diary.
12 File.

SECRET.   Copy No. 6

61st. DIVISIONAL R.E. ORDER No. 119.
                                                           11.9.18.

1.   The Relief of the Advanced Guard Brigade is taking place as follows:-

   (a) On night 10th./11th. instant., one battalion of 184 Inf. Bde. will relieve one battalion of 183 Inf. Bde., and will come under orders of G.O.C. 183 Inf. Bde. until completion of relief on the night 11th./12th. inst.
   Similarly, the relieved battalion of 183 Inf. Bde. will come under the orders of G.O.C. 184 Inf. Bde.

   (b) On the night 11th./12th. inst. the 184 Inf. Bde. (less one Battalion) will relieve 183 Inf. Bde. (less one battalion) and will take over the duties of Advanced Guard Brigade from the hour of relief.

2.   On completion of the above relief 476 Field Co. will come under the orders of G.O.C. 184 Inf. Bde.

3.   476 Field Co. to acknowledge.

Issued at 10 a.m.   Capt. - Adjutant,
11.9.18.   for C.R.E. 61st. Div.

                         Distribution:-
         Copy No.1 to 476 Field Co.   Copy No.5 to 184 Inf. Bde.
          "   2 to 475 Field Co.   "   6 to War Diary.
          "   3 to 477 Field Co.   "   7 to File.
          "   4 to 61st. Divn. 'G'   "   8 to File.

"A" Form.
MESSAGES AND SIGNALS.

Army Form C. 2121.
(In pads of 100.)

Prefix	Code	Words	Charge	This message is on a/c of :	Recd. at .... m.
Office of Origin and Service Instructions.					
SHORT.	Sent At .... m.			.... Service.	Date............ From............
A.R.	To............ By............			(Signature of "Franking Officer.")	By............

TO	476 Field Co.	6i Div G.
	428 Field Co.	6i Div G.
	475 Field Co.	106 Inf. Brigade.

Sender's Number.	Day of Month.	In reply to Number.	AAA
T.34/2	11		

Warning order AAA 476 Field Co will be prepared to follow 475 Field Co tomorrow 12th and to move to billets of 476 Field Co AAA 475 Field Company will be prepared to move to near MERVILLE tomorrow for bath house work AAA 476 Field Co bridging equipment vehicles and equipment to be left behind in charge of 475 Field Co AAA Field Companies to acknowledge AAA Addressed 475, 476 and 475 Field Companies, repeated 6i Div G, 6i Div Q and 106 Inf. Bde.

From: C.R.E.
Place:
Time: 10.5.p.m.

R.E. ORDER NO. 120.

Ref. Maps.
Shts 36a &
36. 1/40000

1. (a) 478 Field Co will relieve 476 Field Co tomorrow the 12th. inst. and on completion of relief 478 Field Co will come under the orders of G.O.C. Advanced Guard Brigade.

(b) On completion of relief, 478 Field Co will be located as follows:-

H.Q & 2 sections.	G.14.a.5.3.
2 sections & part of transport	G.8.a.3.2.
Q.M. Store & remainder of transport.	L.23.b.3.0.

(c) 478 Field Co will take over camps and bridge construction from 476 Field Co.

(d) All other details of relief will be arranged by O's C. concerned.

2. (a) 476 Field Co (less bridging vehicles & equipment) will move tomorrow the 12th. inst. to the neighbourhood of MERVILLE (H.Q. probably at the Factory K.23.c.5.9) where it will be employed on back area work under direct orders of 61 Div Q.

(b) Bridging vehicles and equipment (including drivers and animals) will be attached to 479 Field Co.

(c) O.C. 476 Field Co will detail one section to assist each Infantry Brigade out of the line in the work of improving billeting accomodation. Billets for these two sections to be arranged direct with Brigades concerned.

3. (a) The supply of R.E. material required by Inf. Bdes for billet improvements will be regulated by allotment from this office to Field Companies.

(b) 478 Field Co will supply the Advance Guard Brigade.

(c) 476 Field Co will supply the Brigades out of the line and will in addition supply materials for work carried out under orders of "Q" branch.

4. 476 Field Co will establish a dump at one of the points where light railways cross good roads,- bearing in mind that materials arriving by Light Railway may have to be picked up again by lorry. They will instal an unloading party and be prepared to off-load trains on arrival. They will also be prepared, on receipt of further instructions to take over old R.E. dumps in the Forest and salve contents.

5. All tents and trench shelters will either be moved with units or handed over, and in the latter case, receipts will be obtained and sent to this office.

6. (a) This office No. 8/8 dated 10.9.18 re affiliation of Field Coys to Bdes is cancelled.
(b) My 23/2 dated 9.9.1918 to Field Coys and D.C.L.I (Bridging programme) is being amended.
(c) An amendment to para 6 of my 13/4 (allotment of R.E. Stores) is being issued.

7. Field Coys to ACKNOWLEDGE.

Issued at 61st. R.E. H.Q.
5 p.m.
September 11th. 1918.

Capt. Adjutant.
For C.R.E. 61st. Divn.

Distribution.

Copy No. 1.	476 Field Co.	Copy No. 8.	182 Inf. Bde.
2.	478 Field Co.	9.	183 Inf. Bde.
3.	479 Field Co.	10.	184 Inf. Bde.
4.	1/5 D.C.L.I.	11.	C.E. XI Corps.
5.	61 Div G.	12 & 13	War Diary
6.	61 Div Q		
7.	61 Sig. Co.		

SECRET.   Copy No. 7

Ref. Maps.   R.E. ORDER No. 121.
36 and 36a.
1/40,000.

1.   The 182 Inf. Brigade is relieving the 184 Inf.
     Bde as Advanced Guard Brigade on the nights 14/15th.
     and 15/16th. inst. as follows:-

     (a) On night 14/15th. one battalion of 182 Brigade
          is relieving one battalion of 184 Brigade and
          comes under orders of G.O.C. 184 Inf. Brigade
          until completion of relief on night 15th/16th.
          Similarly, the relieved battalion of 184 Inf.
          Bde comes under the orders of G.O.C. 182nd.
          Inf. Brigade.

     (b) On the night 15th/16th. the 182 Inf. Brigade
          (less one battalion) is relieving 184 Inf.
          Brigade (less one Battalion) and will take over
          the duties of Advanced Guard Brigade from
          the hour of relief.

2.   On completion of relief, 478 Field Co will
     come under the orders of G.O.C. 182 Inf. Bde.

Issued at R.E.H.Q.   Capt. Adjutant.
      9 p.m.   For C.R.E. 61st. Divn.
September 13th. 1918.

Distribution.

Copy No. 1.   476 Field Co.
         2.   478 Field Co.
         3.   479 Field Co.
         4.   182 Inf. Bde.
         5.   184 Inf. Bde.
         6.   61 Div. G.
       7 & 8   War Diary.
         9.   File

SECRET.   Copy No. 8

R. E. ORDER No. 122.

Ref. Maps
36 and 36n.
1/40,000.

1. The 183rd. Infantry Brigade is relieving the 182nd. Infantry Brigade as Advanced Guard Brigade on the nights 20th/21st. and 21/22nd as follows:-

   (a) On night 20/21st. one battalion of 183rd. Infantry Brigade is relieving one battalion of 182nd. Infantry Brigade and will come under orders of G.O.C. 182nd. Infantry Brigade until completion of relief of night 21st/22nd. Similarly, the relieved battalion of 182nd. Infantry Brigade comes under the orders of: G.O.C. 183rd. Infantry Brigade.

   (b) On the night 21/22nd. the 183rd. Infantry Brigade (less one battalion) is relieving 182nd. Infantry Brigade (less one battalion) and takes over the duties of Advanced Guard Brigade from the hour of relief.

2. On completion of relief, 476 Field Co will come under the orders of G.O.C. 183 Inf. Brigade.

                                            [signature]

Issued at 61 R.E.H.Q   Capt. Adjutant.
     11 a.m.
September 16th. 1918.   For C.R.E. 61st. Division.

Distribution.

Copy No. 1.   476 Field Co.
         2.   478 Field Co.
         3.   479 Field Co.
         4.   183 Inf. Bde.
         5.   61 Div G.   Copy No 6 - to 182 Inf Bde
      7 & 8. War Diary
         9.   File.

SECRET.   Copy No. 10

Ref. Maps: R.E. ORDER No. 125.
Sheets 36A.& 36.
 1/40,000.

1.   479 Field Co. will take over work in the Right Brigade area from 476 Field Co. tomorrow, the 21st. inst.

2.   Allotment of work to Field Companies will be as follows:-

   (a) <u>476 Field Co.</u> (H.Q. K.23.c.6.3) employed on back area work. 2 Sections billetted at L.22.d.5.8, employed on billet repairs in Left Brigade area and responsible for water reconnaissance and pump repairs in that area. Bridging section attached to 479 Field Co.

   (b) <u>478 Field Co.</u> attached to Advanced Guard Brigade. Responsible for water reconnaissance and pump repairs in the Advanced Guard area.   Assists Advanced Guard in repairs of billets.   R esponsible for maintenance of bridges - SAILLY Pont Tournant (inclusive) to Northern Divisional Boundary. *One section to assist Div Art in erection of shelters*

   (c) <u>479 Field Co.</u> (Billetted L.26.b.7.3). 2 sections employed on billet repairs for Right Brigade and responsible for water reconnaissance and pump repairs in Right Brigade area.   The Company is responsible for maintenance of bridges - LYS Bridge (exclusive) to SAILLY Pont Tournant (exclusive).

3.   Supply of R.E. materials for billet repairs will be arranged as follows:-

       476 Field Co. supplies Left Brigade.
       478 Field Co. supplies Advanced Guard Brigade.
       479 Field Co. supplies Right Brigade.

   An amendment to stores allotment to Field Companies is being published today.

4.   Field Companies to acknowledge.

Issued at 12.15 p.m.   Capt. - Adjutant,
20th.Sept.1918.   for C.R.E. 61st.Div.

   Distribution:-

   Copy No. 1 to 476 Field Co.
    "   2 to 478 Field Co.
    "   3 to 479 Field Co.
    "   4 to 61st.Div. "G".
    "   5 to 61st.Div. "Q".
    "   6 to 182 Inf. Bde.
    "   7 to 183 Inf. Bde.
    "   8 to 184 Inf. Bde.
    "   9 to War Diary.
    "   10 to War Diary.
    "   11 to File.

SECRET.
FRANCE.
Sht. 36.

Copy No. 13

R.E. ORDER No. 124.

1. (a) The ADVANCED GUARD BRIGADE is ordered to keep vigorous touch with the enemy and to be prepared to advance.

(b) In certain circumstances the Division may bring up another Brigade and advance on a two Brigade front, in which case the Brigades are to be known as the "RIGHT" and "LEFT" Brigades; the inter-Brigade boundary being the East and West grid line through H.19. central.

(c) The Divisional objectives are:-

1st. OBJECTIVE. CROIX BLANCHE - FLEURBAIX - ERQUINGHEM.
2nd. OBJECTIVE. LA BOUTILLERIE (excl) - BOIS GRENIER - RUE MARLE (excl).

2. The Corps Road Policy lays down that Corps will be responsible for making the following roads passable for lorries and heavy guns, building bridges to carry 17 ton axle loads.

(a) GREEN ROAD. ESTAIRES PONT LEVIS - LE NOUVEAU MONDE - SAILLY SUR LA LYS - BAC ST MAUR - FORT ROMPU - FLEURBAIX - BOIS GRENIER.

(b) YELLOW ROAD. LE DRUMEZ - RUE DE PARADIS - LAVENTIE - M.5.b.1.8. - M.6.a.0.3. - G.36.d.7.7. - H.31.c.6.0 H. .d.1.2. - CROIX BLANCHE - N.4.d.8.6. - LA BOUTILLERIE - I.31.a.5.6. - LE BRIDOUX.

(c) BLUE ROAD. LA FLINQUE - FAUQUISSART - RUE TILLELOY - PETILLON - LES CLOCHERS - FROMELLES - LE MAISNIL EN WEPPES.

(d) RED ROAD. PETILLON - CROIX BLANCHE - FLEURBAIX.

3. The Divisional Road Policy is to open up the following roads for first line transport.

(a) YELLOW ROAD. from M.5.b.1.8. forward for Right Brigade.
    GREEN ROAD. For the Left Brigade.
    BROWN ROAD. FLEURBAIX - RUE MARLE for Left Brigade

4. Map showing the above roads is issued herewith as Appendix "A".

5. When the Divisional Advance commences on a two Brigade front

(a) 479 Field Company will place one section under the orders of G.O.C. Right Brigade and 1/5 D.C.L.I. will attach one platoon to this section.

(b) 478 Field Company will place one section under the orders of G.O.C. Left Brigade and 1/5 D.C.L.I. will attach one platoon to this section.

(c) The remainder of the

(c) The remainder of the Divisional R.E and Pioneers will be under the orders of the C.R.E.

(d) 1/5 D.C.L.I. will place 3 platoons under the orders of O.C. 479 Field Co and three platoons under the orders of O.C. 478 Field Co.

(e) 479 and 478 Field Coys (less one section each and with 3 platoons 1/5 D.C.L.I. attached) will operate in the Right and Left Brigade areas respectively, their chief work being:-

  (i) The opening up communications.

RIGHT Field Co.   the YELLOW ROAD.
LEFT FIELD Co.   The GREEN ROAD first and the BROWN ROAD as soon as available labour permits.

The roads shown black will be kept open by Field Companies in their respective Brigade areas until they are relieved by troops from behind.

Whilst it is not the duty of the Division to open up communications for more than first line transport (including Field Artillery) it is always advisable to provide for 5½ ton axle loads and often for 10 ton axle loads where this extra work can be done without hindering the advance of the fighting troops. Pontoons must never be left "in bridge" longer than is necessary and the work of replacing them by a "permanent" structure should be commenced without delay. Many small craters already block the roads ahead of us and it is more than likely that further explosions will occur after we have commenced to use the roads. Every preparation must be made for dealing with these obstructions at once - not only must roads and bridges be made passable but they must be maintained until taken over by some rear organization. Accurate and clear direction boards are essential.

  (ii) Developing Water Supply. The nearest R.A.M.C. officer available should be asked to test likely sources They should then be properly marked and direction boards put up

  (iii) Searching for and rendering inocuous mines.- tank traps - booby traps etc. - The enemy has developed this "art" to such an extent that no dugout, building or cross roads can be guaranteed <u>safe</u> after a reasonably thorough examination. Buildings, dugouts, wells, etc will be examined and marked either

  "DANGEROUS (date)"   or
  "EXAMINED BY (number of Coy and date)".

The date is important and the word "SAFE" should never be used except on the authority of the Company Commander.

No "existing" accomodation in captured territory is to be occupied. - Troops are to use improvised accomodation taken forward.

  (iv) Elaborating and supplementing reconnaissance of forward sections. The functions of the sections attached to Brigades are reconnaissance and the carrying out of hasty work ordered by G.O.C. Brigade. Any important work commenced by this section should be taken over by the Company as soon as circumstances permit, so as to free the Advanced Section for further work. O.C. should decide whether to relieve the section or leave it to complete any special job and place a fresh section under orders of G.O.C. Brigade.

6   The importance

-3-

6. The importance of passing on information in a clear, concise and useful form to all who require it is of paramount importance and is by far our weakest point. Field Company Commanders will personally instruct their officers and N.C.O's in this.

(a) Notice boards <u>and</u> direction boards to water, bridges etc are important and require watching as they have a habit of changing as well as becoming "out of date".

(b) Reports on condition of roads and bridges should make it clear up to what point each class of traffic can go and by what route.

(c) Reports on work required to be done and materials available near the site should make it possible for those behind to send up the correct number of men and quantities of materials to do the job.

(d) Information should always be passed on at once to any troops in the neighbourhood to whom the information may be useful.

(e) Section officers and N.C.O's must get reports to their O.C. as soon as possible and state whom else they have informed.

(f) Field Company Commanders will consolidate reports, check them and inform C.R.E without delay as well as any troops in the neighbourhood to whom the information may be useful. Reports to C.R.E. should make it clear what the O.C is doing with the troops he has available and he should state whom we has informed.

(g) Field Companies are responsible for keeping touch with C.R.E at D.H.Q and should keep runners at the nearest Signal Office - advising C.R.E where he can send their messages.

7. Arrangements have been made at the C.R.E's dump for leaving a guard should a rapid advance take place. Field Coys should at all times be ready to dump all surplus baggage and stores at the C.R.E Dump. In the first instance each Company should leave one man with 7 days rations with these stores. 1/5 D.C.L.I and Signal Company may make similar arrangements if desired.

8. Field Companies and D.C.L.I. to ACKNOWLEDGE.

                                                                               [signature]

Issued at 61st. R.E.H.Q.   Capt. Adjutant.
   11.55 a.m.   For C.R.E. 61 Divn.
September 27th. 1918.

<u>Distribution.</u>   <u>MAPS</u>

Copy No.			
1.	476 Field Co.	2	copies
2.	478 Field Co.	4	"
3.	479 Field Co.	4	"
4.	1/5 D.C.L.I.	4	"
5.	61 Div G.	2	"
6.	61 Div Q.	1	"
7.	61 Signal Co.	1	"
8.	61 Div Art.	1	"
9.	182 Inf. Bde.	2	"
10.	183 Inf. Bde.	2	"
11.	184 Inf. Bde.	2	"
12.	C.E. XI Corps.	1	"
13 & 14.	War Diary.	2	"
15.	File.		

SECRET.   Copy No. 9

ADDENDUM No. 1
to
R.E. Order No. 124.

1.   Para.1 (a) is now inoperative and para.1 (b) has been anticipated as the Division now has two Brigades in line and one in Reserve.
     The R.E. organization for an advance is now a reality and will be completed by O.C. 1/5 D.C.L.I. placing 3 platoons under the orders of each Field Co. in Line the moment the advance commences.

2.   A new Corps Road Policy has been issued, copies of which have been circulated to Field Companies, but as this makes provision for an advance beyond LILLE, it is not proposed to amend the Map issued with R.E. Order No.124 at present. The Divisional Road Policy shown in R.E. Order 124 will therefore hold good until further orders are issued from this office.

3.   <u>Marking of Dugouts, Cellars, etc.</u>
     The instructions contained in Army Routine Order No.3245 are in addition to those contained in paras. 5 & 6 of R.E. Order 124, viz:-

   Dugouts, etc., which have been passed at the first examination will be marked at the entrance with green chalk, the word "examined" and the date and signature of the unit concerned.

   e.g.   ● 4" diam. (Green)
            Examined
            (date)
            (unit)

   After a final examination for delayed action mines has been completed, a white tin sign will be nailed up, lettered in black as follows:-

   >Considered<
   >   Safe   <

   Dugouts, etc., in which booby traps are found, or which are considered dangerous, will be marked either in red chalk as follows:-

            ● 4" diam. (Red).
            Mined. Dangerous.
            (date)
            (unit)

   or will have a red tin sign nailed up, lettered in black as follows:-

   > Mined   <   12" x 4".
   >Dangerous <

   Roads will be marked as follows:-

   12" x 4" [DANGER]   12" x 4" [→ Safe]   Moveable arrow.

   White letters on red board.   This board will be erected
   This board to be erected if   when road has been inspected
   road has not been inspected   and found safe for traffic.
   or has been found mined.

   (b) Tunnellers at present attached to Infantry Brigades are being withdrawn, and as soon as the advance commences 6 tunnellers will be attached to each Field Company in line to assist in reconnaissance for mines and booby traps and for rendering the same innocuous.

(2)

4. **WATER SUPPLY.**

It is the duty of Field Companies to reconnoitre for sources of water in their areas and, as far as their resources permit, they should exploit them.

One chemist from 57 Sanitary Section is now attached to each Field Company in Line for the purpose of examining water and advising Field Companies as to its suitability.

It is anticipated that there will not be sufficient good water available "on the site" and the following resources for (i) rendering unsuitable water pure and (ii) bringing forward suitable water, exist :-

(a) <u>1 Compressor Lorry.</u> This lorry is operated by 351 E.& M. Coy. R.E. under orders of Army Headquarters. It is to be used for forcing water out of bore holes into storage tanks and it is therefore important that information about bore holes should be included in all Field Company reports.

(b) <u>1 Sterilizing Lorry.</u> This lorry filters and chlorinates water and can render potable, muddy water from streams, &c. The lorry is not permitted to work within 10,000 yards of the front line. It can deliver 400 gallons of potable water per hour. Suggestions for sites for sterilizing lorry must take into account the fact that there must be a lorry approach to the source and must be suitable for pulling in water carts.

(c) <u>Alum sedimentation plants</u>, either the same as exist at LYS Bridge or improvised from any available tanks, which will do the same work as a sterilizing lorry but at a much slower rate, and which should be fitted with hand pumps if petrol-pumps are not provided by the E. & M. Company. These plants are not very suitable for use during a rapid advance.

(d) Any pumps on the establishment of Field Companies should be used when required, but must not normally be left behind when Units move. They should be replaced as soon as possible by pumps drawn from the C.R.E's dump, or by repaired captured pumps.

(e) Two lorries, each carrying 150 gallon tanks, are at the disposal of the Division for carrying water forward. Any suggestions from Field Companies as to their use should take account of condition of roads over which the lorries will have to travel.

Issued at 6 p.m.
1st.Oct.1918.

Capt. - Adjutant,
for C.R.E. 61st.Division.

Distribution :-
Copy No.1 to 476 Field Co.
" 2w to 478 Field Co.
" 3 to 479 Field Co.
" 4 to 1/5 D.C.L.I.
" 5 to 61st.Div."G".
" 6 to 61st.Div."Q".
" 7 to C.E. XI Corps.
" 8 to War Diary.
" 9 to War Diary.
" 10 to File.

SECRET.   Copy No. 13

R. E. ORDER No. 125.

Ref. Map
France Sheet 36.   28.9.18.

1.   182 and 184 Inf. Bdes. are relieving 183 Inf. Bde. in
        the line tonight, relief to be completed by 4 a.m.
        Distribution on completion of relief as follows:-

        184 Bde. becomes "Right Brigade" - Brigade H.Q. at
                L.12.c.8.3 - Northern Boundary the East and
                West grid line through H.19.central.

        182 Bde. becomes "Left Brigade" - Bde.H.Q. at G.8.a.8.1.

        183 Bde. becomes "Reserve Brigade" - Bde.H.Q. at
                CHAPELLE DUVELLE, and battalions located in
                the area MAURIANNE FARM, YAM FARM and KENNET
                CROSS.

2.   (a) One Section 479 Field Co. and 1 Platoon 1/5 D.C.L.I. will
         come under the orders of G.O.C. 184 Inf.Bde.

     (b) One Section 478 Field Co. and 1 Platoon 1/5 D.C.L.I. will
         come under the orders of G.O.C. 182 Inf.Bde.

     (c) The remainder of the Divl. R.E. and 1/5 D.C.L.I. are under
         C.R.E's orders.

3.   (a) 479 Field Co. will be employed on improving accommodation
         for the Right Brigade and will commence construction of
         Advanced Bde.H.Q. (including attached Artillery) forthwith.
         The following location is suggested, but will be approved
         by G.O.C. 184 Bde. before work is commenced.
             About G.29.a.8.6 for H.Q. of Infantry and R.A.
             About G.29.c.3.1 for H.Q. personnel.

     (b) 478 Field Co. will be employed on improving accommodation
         for the Left Brigade and will commence construction of
         Advanced Bde.H.Q. (including attached Artillery) forthwith.
         The following location is suggested, but will be approved
         by G.O.C. 182 Bde. before work is commenced.
             About G.23.c.7.7 for H.Q. of Infantry and R.A.
             About G.23.d.4.8 for H.Q. personnel.

     (c) 476 Field Co. will take over maintenance of Bridges over
         the METEREN BECQUE. With the exception that 478 and 479
         Field Coys. responsibility for bridge patrol remains as at
         present.

     NOTE:- The attachment of 3 platoons of Pioneers to 478 Field
         Co. and 3 platoons to 479 Field Co. vide R.E. Order No.124
         para. 5 (d) does not come into operation until the advance
         commences

4.   (a) 476 Field Co. (with attached Pioneers) will move tomorrow,
         the 29th.inst. from MERVILLE to the area L.15.16.21.22
         (exact location to be notified later).

     (b) 476 Field Co. Bridging Section will rejoin its Company from
         479 Field Co.

     (c) 476 Field Co. will take over all work west of the Corps
         Battle Line, except work for Right and Left Brigades; and
         will continue to take orders direct from "Q" Branch.

(2)

4. (contd.)   (d) 476 Field Co. will ration all details at present rationed by 479 Field Co., including Divisional R.E. dump party.

5.   478 and 479 Field Companies will form forward dumps of bridging stores etc. forthwith. Selected sites should, if possible, be close together and locations will be reported to this office. Separate instructions are being issued as to contents of dumps.

6.   Field Companies and 1/5 D.C.L.I. to acknowledge.

Issued at 1.30 p.m.
28th. Sept. 1918.

Capt. - Adjutant,
for C.R.E. 61st.Div.

Distribution:-

Copy No. 1 to 476 Field Co.
" 2 to 478 Field Co.
" 3 to 479 Field Co.
" 4 to 1/5 D.C.L.I.
" 5 to 61st.Div. "G".
" 6 to 61st.Div. "Q".
" 7 to 61st.Div.Signals.
" 8 to 61st.Div. Arty.
" 9 to 182 Inf. Bde.
" 10 to 183 Inf. Bde.
" 11 to 184 Inf. Bde.
" 12 to C.E. XI Corps.
" 13 to War Diary.
" 14 to War Diary.
" 15 to File.

War Diary.
(ORIGINAL.)
for SEPT 1918.
C.R.E. 61st DIVN.

APPENDIX 3

Work Orders & Instructions

"A" Form
MESSAGES AND SIGNALS.

Army Form C. 2121
(In pads of 100.)

No. of Message..............

Prefix...... Code.......m	Words	Charge	This message is on a/c of:	Recd. at.........m
Office of Origin and Service Instructions	Sent		..........................Service.	Date.................
....	At.........m			From...............
....	To			
	By		(Signature of "Franking Officer.")	By.................

TO { 61st. Div. "G".   HJEU
     61st. Div. "Q".   HUFU   C.E. XI Corps.
     C.R.A.   HUTU

Sender's Number.	Day of Month.	In reply to Number,	AAA
T.23/2	1st.		
with	the	exception	of
two	bad	places	at
L.9.d.9.1	and	L.10.c.9.1	road
is	fit	for	field
guns	and	limbers	to
L.10.b.7.8	and	L.11.c.7.3	via
WILLOT	FARM	BDY	BERQUIN -
and	MONTIGNY	SELSEY	FARM
and	Guns	can	get
right	through	now	in
daylight	and	the	two
bad	patches	will	probably
be	passable	by	tomorrow
evening	AAA	CHAPELLE	DUVELLE
road	is	now	fit
for	field	guns	as
far	east	as	L.20.a.0.7

From   AAA Added. G.   Q.   C.R.A. C.E. XI Corps
Place   and 3 Inf. Bde.
Time   from   G.H.Q.

The above may be forwarded as now corrected. (Z)

....
               Censor.   Signature of Addressor or person authorised to telegraph in his name.

* This line should be erased if not required.

476 Field Co.
478 Field Co.
479 Field Co.

    1. Field Companies are reminded that they must always be prepared to carry out bridging operations with their bridging equipment.

    2. At the present moment it is not deemed necessary to issue orders that bridging equipment should be loaded each time wagons return to their horse lines, but Companies should always be prepared to load their bridging equipment without undue delay.

    3. It will probably be necessary to throw pontoon bridges across the LYS CANAL E. of ESTAIRES and the policy will be to replace these as soon as possible with timber bridges, so as to bring the technical equipment into reserve for further use.

    4. The two reserve sections of 479 Field Co may be used by O.C. 479 Field Co for reconnaissance, which should include suitable places for pontoon bridges across the LYS E. of ESTAIRES as soon as our line enables reconnaissance to be carried out.

    5. 479 Field Co should also make dumps of salved timber suitable for bridging, and it is suggested that this work be done forthwith in MERVILLE, such dumps should, of course be so located that transport can get at them to load, and locations and approximate quantities should be notified to this office without delay.

    Should O.C. 479 Field Co require Pioneer assistance in this connection, he should report number of men, time and place required.

    Capt. Adjutant.

Sept. 1st. 1918.   For C.R.E. 61st. Division.

476 Field Co.
478 Field Co.
479 Field Co.
61st. Div G.
61st. Div Q.
1/5 D.C.L.I.
G.S. XI Corps.

23/2/2

1. (a) Patrols found the Western portion of ESTAIRES unoccupied today and there are indications that our line will advance comparatively rapidly during the next two days.

(b) 479 Field Co has been instructed to reconnoitre for crossings over the LYS E. of ESTAIRES as soon as the situation permits; the policy being to construct bridges in the first instance with bridging equipment, and to replace these as soon as possible with timber bridges.

2. All Field Company bridging equipment will be loaded by 6 p.m. tomorrow the 2nd. inst and will not be off-loaded again without reference to this office.

3. The following moves will take place tomorrow 2nd. inst.

(i) 479 Field Co (less 2 sections attached to the outpost Brigade) including transport, to the area about K.23 - K.24. - K.30. - L.25.

(ii). "A" Company 1/5 D.C.L.I. from APPLE HOUSE to about CHAPELLE DUVELLE (remains attached to 479 Field Co)

(iii) "C" Company 1/5 D.C.L.I from present quarters to APPLE HOUSE.

4. Field Companies and Pioneers will be employed tomorrow 2nd. inst as follows:-

(a) <u>476 Field Co.</u>   2 sections billets repairs D.H.Q.
                         2 sections billet repairs LE PARC and RUE DES MORTS.

(b) <u>478 Field Co.</u>   Necessary R.E. supervision with all attached PORTUGUESE troops on repair of Road LE SART - K.28.a. - K.29.b.7.9.
                         Remainder of Company on construction of weather-proof shelters in M.L.R & work in hand in back areas.

(c) <u>479 Field Co.</u>   2 sections with Advance Guard.
                         2 sections reconnaissance etc according to circumstances.

(d) 1/5 D.C.L.I.   One Company attached 479 Field Co
                         2 strong platoons repairs to road TRENT FM - GREVE FARM.
                         2 strong platoons moving mud from surface of (and repairing) road GREVE FM → NEUF BERQUIN. Remainder of Battn as available on billet repairs at RUE DES MORTS.

(e) The platoons of D.C.L.I. at present employed at HARTSTONE Dump will rejoin its company tomorrow after detailing 10 men to remain behind for work at the dump. Adjustment of rations etc to be made direct between O.C. D.C.L.I and 479 Field Co.

1.9.1918.

Capt. Adjutant.
For C.R.E. 61st. DIVN.

476 Field Co.
478 Field Co.
479 Field Co.
1/5 D.C.L.I.
61st.Div. "G".
61st.Div. "Q".
C.R.E II Corps.

The employment and moves of Field Companies and 1/5 D.C.L.I. for tomorrow, 3rd.inst.,will be as follows :-

1. **476 Field Co.**
   (a) 2 Sections billet repairs B.H.Q.
   (b) 2 Sections prepare accommodation neighbourhood – GRAVE FARM – ROBERMETZ.
   (c) 476 Field Co. (less 2 sections) will move to this area tomorrow; move to be completed by 6 p.m.

2. **478 Field Co.**
   (a) 1 Section continue work at present in hand in back area.
   (b) 2 Sections working with Portuguese on roads:
       (i) LE SART - K.29.b.3.9 - Cross roads K.29.b.1.5;
       (ii) LE SART - Road Bridge K.29.c.5.2.
   (c) Spare R.E. labour to be employed on erecting weather-proof accommodation in the M.L.R.

3. **479 Field Co.**
   (a) 2 Sections with Advanced Guard.
   (b) Remainder constructing foot and first line transport bridges across the LIS CANAL at K.29.d.8.5.

4. **1/5 D.C.L.I.**
   (a) "A" Coy. employed under orders of O.C. 479 Field Co.

   (b) "B" Coy. - 1 platoon to report to O.C. 479 Field Co. at the College, MERVILLE, K.23.d. at 8 a.m. to salve timber for bridging.
          Remainder under orders of O.C. 1/5 D.C.L.I.

   (c) "C" Coy. - 2 Platoons clearing NEUF BERQUIN - ESTAIRES Road from road junction L.13.b.95.05 towards ESTAIRES.
          2 Platoons on road from GRAVE FARM to Road junction L.13.b.95.05.

2nd.Sept.1918.

Capt. - Adjutant,
for C.R.E. 61st.Div.

61st. Division, "G".
182 Inf. Bde.
479 Field Co.
C.R.E. XI Corps.

RECONNAISSANCE REPORT - 2.9.18.

1.(a) L.29.d.95.30 - Pont Levis bridge destroyed. Patrols can cross on debris. Footbridge under construction tonight; first line transport bridge will be constructed tomorrow.

1.(b) L.29.d.15.00 - Destroyed trestle transport bridge. Footbridge can be constructed quickly on remains of piles.

2. L.35.a.05.65 - Duckboard raft, secured to north bank; would carry 3 or 4 men.

3. L.34.b.90.65 - Remains of a large dump on south bank; contains - duckboards, angle iron pickets, wood pickets, decauville track and round iron.

4. L.34.b.85.70 - Light railway bridge destroyed; otherwise Rly. in good condition. Small amount of timber on north bank, including 3" and 2" stuff suitable for decking.

5. L.34.b.60.65 - Footbridge destroyed.

6. L.34.b.50.80 - Road bridge destroyed; masonry abutments in good condition. 59th.Div.R.E. erecting footbridge. Some timber on site, including baulks in 12ft. lengths.

7. L.34.b.25.85 - Footbridge destroyed.

8. L.28.c.90.20 - Dump on north bank. 300 to 400 coils Bosch barbed wire, long & medium screw pickets, about 600 concertinas, plain wire, and angle iron pickets with footplates.

9. L.28.c.60.25 - Ballast and stone dump.

10. L.28.c.10.60 - Destroyed footbridge.

11. L.27.d.90.60 - Barge sunk 1oft. clear of north bank.

12. L.27.d.70.45 - Ballast dump and about 10 tons of coal.

13. L.27.d.45.35 - 50 duckboards in a hut.

14. L.27.d.30.15 - Barge stranded, 15ft.clear of north bank, laden with coal.

15. L.27.d.20.00 - Destroyed road bridge & 25oyds. timber road on north bank, 3" stuff, 9ft.lengths.

2nd.Sept.1918.

Lieut.-Colonel, R.E.
C.R.E. 61st.Division.

475 Field Co.
476 Field Co.
479 Field Co.
1/5 D.C.L.I.
61st.Div. "G".
61st.Div. "Q".
O.C. XI Corps.

The employment and moves of Field Companies and 1/5 D.C.L.I. for tomorrow, 4th.inst., will be as follows:-

1. **475 Field Co.** Under orders of G.O.C. Advanced Guard.

2. **476 Field Co.** (a) Billet improvements at D.H.Q., HAVERSKERQUE, LE PARC, and RUE DES MORTS.
   (b) Superintending Portuguese working parties on roads.

3. **479 Field Co.** (a) 2 Sections in Reserve, on completion of work on bridges tonight.
   (b) Construction of first line transport bridge at L.20.c.0.4.

4. **1/5 D.C.L.I.** (a) "A" Coy.- employed under orders of O.C. 476 Field Co. repairing road at L.11.c.9.4. clearing FAGOOT FARM - ESTAIRES - NEUF BERQUIN Roads in ESTAIRES.
   (b) "B" Coy.-
   (i) 1 Platoon working with 479 Field Co. on bridge at L.20.c.0.4. O.C. 479 Field Co. will arrange time and rendezvous.
   (ii) 3 Platoons improving NEUF BERQUIN - MONTIGNY - SELBNY FARM Road.
   (c) "C" Coy.-
   (i) Improving LES PUREBEBOQUE - MERVILLE Road in K.23.c. and K.29.a.
   (ii) Improving MERVILLE - NEUF BERQUIN Road, particularly in K.29.a. & b.
   (iii) Improving ESTAIRES Road in the neighbourhood of L.25.central.

3rd.Sept.1918.

Capt. - Adjutant,
for C.R.E. 61st.Div.

476 Field Co.
478 Field Co.
479 Field Co.

NOTES on RECONNAISSANCE - 4.9.18.

1. G.26.d.4.3 - 3 bridges destroyed - no material.

2. G.27.c.3.4 - 3 bridges destroyed; good approach to left bank.

3. G.27.c.5.8 - Destroyed footbridge; some material on site; large stone dump on left bank.

4. G.21.d.9.9 - 2 road bridges destroyed; material on site. Footbridge (indifferent) 100yds. up stream.

5. G.21.b.95.70 - Destroyed heavy footbridge; some material.

6. G.22.a.2.9 - Destroyed light footbridge; no material.

7. G.16.b.65.65 - Road bridge demolished. Embanked sleeper road approach to right bank, but there is a second gap on this road.
Light railway bridge demolished on down-stream side of road bridge.
There is a second light railway bridge destroyed 80 yds. down-stream. The towing path bridge (left bank) is destroyed here; otherwise, the towing path is passable for transport from ESTAIRES to this point. There are a few awkward shell holes in it near ESTAIRES. O.C. 476 Field Co.should arrange with A.Coy. D.C.L.I. to fill these.

4th.Sept.1918.

Lieut.-Colonel, R.E.
C.R.E. 61st.Division.

"A" Form.
MESSAGES AND SIGNALS.

Army Form C. 2121.
(In pads of 100.)

TO	61 Div G.	C.E. XI Corps	
	61 Div Q	182 Brigade	
	61 Div Art	183 Brigade	184 Brigade

Sender's Number.	Day of Month.	In reply to Number.	
*T.588	5		AAA

Following	bridges	have	been
completed	aaa	G.16.c.8.6.	pontoon
bridge	aaa	G.16.c.7.9.	trestle
bridge	aaa	G.21.d.8.8.	pontoon
bridge	aaa	G.27.a.9.4.	packanimal
bridge	aaa	G.26.c.15.30	Road
diversion	round	dry	stream
aaa	G.26.c.0.5	trestle	bridge
aaa	L.17.d.4.8.	bridge	oevr
Meteren	Becque	aaa	addressed
61 Div G	61 Div Q	61 Div Art	182
Brigade	183 Brigade	184 Brigade	and
C.E.	XI	Corps.	

From C.R.E.
Place
Time 9.50 a.m.

476 Field Co.
478 Field Co.
479 Field Co.

1. Failing receipt of orders to carry out any more important works, Field Companies will be employed on the following:-

   479 Field Co. - Lorry bridge NOUVEAU MONDE, and

   First line Transport Bridge ROUGE MAISON.

   476 Field Co. - Lorry bridge at O.16.b.5.5, if approach on right bank can be made suitable for M.T. after bridging gap over stream at O.16.b.6.3; and

   Reconnoitre for First Line Transport or Lorry bridge in neighbourhood of BAC ST. MAUR. Town to be avoided, if possible.

2. Lorry bridges are to take a minimum axle load of 5½ tons.

3. Pontoons will not be taken out of the water until receipt of definite orders to do so from this office.

5th. Sept. 1918.

Capt. - Adjutant,
for C.R.E. 61st. Div.

Copies to:-
61st. Division, "G".
61st. Division, "Q".
61st. Div. Art.
C.R. XI Corps.
1/5 D.C.L.I.

"A" Form.
MESSAGES AND SIGNALS.

Army Form C. 2121.
(In pads of 100.)

Prefix......Code.......m.	Words.	Charge.	This message is on a/c of:	Recd. at.......m.
Office of Origin and Service Instructions.	Sent			Date...........
	At........m.		........Service.	From...........
	To........			
	By:.......		(Signature of "Franking Officer.")	By........

TO – ~~HQU~~ 478 Fd Co   ~~NOR~~ 184 Bde
    ~~NOBO~~ 182 Bde   ~~XCO~~ Div Art
          183 Bde

Sender's Number. | Day of Month. | In reply to Number. | AAA
~~T.592~~ | 5 | |

It	is	~~reported~~	~~that~~
the	2	~~pontoon~~	~~bridges~~
have	been	~~destroyed~~	~~are~~
you	will	~~construct~~	a
medium	pontoon	~~bridge~~	forthwith
at	about	~~C.21.d.6.2~~	~~are~~
completion	and	route	for
traffic	to	be	reported
to	Infantry	Brigades,	Div
Arty	and	this	office
as	early	~~as~~	possible
~~soon~~	addressed	478 Fd Co	repeated
182	183	184 ~~HQU~~	and
~~NOBO~~ Div Art			

From
Place   MEBO
Time   13.5

The above may be forwarded as now corrected. (Z)

Censor. Signature of Addressor or person authorised to telegraph in his name.

* This line should be erased if not required.

"A" Form.
MESSAGES AND SIGNALS.

Army Form C. 2121.
(In pads of 100.)

Prefix......Code........ m	Words.	Charge.	This message is on a/c of:	Recd. at.........m
Office of Origin and Service Instructions.	Sent			Date...........
	At..........m.		..............Service.	From..........
	To.........			By............

TO { 478 Hdts ~~~~ 184 Bdt
      182 Bde ~~~~ Div Art
      183 Bde

Sender's Number.	Day of Month.	In reply to Number.	AAA

* ~~No?~~ ~~~~ ~~T.512~~ ~~pontoon~~
~~bridge~~ ~~at~~ ~~G.21.c.8.7.~~ ~~is~~
~~intact &~~ ~~but~~ ~~the~~ ~~pontoon~~
~~bridge~~ ~~at~~ ~~G.16.c.7.6.~~ ~~has~~
~~been~~ ~~destroyed.~~ ~~and~~ ~~advanced~~
~~post piquets~~ ~~of~~ ~~T.100~~ ~~and~~
61 Div @

From CRE
Place 10.25 a.m.
Time

SECRET.   Copy.

61st. DIVISION INSTRUCTIONS No.T-1.
OPERATIONS.

1. The enemy's continued withdrawal, and the distance which the Advanced Guard Brigade has now gained necessitates the following revision of plans for future operations.

Advanced Guard Brigade. 2. The Advanced Guard Brigade will continue to maintain contact with, and act vigorously against, the enemy rearguards, and be prepared to take advantage of opportunities created by success elsewhere.

Objectives. 3. Objectives to be reached by the Advanced Guard Bde will be given from time to time, but in the event of a very rapid advance, contact will continue to be made even though the advance is made beyond the objective line laid down by the Division.

Outpost Line of Resistance. 4. An Outpost Line of Resistance, to which the Advanced troops of the Advanced Guard Bde will fall back in event of heavy hostile counter-attack, and upon which the Advanced Guard Brigade and supporting artillery will resist and break up an enemy counter-stroke, will be selected & notified to Div H.Q from time to time.

Corps Battle Line. 5. A Corps Battle Line, usually some 3000 to 5000 yds in rear of the objectives to be reached by the Advanced Guard Brigade will be selected and notified to all concerned.
This Corps Battle Line will represent the front of the position on which the Division will stand and fight in the event of a heavy hostile counter-attack, and its selection will therefore regulate the forward movement of the main body of the Division and Heavy Artillery.

Method of holding Corps Battle Line. 6. The Corps Battle Line on this Divisional front will be held with two Infantry Brigades in the Line covered by one Field Artillery Brigade and Heavies.
The Advanced Guard Brigade will be brought into Divisional Reserve on being forced to withdraw.
The inter-Brigade boundary will be notified, together with the publication of the Corps Battle Line.

Dispositions. 7. The above dispositions for defence will, for the future modify those of the two Infantry Bdes forming the main body of the Division. These two Brigades will now be disposed in depth in three excelons. Each Brigade will be disposed with one battalion forward, on or in close proximity to the existing Corps Battle Line; one battalion within supporting distance in rear of the Corps Line, and the third battalion in Reserve.
The necessary orders in regard to these dispositions will be issued.

Accomodation of troops. 8. This arrangement will facilitate the question of accomodation, battalions improving the accomodation for the successive moves forward of battalions in rear.
The importance of the improvement of accomodation in the area vacated by the enemy is emphazised. All units will make every endeavour to prepare and repair the houses they may be temporarily occupying, as well as those in the vicinity that can be made habitable.
At the same time, advantage will be taken of the excellent facilities for training in the present area by battalions and other units not operating with the Advance Guard.

P.T.O.

-2-

Defences.	9. Infantry Brigades concerned will be responsible for siting in detail of the line to be held in case of counter-attack.

It is not the intention to construct new systems of defence until the line stabilises, but it will be necessary to strengthen localities, and to improve and adapt such defences as exist and are suitable.

In order to save time, and labour, the fullest use will be made of existing wire entanglements.

Machine Guns. 10. Two Companies Machine Gun Battn will be prepared to occupy the Corps Battle Line, one Company being allotted to the defence of each Brigade sector, and to come under the orders of the G.O.C. Infantry Brigade concerned.

The O.C. 61st. Bn. M.G.C. will, on receipt of the notification of the Corps Battle Line, detail one Company to each Infantry Brigade and will notify all concerned.

These Companies will be accomodated in the area allotted to the forward battalions of Brigades, under arrangements to be made by Brigadiers concerned, and will be in a position to man their battle positions immediately on the receipt of orders.

The Machine Gun Company Commander will carry out the necessary reconnaissances on the Brigade sector of the Corps Line under the Orders of the G.O.C. Brigade.

Artillery. 11. The Advanced Guard Artillery Brigade will be disposed to cover the outpost Line of Resistance, and to assist the forward movement of the advanced troops.

The remaining F.A. Brigade will be prepared to occupy previously reconnoitred positions to cover the Corps Battle Line, under orders of the C.R.A.

Communications. 12. Signal communications will be run upon the lines laid down in S.S. 191 Chapter III. To this end, the XI Corps will determine, in consultation with Divisions, a succession of points on the line of advance of the Division.

These points are to be the most likely positions of Brigade and Divisional Headquarters, and Signals will make all such points communication centres.

All telephone lines will be laid to these communication centres, and very early information as to their positions will be necessary to enable Signals to establish and equip them for Signal traffic as soon as they are needed.

13 ACKNOWLEDGE.

(Sd) ? WETHERLEY.
Lieut-Col.
5.9.1918. G.S. 61 Division.

476 Field Co.
478 Field Co.
479 Field Co.
1/5 D.C.L.I.

1. The function of the Advanced Guard Engineers is:-

(a) To open up communication for the Advanced Guard under instructions received from the Commander of the Advanced Guard.

(b) To carry out Engineer reconnaissance to include

Condition of roads.
Reconnaissance of rivers and canals, with special reference to suitable sites for pontoon and trestle bridges.
Water Supply.
Situation and description of Engineer material including rough estimate of contents of dump.

(c) Report all work proposed, in hand, and completed to C.R.E.

N.B. The object to be aimed at on Engineer Reconnaissance is to send back such information as will enable the C.R.E. to decide what work is necessary for the advance of the Division, and to put this work in hand with the least possible delay.

2. To assist the O.C. Advanced Guard Engineers in opening communications, one Company 1/5 D.C.L.I. will be placed at his disposal for work.
This Company should move forward with the Advanced Guard.

3. In addition to providing for the requirements of the Advanced Guard, certain work will from time to time be allotted the Advanced Guard Engineers by the C.R.E. The requirements of the Advanced Guard Commander will however at all times take precedence over any such additional work.

4. Copy of Divisional Instructions (Operations) dated 4.9.1918 is circulated herewith to Field Coys.

6.9.1918.

Lieut-Colonel, R.E.
C.R.E. 61st. Division.

182 Inf. Bde.
183 Inf. Bde.
184 Inf. Bde.
475 Field Co.
476 Field Co.
479 Field Co.
   Copy to 61 Div G.

      Ref. para 9 of 61st. Divisional Instructions (Operations) dated 4.9.1918.

      The O.C. 475 Field Co will give technical assistance required by Infantry Brigades in siting the Corps Battle Line.

      Will Brigades please communicate direct with him, if they require his assistance.

6.9.1918.

                              Lieut-Colonel, R.E.
                              C.R.E. 61st. Division.

CONFIDENTIAL.

O.C. 476 Field Co.
O.C. 478 Field Co.
O.C. 479 Field Co.

I wish to draw attention to the following points in view of recent operations.

1. BRIDGES.

(a) In certain cases no maintenance parties have been left on bridges after they have been completed. This was even the case with a pontoon bridge. Maintenance parties must always be detailed for road bridges. These may subsequently be withdrawn after the bridges have settled down to their work, and be replaced by patrols.

(b) Absence of notice boards on bridges: this is in the nature of a military crime.

(c) I can't help thinking that sufficient care is not taken when measuring up gaps and that sections of the gap, and soundings for footings of trestles, are too hurriedly done, or not done at all, thereby causing serious subsequent delay. Thorough measurement of a gap is even more essential these days when such great use is made of framed trestles.

2. OPEN WARFARE.

Trench warfare has had its blighting effect on us as on every other branch of the service. We must continually fight against this if we are to be efficient. The following points have been noticed.

(a) Tendency to seek out billets and spend valuable labour and material on their repair, when a bivouac for the night would have been sufficient.

(b) The same thing applies to horse lines.

(c) One Company sent forward its bridging equipment 10,000 yds. and having got it there proposed to send the animals back whence they came.

(d) Engineer reconnaissance has not been good. Since the advance commenced the information sent back has been generally meagre and at times misleading.

Every effort must be made towards greater efficiency in open warfare. Company Commanders must continually strive to get the right spirit and the right form of knowledge into the junior officers and senior N.C.O's. especially.

In making the above observations I do not wish in the least to disparage the good work done by the Field Companies. The breaking away from trench warfare and getting going in open warfare constitutes a most difficult phase of operations. It is, however, by noting our failures that we learn most.

6th.Sept.1918.

Lieut.-Colonel, R.E.
C.R.E. 61st.Division.

O.C. 257 Tunnelling Co. R.E.

      1. The road from NEUF BERQUIN, L.14.c.9.6 via Rue MONTIGNY and SELSEY Farm to road junction L.11.a.35.85 was repaired by the Division to carry first line transport.

      2. It has been rendered impassable for limbers by Corps lorries

      3. I have no one available to carry out repairs again although the road is very important for supplying our left.

      4. C.E. has asked me to arrange direct with you for the road to be made passable.

      5. An alternative route would be from road junction L.13.b.2.7. (S. of COCHIN CORNER) via Rue PROVOST to ACTON CROSS L.4.a.8.2.
      If this road is in better condition there is no objection to its being made passable in lieu of that through Rue MONTIGNY.

Lieut-Colonel, R.E.

9.9.1918.   C.R.E. 61st. Division.

476 Field Co.
478 Field Co.
479 Field Co.
1/5 D.C.L.I.

1. Bridging programme over LYS CANAL is as follows:-

476 Field Co.

(a) Complete heavy bridges now under construction.

(b) Construct medium trestle bridge at site selected E. of heavy bridge, in consultation with Brigade.

(c) Construct further pack bridges E. of SAILLY PONT TOURNANT (exclusive)

478 Field Co.

(a) Complete bridges in hand.

(b) Replace ROUGE MAISON Pontoon bridge with medium trestle bridge.

(c) Construct additional pack animal bridges at ~~SAILLY PONT TOURNANT~~ and between LYS bridge & ESTAIRES Pont Levis

479 Field Co.

(a) Complete heavy bridge at NOUVEAU MONDE.

(b) Replace pontoon bridge with medium trestle bridge.

(c) Construct additional pack animal bridges between ESTAIRES PONT LEVIS and SAILLY PONT TOURNANT exclusive.

2. B. and C. Companies, D.C.L.I. will furnish parties to assist in construction of above bridges under arrangements made direct between O.C. D.C.L.I. and O's C. Field Coys.

3. A Company and Platoons of B. and C. Coys not required for work as in 2 above will be employed on roads under the orders of O.C. 1/5 D.C.L.I.

4. On the advance of the Division being resumed however, one Company will again be employed with the Field Company attached to the Advanced Guard.

Lieut-Colonel, R.E.

9.9.1918.   C.R.E.   61st. Division.

S E C R E T.

476 Field Co.
478 Field Co.
479 Field Co.
1/5 D.C.L.I.

BRIDGING PROGRAMME - LYS CANAL.

Para. 1 of my No. 23/2 dated 9.9.18 will be amended as follows:-

478 Field Co.
    (a) Complete heavy bridges now under construction by 476 Field Co.

* (b) Construct additional pack and footbridges E. of SAILLY PONT TOURNANT, exclusive.

    (c) Complete medium trestle bridge to replace pontoon bridge.

* (d) Construct medium trestle bridge East of G.17.b.

* Sites to be selected in consultation with Advanced Guard Brigade.

479 Field Co.
    (a) Complete medium trestle bridge to replace pontoon bridge.

    (b) Construct additional pack and footbridges between LYS bridge and SAILLY PONT TOURNANT, inclusive (to include 4 bridges between the LYS bridge and ESTAIRES PONT LEVIS and a pack bridge at SAILLY PONT TOURNANT.)

11.9.18.

Lieut.-Colonel, R.E.
C.R.E. 61st.Division.

476 Field Co.
478 Field Co.
479 Field Co.

    Two sites for emergency pontoon bridges have been selected as below.

    Companies should keep the following particulars handy for use in emergency.

SITE B. Emergency Pontoon Bridge. G.16.b.6.6.

(a)	(b) Distance	(c) Total height to top of transoms.	(d) Camber all^d for in (c)	(e) Remarks.
West side & commencing S. shore. Bottom hard.	15' 30' 45' 60'	6' 7" 9' 11" 9' 9" 8' 7"	6" 1' 10" 1' 6"	) No allowance) is made for) sinkage:-) 6" is suggested) Shore transomes) have been) fixed.
East side & commencing S. shore	15' 30' 45' 60'	7' 2" 8' 5" 10' 5" 8' 8"	6" 1' 1' 6"	))))

SITE A. Emergency Pontoon Bridge. G.21.b.75.50.

South side & commencing S. shore. Bottom mud.	15' 30' 45' 60'	8' 6" 12' 1" 14' 9" 8' 7"	6" 1' 1' 6"	) No allowance) is made for) sinkage:-) 12" is suggested.) Shore transomes) have been) fixed.
North side and commencing S. shore	15' 30' 45' 60'	8' 3" 13' 10" 14' 4" 8' 3"	6" 1' 1' 6"	))))

11.9.1918.

              Lieut-Colonel, R.E.
            C.R.E.   61st. Division.

PRESSING.

479 Field Co.

> C.R.E.
> No. 8/3
> 13 SEP. 1918
> 61st (S. Midland) Division

You will carry out the reconnaissance required in 61st.Div. G.C.16/2/1 dated 12.9.18, attached.

If possible, 3 reconnoitring parties should be sent out so as to obtain the information required as soon as possible.

4 copies of Sheet 36 S.W. 1/20,000 and 1/40,000 showing generally the position of British defences before the withdrawal are attached. One copy of each of these should be kept by you as an office copy and returned to me with your report.

If possible, different colours should be used to denote the following:-

    (a) Original British defences.
    (b) British defences converted by the enemy.
    (c) Enemy defences.

The preparation of the 1/10,000 map can be done in this office if preferred.

The Corps Battle Line may be taken as G.33.central - NOUVEAU MONDE - line of LYS CANAL and STILBECQUE. The W. boundary of the reconnaissance will therefore be:- Grid line N. through G.33.central to its junction with LYS CANAL - along Canal to junction with STILBECQUE G.16.b.9.7 - along latter stream to Northern Divisional Boundary.

If it would be any assistance, 476 Field Co. can place Lieut. RIGDEN at your disposal to assist in carrying out the reconnaissance. Please arrange direct with O.C. 476 Field Co. if you would like his services.

13.9.18.

Lieut.-Colonel, R.E.,
C.R.E. 61st.Division.

SECRET.   Copy No. 4

Extracts from
61st. Divisional Instructions No. 4 (OPERATIONS).

Advanced Guard Bde. 1. The Advanced Guard Brigade to act vigorously against the enemy with a view to obtaining information about his dispositions and intentions; schemes for maintaining contact should he again withdraw to be always ready and handed over at reliefs. Enemy raids to be guarded against and locations of advanced posts to be changed frequently.

Objective. 2. In event of the enemy continuing his withdrawal at any moment, the objective to be reached by the Advanced Guard Brigade will be the line CROIX BLANCHE - FLEURBAIX - ERQUINGHEM (H.4.d.9.7).

Corps Battle Line. 3. The 61st. Divisional Sector of the Corps Battle Line is known as the Left Divisional Sector and remains the line - MUDDY LANE POST (excl.) - NOUVEAU MONDE - thence line of LYS to G.16.b.6.7 and line of STILBECQUE to G.10.b.6.0.

Brigade Sections: - Right Brigade - NOUVEAU MONDE Sectn.
                  Left Brigade - SAILLY Section.

Inter-brigade Boundary:- The grid line between L.13 and L.19, Eastwards to L.17.d.0.0, thence in a straight line to G.22.central.

Nucleus Garrison Posts. 4. Nucleus garrisons - 1 Section to 1 platoon with M.Gs. to cover the following important points and main lines of approach:-

NOUVEAU MONDE Section:
(i) MUDDY LANE POST (G.33.a.1.5 & G.33.c.1.7) - Road.
(ii) NOUVEAU MONDE (G.27.c.7.2) - 2 roads.
(iii) G.27.a.4.5 - Road Bridge.
(iv) On high ground immediately East of Canal at G.21.d.70.
(v) G.21.d.8.6 - 2 road bridges.
(vi) G.16.c.6.6 (Pt. TOURNANT) - road bridge.
(vii) G.16.b.6.6 - road bridge.
(viii) G.10.d.75.45
(ix) House G.10.b.0.1.

5. ACKNOWLEDGE.

                                              [signature]
                                              Capt. - Adjutant,
15.9.18.   for G.R.E. 61st.Div.

Distribution:-

Copy No.1 to 476 Field Co.
"   2 to 478 Field Co.
"   3 to 479 Field Co.
" 4 & 5 to War Diary.
"   6 to File.

SECRET.   COPY NO. 4

Extracts from
61st. Division Instructions No.5.
DEFENCE AGAINST GAS.

1. The general instructions regarding defence against gas are contained in S.S. 534 - "Standing Orders for defence against Gas", and the following notes are supplementary to, or in amplification of, these instructions.

2. The ALERT ZONE is the area forward (Eastward) of a line running approximately 6,000 yards West of the most advanced troops.
   The present western boundary is as follows:-
   G.25.d.8.8 - G.19.b.7.7 - G.8.d.8.5.

3. The READY ZONE is the area between the Western edge of the ALERT ZONE and a line about 10,000 yards West of that Zone.
   The present Western limit of the READY ZONE is:-
   The general line RIEZ-du-VINAGE - RUE-des-VACHES - CALONNE CHURCH - Pt.TOURNANT (K.15.d.) - ARREWAGE-CAUDESCURE (all inclusive).

4. Box respirators will always be worn in the "ALERT" position by everyone in the ALERT ZONE.
   Box respirators will be carried by everyone when in the READY ZONE.

5. Attention is drawn to S.S. 212, which deals with YELLOW CROSS GAS and measures to be taken to counteract its effect.

6. A large percentage of casualties from gas shelling are due to either carelessness or ignorance, and are preventable.
   Casualties can be reduced to a minimum by:-
   (a) Rigid gas discipline.
   (b) Giving all ranks a thorough knowledge of the properties of the various gasses, their effect, and the measures which must be taken to counteract them, with special reference to the persistency of YELLOW CROSS GAS, and its habit of reappearing after dawn under the influence of the sun. The imparting of this knowledge should be the duty of all Officers.

7. In order to reduce casualties to a minimum, all Commanders will ensure that the responsibilities of all concerned for successful anti-gas measures are fully realised and acted upon.
   All gas casualties to be investigated by O.Cs. as soon as possible after they occur, in order to ascertain that all reasonable precautions were taken by officers, N.C.Os, or/men, either for their own protection or for that of the men under their charge. Neglect of these precautions to be severely dealt with.
   Results of these investigations, together with any suggestions, to be forwarded to D.H.Q. through the usual channels, in order that as much information as possible may be available on the subject to assist the troops in the Division.

8. Arrangements to be made previous to bombardment:-

   (a) Every unit to have a scheme ready for evacuation of a gassed area should the tactical situation permit. Evacuations not to take place down wind.

   (b) Supplies of spare clothing and stocks of chloride of lime and bi-carbonate of soda to be held by all units, if possible.

   (c) Orders to be issued to prevent dugouts, or other protected places from becoming contaminated during bombardment by anyone

-2-

who has been in contact with gas entering and bringing in gas on their clothing, etc.

This especially refers to YELLOW CROSS GAS, as the presence of dangerous quantities of GREEN or BLUE Cross can be noticed.

9. Action to be taken at the commencement of a bombardment:-
The alarm will be streaded as laid down in S.S. 534.

   (a) All instances of gas shelling to be reported to the D.G.O. & immediately, giving location and approximate number of rounds fired.

   (b) Should the bombardment exceed approximately 500 rds., all units within 2,000 yds. of affected area to be warned by unit in whose area the shelling occurs, giving area affected. The next higher formation to be informed by wire, stating area affected, nature of gas, and approximate number of rounds.

      The affected area will be picqueted in order to prevent other troops entering the gassed area.

      When informing Division, the wire will be repeated to the D.G.O., who will advise Units as to protective measures to be adopted.

   (c) Plans for evacuating affected areas to be put into practice if necessary and possible.

10. Units in whose area gas shells have fallen, are responsible that the contaminated area is plainly marked with notices and picqueted to prevent other troops entering it until free of gas, and that the earliest opportunity is taken to fill in all gas shell holes.

11. Company Gas N.C.O's. not to be detailed for any other than Anti-Gas duties when their unit is in the ALERT ZONE.

12. CLOUD GAS ATTACK.
Attention is directed to S.S.534, Appendix IV, Section 5, the provisions of which will be strictly adhered to.
Units will arrange to warn:-
        (a) all troops in their area,
        (b) troops on their flanks,
        (c) Div. H.Q. repeating to D.G.O.

13. The "Cloud Gas" warning message is :-
       G.A.S. (name of part of front from which the message originates).

Strombos horns will be sounded.

15.9.18.

                Capt. - Adjutant,
                for C.R.E. 61st.Divn.

Distribution:

Copy No.1 to 476 Fld.Co.
  " 2 to 478 Fld.Co.
  " 3 to 479 Fld.Co.
  " 4 & 5 to War Diary.
  " 6 to File.

476 Field Co.
478 Field Co.
479 Field Co.

        Further to my 8/7 dated 11th. inst.
Site "C" for Emergency Pontoon Bridge has now been selected as under:-

        Site "C" Emergency Pontoon Bridge. N.13.a.4.3.

        Total height to top of roadway.

Trestle.	Down stream side.	Upstream side.
1.	6' 2"	6' 2"
2.	14' 8"	14' 2"
3.	16' 5"	16' 8"
4.	13' 8"	14' 2"
5.	3' 6"	3' 8"

Readings commence from Northern Bank.

15' bays.   Total span from bank to bank 80'
Calculations include allowance for mud & camber.

                              Lieut-Colonel, R.E.
15.9.1918.   C.R.E.   61st. Division.

```
182 Inf.Bde.      61st.Div.Art.              C.R.E.61st.Div. No. 6/5.
183 Inf.Bde.      A.D.M.S.
184 Inf.Bde.      61st.Div."Q" (for information).
```

1. It is necessary to concentrate labour, as far as possible, on essential roads, both as regards repair and maintenance.

2. Would Formations therefore insert on attached map the roads considered essential by them.

3. A scheme for road repair and maintenance will then be made out embodying, as far as possible, the general requirements of all Formations in the Division.

4. In forwarding their requirements, would Formations kindly bear in mind the fact that the recent bad weather and the approach of winter make it desirable to maintain as few roads as possible and that the facilities at the disposal of the Division for this work are strictly limited.

5. Any information with regard to roads most suitable for use in the event of a further advance would also be of value.

15th.Sept.1918.

Lieut.-Colonel, R.E.,
C.R.E. 61st.Division.

SECRET.   URGENT.

Engineer in Chief,
G.H.Q.

TANK MINEFIELDS N.W. of ST. QUENTIN.

1. It is regretted that no records now exist with this Division as to the number of bombs laid or the exact position of the minefields.

2. I attach a map however which shows the neighbourhood of the minefields.
    These areas should be treated with extreme caution.

3. The mines consisted of 2" T.M. Bombs, laid as suggested in the G.H.Q. circular on the subject issued early in March last, of which I have not now a copy.
    The bombs were fitted with Newton fuzes, specially adapted with brass shearing wires.

4. The laying of the bombs was discontinued after it was found that the fuze was highly dangerous.

5. There were several instances of fuzes firing by the weight of a man treading on them. Two men were killed traversing the southern minefield at night.

6. There is no safety arrangement by which the fuzes can be rendered inoperative during the work of raising the minefield.

7. All the minefields were enclosed by special wire fences as under:-

The intervals and distances between picquets are according to my recollection and may not be accurate.
I think long screw pickets were used. There was no other wiring similar to this on the Divisional front. The idea of this form of fence was that it would be distinctive to our troops in the dark, but its peculiar form would not be noticed by approaching tanks.

8. It was intended that each minefield should consist of four rows of mines, but to the best of my recollection, not more than two rows were laid anywhere except in the Southern of the three minefields, weere, I think, two belts of two rows each were laid in the road.

Sept. 15th. 1918.

Lieut-Colonel, R.E.
C.R.E. 61st. Division.

476 Field Co.
478 Field Co.
479 Field Co.

No houses or cellars, or concrete shelters etc. E. of the enemy belts of wire L.27.c.9.5. - TROMPE BRIDGE - L.14.b.central. - L.8.a.central will be occupied until further orders.

All ranks will vacate existing accomodation of this nature as soon as possible, and in no case later than noon tomorrow 17th, but such accomodation should be earmarked for future use.

Tents have been applied for and I can supply C.I. straight and curved.

During any further advances we shall probably have to rely entirely on bivouacing in accomodation of our own construction.

Field Companies should therefore make light shelter frames which can be taken forward by them and should be prepared to camp entirely under canvas.

Lieut-Colonel R.E.
C.R.E. 61st. Divn.

16.9.1918.

61st. Div Q.

LIGHT RAILWAYS.

Reference XI Corps Q.J. 4. dated 17.9.1918

1. C.R.E's present dump is at L.28.d.1.3. but as the Railway Bridge at L.35.a.4.3. is broken and the Light Railway Line to the dump is not suitably arranged, I am moving my dump to L.35.a.4.2. (a proposal to which both the C.E. XI Corps and the C.R.E. 59th. Division have agreed)

2. The C.R.A's first proposal (viz a line via NEUF BERQUIN - L.18 - G.20) would be useful as it would deliver road stone to the north of the Divisional back area, but in view of the probability of an advance, I think that the Southern route would be the best one to develope.

3. My suggestions are therefore as follows:-

(a) Operate the spur from L.35.c.2.1. to L.35.a.4.2. which is in good condition except for two breaks which I am repairing.

(b) Repair the line from L.36.a. to G.26.d.5.0 making a spur here for an advanced R.E. Dump and stone siding.

(c) Continue this line on to G.20.d.central and put in a spur for a stone siding.

(d) Repair the line M.4.a. - M.5.b. - H.31.c. - G.30. to BAC ST MAUR putting in a spur near the main road where I propose opening a dump when the situation permits.

Lieut-Colonel, R.E.
C.R.E.   61st. Division.

18.9.1918.

476 Field Co.
478 Field Co.
479 Field Co.

MAINTENANCE OF BRIDGES, etc.

1. Bridges will be identified as follows:-

    Medium and Heavy Bridges by Names.
    Pack and Foot Bridges by Numbers.

2. Bridges over RIVER LYS.
    Reading from West to East:-

    No. 1............................- Pack bridge at L.29.d.2.0.
    "MEUSE DIVERSION"............- Heavy bridge at L.29.d.8.3.
    No. 2............................- Pack bridge at L.30.c.4.4.
    No. 3............................- Footbridge at G.25.d.9.4.
    "PONT LEVIS DIVERSION"........- Heavy bridge at G.26.c.0.4.
    No. 4............................- Pack bridge at G.26.c.4.5.
    No. 5............................- Pack bridge at G.26.d.4.3.
    "NOUVEAU MONDE"..............- Heavy bridge at G.27.c.4.5.
    No. 6............................- Pack bridge at G.27.b.0.4.
    "DE LA JUSTICE"...............- Medium bridge at G.21.d.7.2.
    No. 7............................- Pack bridge at G.21.d.8.4.
    "ROUGE MAISON"...............- Medium bridge at G.21.b.9.0.
    No. 8............................- Pack bridge at G.21.b.9.4.
    No. 9............................- Diversion bridge at G.16.a.7.7.
    No.10............................- Pack bridge at G.16.c.8.6.
    No.11............................- Pack bridge at G.16.b.3.3.
    "G.16.b."........................- Heavy bridges at G.16.b.8.7 and)
                                                       G.16.b.9.4.   )
    "TOWPATH"........................- Medium bridge at G.16.b.9.9.
    No.12............................- Pack bridge at G.17.b.5.7.
    "BAC ST. MAUR"...................- Medium bridge at G.18.a.5.4.
    No.13............................- Pack bridge at G.18.a.6.3.
    No.14............................- Footbridge at G.18.b.2.0.
    No.15............................- Footbridge at H.13.a.3.4.
    No.16............................- Pack bridge at H.13.a.9.8.

Contd.

-2-

Bridges over RIVER LYS (contd.).

    No.17. .. .. - Pack bridge at H.7.d.3.3.

    No.18. .. .. - Footbridge at H.7.d.4.4.

                                           Ferry at H.7.b.8.2.

Bridges over STILBECQUE.

    "LA BOUDRELLE". .. .. .. - Medium bridge at G.10.d.7.5.

Bridges over METEREN BECQUE.

    "POIVRE" .. .. - Heavy bridge at L.24.c.9.4.

    "PETIT BOIS" .. .. - Heavy bridge at L.17.d.4.8.

    "KENNET" .. .. - Heavy bridge at L.11.c.9.0.

3.   The above names and numbers will be painted on small bridge notice and direction boards.

4.   Bridge guards will be replaced by maintenance patrols on 21st.inst. as follows :-

    LYS Bridge (exclusive) to SAILLY Pont Tournant (exclusive) - 479 Field Co.

    SAILLY Pont Tournant (inclusive) to Northern Divisional Boundary - 478 Field Co.

5.   Maintenance patrols must be of sufficient strength to enable them to carry out minor repairs to bridges, approaches, and notice and direction boards.   They will be given orders to report immediately to Company H.Q. any case of breakdown which they cannot repair themselves within a reasonable time. A bicycle must always be available at the patrol billet for this purpose.

    Bridges will be patrolled at daylight, midday and evening. It is the duty of patrols to report immediately to Company H.Q. any case of improper use of bridges and to obtain sufficient information to identify the offender.

    Each patrol will be given a plan shewing the bridges and approaches for which it is responsible and the position of notice and direction boards.   This plan is to be marked "Secret" and handed over on relief.

19.9.18.

                                                 Lieut.-Colonel, R.E.,
                                                C.R.E. 61st.Division.

WAR DIARY.
(ORIGINAL.)
for SEPT 1918.
C.R.E. 61ˢᵗ DIVⁿ.

APPENDIX 4

NOMINAL ROLLS

NOMINAL ROLL OF UNIT.

1st. Sept. 1918.

Officers.

Lieut-Colonel	G.E.J. DURNFORD, D.S.O.		C.R.E.
Captain	M.E.W. FITZGERALD.		Adjutant.
Captain	J.K. RENNIE, M.C.		M.O. (RAMC)
		(attached 476 Field Company)	

Other Ranks.

52959	R.S.M.	H. DEYERMOND, D.C.M.
500121	Sergt.	W.A. FEATHERSTONE.
500336	L/Cpl.	A. SKINNER
498197	L/Cpl.	F. HAYCRAFT.
99315	Sapper	G. BOLLAND
500171	Driver	L. WATTS
500303	Driver	J. GREGORY.
56185	Driver	A. DAVIES
61497	Driver	G. PATTEN

T/4/ 248151   Driver E. LORTON   (A.S.C)

Attached.

Officers.

Lieut. GCHH SIMMONS, M.C.   479 Field Co.

476 Field Co.   Other Ranks.

498134	L/Cpl.	A.L. MOTT.
498276	Sapper	T.A. ELLISON.
498223	Sapper	J. COLLINS.
84339	Driver	G. KING.

478 Field Co.

496773	Corpl.	F.L. PENNY.

479 Field Co.

494375	Sapper	H. TALBOT
488601	Sapper	E.S. NEWTON
494779	Driver	G. DOLLING.

French Mission.

Interpreter GUEUX

Detached.

Driver F. FOXON   to   479 Field Co R.E.

War Diary.
(ORIGINAL.)
for SEPTEMBER 1918.
C.R.E. 61st DIVN.

APPENDIX 5

R.E. Stores & Dumps

475 Field Co. Copies to:-
476 Field Co.   1/5 D.C.L.I.
479 Field Co.   C.R.E.O.
R.E.M.   C.E. XI Corps.
                  Traffic, 61 Div. "Q".

R.E. DUMPS.

1. It has not yet been possible to arrange for any Corps units to follow us up and take over dumps, whereas our present dumps are rapidly becoming too far back to be of much value.

2. (a) The C.R.E's dump will move tomorrow, the 3rd.inst., from HARTSTONE to MEREDITH.

   (b) The R.E.M. will arrange direct with O.C. 479 Field Co. as to when 479 storemen may be withdrawn from MEREDITH.

   (c) R.E.M. will detail 2 men to remain behind and guard HARTSTONE dump and he will send them rations daily.

3. Companies will remain responsible for guarding dumps as under, whilst any stores remain at these spots. As soon as any dump becomes of no further value to the Division, by reason of its location, the Company concerned will arrange to move the stores either to a new Company dump forward, or into the C.R.E's dump.

   475 - CROIX MARMAISSE and DUNGAN.
   476 - CANADA - KARK - BOOM - GUENAND, etc.
   479 - PUKEBROUCK.

4. Local moves of small quantities of stores by rail should be arranged by Companies direct with Traffic Officer at 61st. Division. "Q". who controls Foreways' trains.

5. Movement of quantities exceeding about 10 tons by rail can be carried out by Light Railway trains, providing particulars reach R.E.H.Q. by noon the previous day.

6. The same principle will hold good as we go forward. The Light Railway will probably not keep pace with the Division, but dumps formed by road transport should be located, as far as possible, on routes for Light Railways. If close to motor lorry routes so much the better.

7. The Light Railway programme of construction as far as it is known at present will form junctions of rail and road as below; order of value from an R.E. dump point of view is as follows :-

               GRENE FARM.
               K.30.d.6.4.
               K.30.b.5.5.
               K.24.a.2.5.

                              Capt. - Adjutant,
                              for C.R.E. 61st. Div.
2nd.Sept.1918.

476 Field Co.   R.S.M.
476 Field Co.   Cpl. Penny.   13/4/1
479 Field Co.

DUMPS.

1. R.S.M. will take over the dumps at CANADA, CHAPELLE BOOM and TANK. Field Coys. to arrange details direct with the R.S.M. at MEREDITH. R.S.M's. daily stock list sent to this office will include stocks at MEREDITH, CANADA, CHAPELLE BOOM and TANK.

2. 476 Field Co. will take over FURESBECQUES dump from 479 Field Co.

3. 479 Field Co. will establish a dump (which will probably become C.R.E's dump eventually) near CHAPELLE DUVELLE. Along the main road in L.28.c. is suggested as a likely place as being suited for communications in all directions. This dump should be clearly labelled "R.E. DUMP".

4. The C.R.E. will endeavour to push up materials most urgently required forward to DUVELLE by lorry; 479 arranging to unload and issue to 476 and 478.

5. Tomorrow the 5th.inst.:

   (a) Trains will leave LA LACQUE dump at 9 a.m. for MEREDITH. On arrival the R.S.M. will take them over and use them until 5 pm for salving CANADA and TANK, running stores forward either to MEREDITH or FURESBECQUES.

   (b) Lorries will take supplies from LA LACQUE to CHAPELLE DUVELLE with Cpl. Penny i/c.; 479 to have 3 guides at K.30.d.2.3 at 10 a.m. to guide lorries to the new dump. On arrival at 479 dump any Field Co. may take charge of one lorry for special work during the remainder of the day. Surplus lorries under Cpl. Penny will be employed for the rest of the day salving stores into 479 Field Co. dump. 479 will furnish 6 men for loading. Stores to be salved are as follows :-

   (i) Any special requirements of 479 Field Co.
   (ii) 24ft. footbridges dumped near roadside between CORBIE and LE SART.
   (iii) Timber collected from MERVILLE by 479 for forward bridging.
   (iv) Thin boarding from K.1.c.8.2.
   (v) Wiring stores, bridges and camouflage from MEREDITH.

   (c) One lorry (detailed by Cpl. Penny) will remain with 479 tomorrow night and will be at disposal of O.C. 479 until further orders.

6. Field Companies are again reminded of the advantages of wiring their stocks through early each evening, for the next days deliveries are based upon this information.

   The wire should include stocks of all stores likely to be required anywhere in the area for urgent work; i.e. - Bridges all sizes and kinds (stating sizes), wiring stores, heavy timber, C.I., felt, shelters, shovels, picks, etc.

4.9.18.

Capt. - Adjutant,
for C.R.E. 61st.Div.

APPX. 6

DRAWINGS ISSUED
DURING
MONTH

SKETCH OF TRESTLE BRIDGE, ESTAIRES.

SKETCH SHOWING SITE FOR ABOVE BRIDGE.

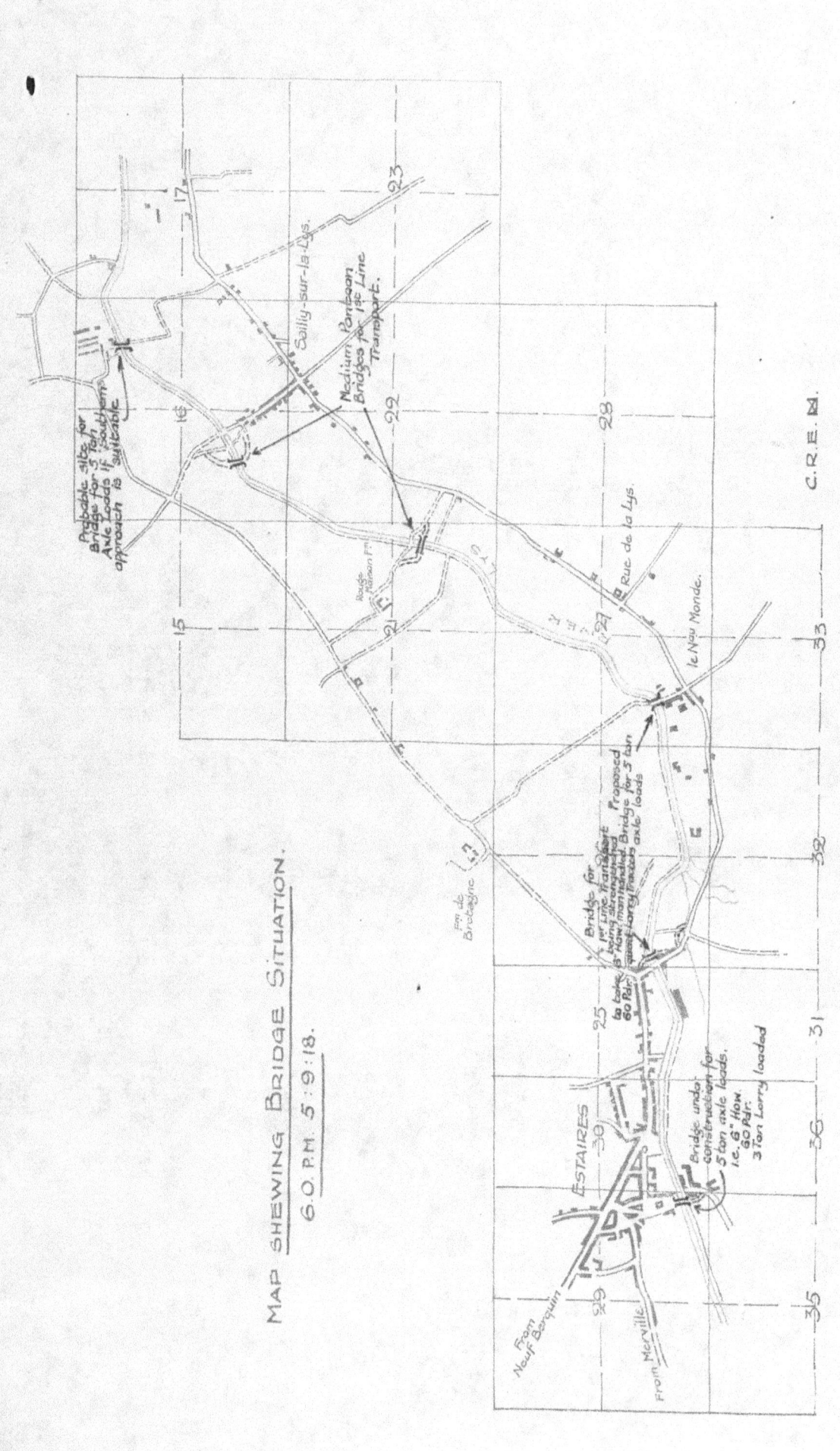

SPLINTER PROOF SHELTER MADE IN A RUINED VILLAGE.

Build the walls at least 9" brick or 18" bricks bedded in mortar made from clay, when the walls are 5 feet high put wall plates on — these can be soaked "H" Girders.

4 Sheets of "Boadi" Corrugated Iron Shelter are required to roof a villa with the dimensions shown — place them in position, work in any available window and finish off H's and walls. A layer of bricks on the roof will make it splinter proof.

X Width inside should be 6 feet for sheets of Large English Shelter which will carry weight of bricks on top. For C.I. Bivouac Sheets width inside will be 7ft. but only 3" of earth can be carried on top.

Road Land Mine

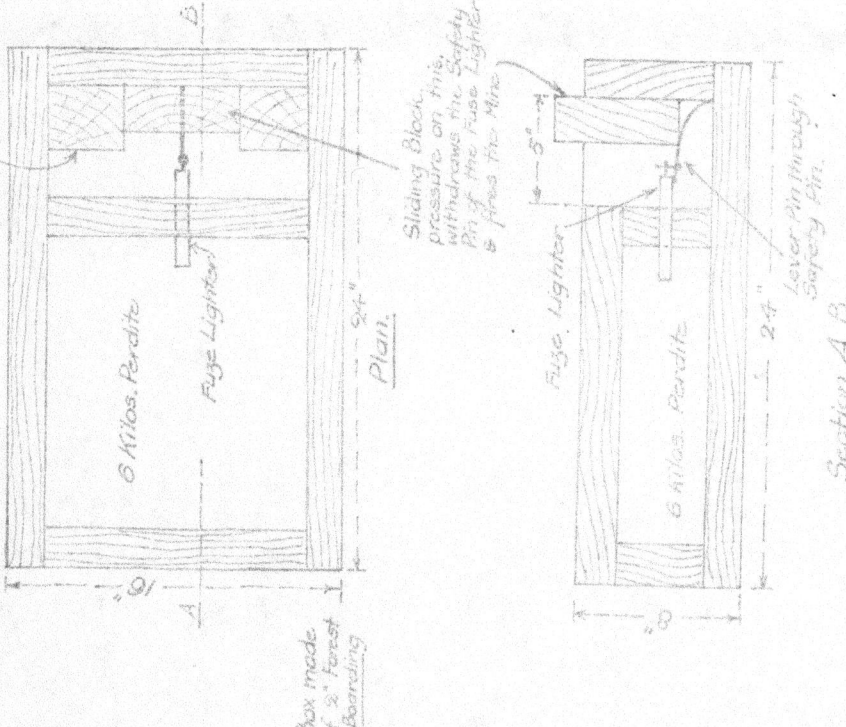
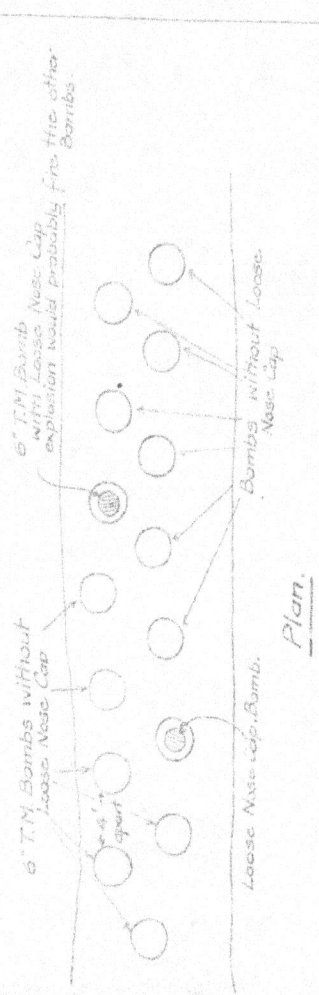

German Contact Mine in Trench.

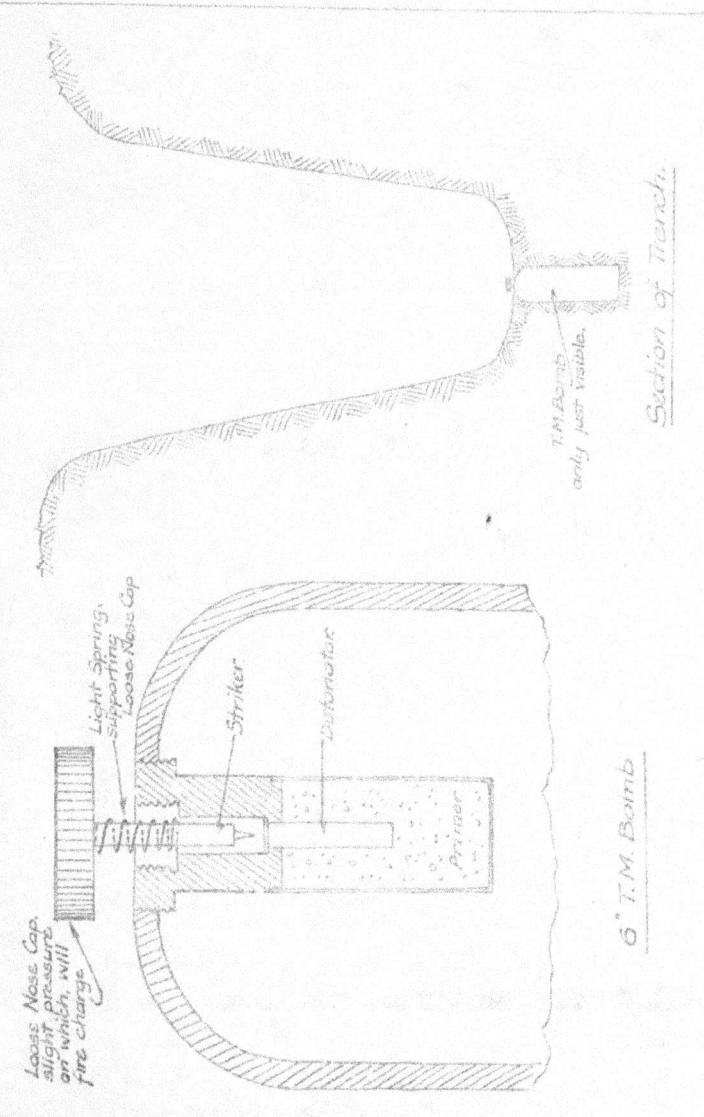

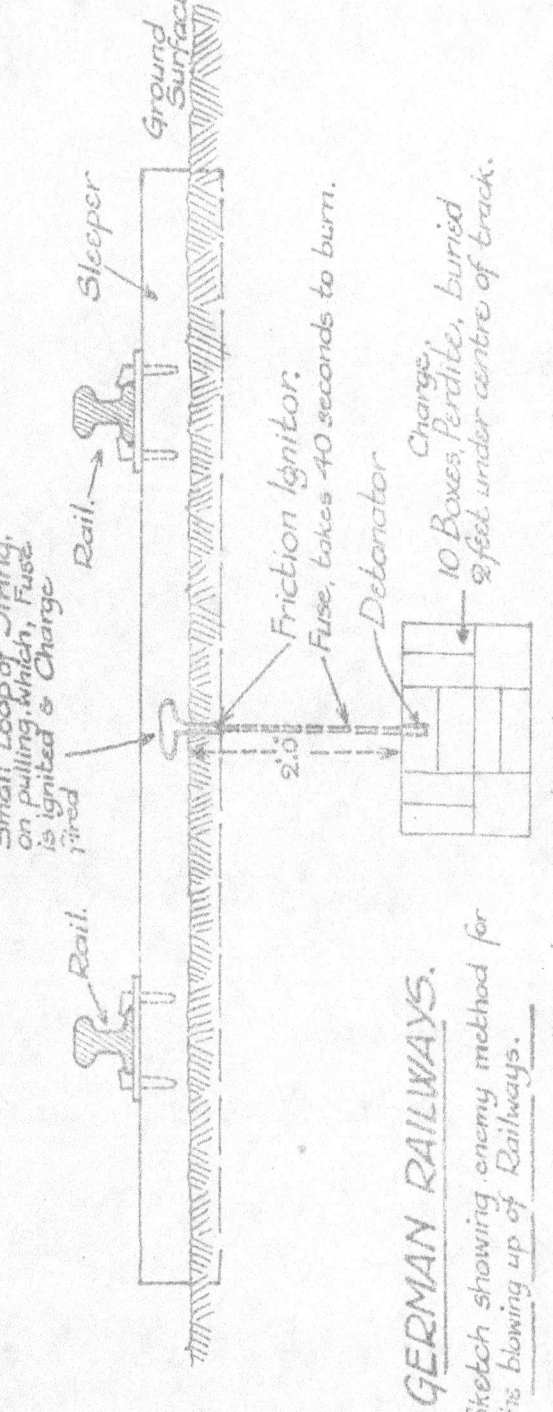

Vol 30

WAR DIARY
of
H.Q. 61ST (S.M.) DIV. R.E.
for month of
OCTOBER 1918

Vol XXX

Army Form C. 2118.

WAR DIARY
or
INTELLIGENCE SUMMARY

(Erase heading not required.)

HEADQUARTERS 61st DIVISION ROYAL ENGINEERS
Vol XXX
Page 1

OCTOBER 1918

Instructions regarding War Diaries and Intelligence Summaries are contained in F. S. Regs., Part II. and the Staff Manual respectively. Title pages will be prepared in manuscript.

Place	Date	Hour	Summary of Events and Information	Remarks and references to Appendices
L.27.d.8.4	1st		Nominal Roll of Unit	
			Received instructions by telephone from "Q" to resume work on "Q" camp and push ahead as quickly as possible.	Appx 4
		10.00	A/C.R.E. saw G.1 and learnt that Division will shortly be relieved.	
		11.00	A/C.R.E. saw 476 Field Co and arranged for work at "Q" camp.	
		15.40	Received 61 Div Order 209 re operation by Right Brigade	
		17.01	Received 61st Div Order 210 re relief of 61st Division by 59 Division 2/5th October.	
		21.45	Received 184 Bde Order 233 re Battalion relief	
		21.45	Received 184 Bde Order 234 re attack by 2/4th Berks	
		21.45	Received 183 Bde Order 254 re Divisional Relief	
	2nd	00.15	Received 61st Div Order 211 re Divisional Relief	
		10.00	G.S.O1 telephoned that Brigades are advancing through FLEURBAIX	
		10.15	C.R.E. 59th Division called with reference to taking over. Arranged for O's C 59th Division Field Companies to see O's C Companies this afternoon.	
		18.00	Issued R.E. Order 126 re relief of Div R.E by 59 Div R.E on 3rd	Appx 2
		19.00	Issued Routine Order 127:- Major M. WHITWILL, D.S.O., M.C. assumes command of 61st Div R.E on his return from leave.	Appx 1
LA LACQUE	3rd		Received 59 Div R.E. Letter K: 7645 re Relief R.E.H.Q moved to LALACQUE after handing over to C.R.E. 59th Divn	
	4th		Received 183 Bde Order 255 re move from STEENBECQUE to DOULLENS Area Advance D.H.Q moved to LALACQUE after handing over to 59th Division	
	5th.		Setting out office	

Army Form C. 2118.

WAR DIARY or INTELLIGENCE SUMMARY

(Erase heading not required.)

HEADQUARTERS 61st DIVNL ROYAL ENGINEERS.

Vol XXX

Page 2

OCTOBER 1918

Instructions regarding War Diaries and Intelligence Summaries are contained in F.S. Regs., Part II and the Staff Manual respectively. Title pages will be prepared in manuscript.

Place	Date	Hour	Summary of Events and Information	Remarks and references to Appendices
DOULLENS.	6th		Received orders for Major M, WHITWILL, D.S.O, M.C. to report as C.R.E. 73rd Division. R.E.H.Q. moved to DOULLENS - Major WHITWILL and Adjutant calling on C.E. 3rd Army en route. Remainder of R.E.H.Q. moved by train.	
	7th		Received Special Divisional Order expressing thanks of The Fifth Army Commander (General Sir W.R. BIRDWOOD) for work of 61st Division.	Appx 5
		08.00	Received 61st Div Order 213. Division to be prepared to move 8/9th by train.	
		12.30	Recd 61 Div Order 214 giving details of moves by train and road.	
			Recd 183 Bde Order 256 re move of Bde Group	
		22.15	Recd 184 Bde Order 238 re move of Bde Group	
			Major WHITWILL left the Division and Major H.S. DAVIS, M.C. assumed command of Divnl R.E.	
	8th		Issued Orders for move of R.E.H.Q. tomorrow Received Camp Commandants Order re move of D.H.Q. tomorrow Received 184 Bde Order G.53 enclosing movement table for tomorrows move Lieut. Col G.E.J. DURNFORD, D.S.O. returned from leave and resumed command of Divnl R.E.	Appx 2
Sht 57c. LAGNICOURT C.24.c.2.2	9th.		R.E.H.Q.rs moved to LAGNICOURT, partly by road and partly by train to FREMICOURT. We are now Reserve Division of the XX 17th Corps; 17th Corps being the Northern Corps of the Third Army.	
	10th	13.20	61 Div Order 215 Recd. Enemy carrying out retirement on large scale - giving Corps boundaries	
		13.20	61 Div Order 216 recd. Bde to move forward today to conform to advance on Corps front	
		16.15	61 Div Order 217 Recd. Further Orders re Divisional moves.	
		17.45	Issued R.E. Order 127 Advising Field Coys of Corps boundary; 478 Field Co to be Advance Guard Engineers in event of Division becoming Leading Group. Recd 184 Bde Order re move of Bde Group. Placed Capt HOLBROW in charge of 478 Field Co pending the return from leave of Major HUMPHREYS who is taking command of 478 Field Company	Appx 2

Army Form C. 2118.

WAR DIARY
or
INTELLIGENCE SUMMARY.

(Erase heading not required.)

HEADQUARTERS
61st DIVNL ROYAL ENGINEERS
Vol XXX

Page 3

OCTOBER 1918

Instructions regarding War Diaries and Intelligence Summaries are contained in F. S. Regs., Part II. and the Staff Manual respectively. Title pages will be prepared in manuscript.

Place	Date	Hour	Summary of Events and Information	Remarks and references to Appendices
LAGNICOURT	11th	09.30	Issued Routine Orders 128-129. Lieut-Col G.H.T. DURNFORD assumes command on Divl R.E. Recd 183 Bde Order 257 re enemy withdrawal. Received instructions to make a dry weather track from the CANAL du NORD to CAMBRAI to relieve congestion of traffic on the main road. C.R.E and Adjutant reconnoitred the area & arranged for each Field Company to have ones Company of Infantry to commence work forthwith.	Appx 1
	12th	10.05	Recd 61 Div Order 219 Warning Move of Division. Received Camp Commandants move orders. C.R.E. visited all Companies and work on dry weather track.	
NOYELLES sur L'ESCAUT	13th		R.E.H.Q moved to NOYELLES (S.W. of CAMBRAI) C.R.E., and Adjutant visited Field Coys and inspected dry weather track which is nearly completed.	
	14th	12.00	Gave C.E. XI Corps list of principal work on roads & bridges when in MERVILLE area. Parade of R.E.H.Q and C.R.E. read Divnl letter pointing out that Peace Talk was not to affect the conduct of the war. During the afternoon R.E.H.Q. carried out Musketry Exercises on 25 yard range. C.R.E. and Adjutant road to AWOINGT to get a Birds Eye View of the country.	Appx 3
	15th		C.R.E. visited Field Companies. R.E.H.Q continued rifle practice.	
	16th	17.00	Conference of Field Company Commanders at R.E.H.Q.	Appx 3

Army Form C. 2118.

WAR DIARY
or
INTELLIGENCE SUMMARY
(Erase heading not required.)

HEADQUARTERS.
61st. DIV. ROYAL ENGINEERS.

Vol. XXX   Page 4.

Place	Date	Hour	Summary of Events and Information	Remarks and references to Appendices
NOYELLES sur L'ESCAUT.	17th	13.00	Recd. 51 Div Order - Division to become supporting group.	
		19.20	Recd. 61 Div Order 221 re move of Division to S. of CAMBRAI tomorrow. Received 184 Bde. Order 240 re move to South of CAMBRAI tomorrow. Received 183 Bde Order 258. re move to South of CAMBRAI. Received wire from Division instructing Capt. FITZGERALD (adjutant) to report to C.E. Vth. Corps forthwith (Auth. XVII Corps a wire No. A.422 dated 16.10.1918) Lieut. G.H. SIMMONS, M.C. taking over duties as Adjutant. M.O. Capt. RENNIE, M.C. R.A.M.C. ordered to report to 2/3rd. Field amb. when relieved. Lieut. STONE, R.A.M.C. reported to relieve Capt. RENNIE.	
		15.00		
	18th	21.00	Received 61 Div Order 222 re move forward of Division C.R.E. interviewed two candidates for R.E. Commission. Capt. FITZGERALD left for Vth. Corps to take up appointment as S.O. to C.E. Lieut. SIMMONS, M.C. assumed duties as Adjutant, 61st. Div. R.E.	
RIEUX.	19th	07.50	Received 184 Bde. Order 241 re forward move. Division moved into Support with 19th. Division in line. R.E. HEADQUARTERS moved to RIEUX. C.R.E. interviewed three candidates for R.E. Commission.	Appx 1
	20th		Issued Routine Order 130. Capt. LONG to be a/Major. Received 183 Bde. Order 259 re move forward	
	21st	10.50	Received 61 Div Order 223 warning of attack by Division. C.R.E. attended conference at D.H.Q re attack on the ECAILLON River to be carried out by this Division on the 24th. C.R.E. visited C.R.E. 19th. reference foot bridges used over R. SELLE, went on to MONTRECOURT and inspected two of these 30 foot bridges;- Too heavy. - Conference of Company Commanders at R.E.H.Q and made arrangements to commence making footbridges tomorrow.	
		15.50	C.E. XVII Corps called reference Corps bridge policy over ECAILLON.	

Army Form C. 2118.

WAR DIARY
or
INTELLIGENCE SUMMARY

HEADQUARTERS
61st. DIV. ROYAL ENGINEERS.
Vol. XXX.

Page 5

OCTOBER 1918.

(Erase heading not required.)

Instructions regarding War Diaries and Intelligence Summaries are contained in F. S. Regs., Part II. and the Staff Manual respectively. Title pages will be prepared in manuscript.

Place	Date	Hour	Summary of Events and Information	Remarks and references to Appendices
			FRANCE.	
RIEUX	22nd	14.00	C.R.E. attended conference at D.H.Q.	
		14.30	Received 61 Div Order 224 re forward move of Div. preparatory to attack on 24th.	
		17.30	Conference of Company Commanders. Reported 10 bridges made and discussed means of getting them forward.	
		21.00	Issued R.E. Order 128 giving moves of Field Companies.	Appx 2
		23.50	Received 61 Div Order 225 re operation by the Division on morning of 24th.	
			C.R.E. and Adjutant visited "DUFOUR" Dump supervising construction of 30' footbridges.	
Sht. 51a.				
ST AUBERT	23rd	09.00	Box car reported to remain for attachment.	
		09.50	Received 184 Bde. Order re forward move of Brigade.	
			Received letter from C.E. XVII Corps (C.E. 247) giving details of bridge work in connection with operations on morning of 24th.	
		11.15	Issued R.E. Order 129 re operation on 24th. giving work to be done by Field Companies	Appx 2
			Recd. 19th. Div. R.E. Order 91. re the Relief.	
		14.00	Corpl. PENNY attached to Corps R.E. Dump "DUFOUR". For 2 days.	
		14.30	R.E. Headquarters moved to ST AUBERT.	
		17.30	C.R.E. attended conference at D.H.Q reference progress made by 19th. Div.	
			Conference of Field Coy Commanders and C.O. 1/5 D.C.L.I.	
		✗	C.R.E. and Adjutant at "DUFOUR" dump and arranged transport for getting bridges forward - 20 bridges completed by 12.00 hours.	
			Detailed one section 479 Field Co and one platoon 1/5 D.C.L.I. for attachment to each rear Brigade.	
		20.40	Recd. 61 Div Order 228 re extension in depth of tomorrows operation in view of satisfactory progress made today.	
		21.00	Recd. 184 Bde. Order re tomorrows attack.	
			Recd. 183 Bde. Order re tomorrows attack.	

WAR DIARY
or
INTELLIGENCE SUMMARY

(Erase heading not required.)

Army Form C. 2118.

HEADQUARTERS
61st. DIV. ROYAL ENGINEERS
Vol. XXX.
Page 6

Place	Date	Hour	Summary of Events and Information	Remarks and references to Appendices
ST AUBERT & MONTRECOURT	OCTOBER 1918. 24th	04.00	FRANCE. Sht. 51a. 1/40000. Zero Hour.	
		12.00	Advance R.E.H.Q. moved to MONTRECOURT by box car, and collided en route with motor ambulance	
			Inspected 479 Field Co and 1/5 D.C.L.I. en route.	
		13.15	Arrived MONTRECOURT.	
			Operation not a complete success owing to opposition from VENDEGIES,- footbridges placed across in this vicinity are either captured or smashed. Ordered up 6 bridges from 19th. Division Dump at P.34.c. to be put in tonight.	
			Instructed Detachment 178 Tunnelling Co attached 61 Division to remove charges in abutments of bridge over ECAILLON River at Q.21.d. and to examine all bridges.	
			Advised all concerned that pumps in working order and yielding water are at Fme de RIEUX (W.2.b.7.7), house near Mill (Q.26.d.2.4) and Fme D'ORCHIVAL (Q.26.b.1.4.)	
			Instructed D.C.L.I. to clear ford across River HARPIES at W.2.d.6.6. which is reported impassable.	
			Advised all concerned that pack animal bridge at Q.32.b.1.5. erected and that heavy bridge at Mill Q.26.d.2.3. under construction.	
			Reported that repairs to medium bridge at V.4.d.1.5. completed.	
		15.00	G.O.C. sent for C.R.E.	
		19.50	C.R.A. called reference bridge at Fme de RIEUX.	
		20.15.	Instructed 478 Field Co to erect medium bridge at Fme de RIEUX as it is required urgently for field guns.	
		22.15	Stock list of Corps R.E. Dump "DUFOUR" shows no bridging timber available.	
		23.55.	Advised all concerned that ford at W.2.d.6.6. now passable for field guns (2' water over it)	

WAR DIARY
INTELLIGENCE SUMMARY

HEADQUARTERS 61st. DIV. ROYAL ENGINEERS.

Army Form C. 2118.

Vol. XXX

Page 7.

OCTOBER 1918.

FRANCE. Sht. 51a. 1/40000

Place	Date	Hour	Summary of Events and Information	Remarks and references to Appendices
MONTRECOURT & VENDEGIES		0.105	Received message from 61 Div G (G.183):- essential for touch to be maintained with enemy 184 Bde to be prepared to resume advance and clear up situation at VENDEGIES; in event of enemy withdrawal, touch will be maintained by Corps mounted troops.	
		04.1a	Instructed Lieut. RIGDEN (476 Field Co) to report to 182 Bde H.Q. re construction of medium bridge at SOMMAING.	
	25th	07.30	VENDEGIES captured and our troops are beyond their objective.	
		07.50	Advised G, and Div Art. that bridge to carry guns and first line transport at Fme de RIEUX completed at 04.00 hours.	
		10.00	C.R.E. went to G. and arranged to wash out the consolidation of the village line. Ordered troops concerned to salve and replace foot bridges and to clear roads instead. Instructed Field Companies to move as follows:- 476 Field Co to VENDEGIES 478 and 479 Field Coys to BERMERAIN. Transport to MONTRECOURT and HAUSSY respectively.	Appx 6.
		12.30	Rear R.E.H.Q moved up. To MONTRECOURT	
		14.45	Adv. R.E.H.Q. moved to VENDEGIES. C.R.E. rode over and inspected work along ECAILLON. Noted the great strength of enemy position round SOMMAING and VENDEGIES. asked Div Q for transport for heavy bridging material, but could not be supplied owing to getting ammunition forward. Wired C.E. XVII Corps for bridging timber.	
		17.15	Advised Div G, Div Art, and C.E. XVII Corps that Field Artillery and First Line Transport bridge completed at Q.7.d.25.30 and pack bridge at Q.13.b.9.5.	
		18.50	Advised G, Div Art, and C.E. (G.206) 184 Bde. that pack mule bridge completed at Q.21.d.2.7.	
		21.05	Received message from Div G. (G.183). to continue operation as in wire G.183. If heavy opposition met, Adv. Guard Commander to confine himself to reconnaissance. Early information re bridges and crossings required. Sent all concerned copies of reconnaissance of water supply in Div. Area. Issued work orders for tomorrow Received from Major H.S. DAVIS (476 Field Co) report of footbridging operations in connection with attack on VENDEGIES. Reported all roads passable up to 2000 yards E. of the villages. Reported charges withdrawn from four bridges at BERMERAIN.	Appx 3

Army Form C. 2118.

WAR DIARY

Intelligence Summary (*Erase heading not required.*)

HEADQUARTERS
61st. DIV. ROYAL ENGINEERS.
vol XXX

Page 8

Place	Date	Hour	Summary of Events and Information	Remarks and references to Appendices
FRANCE. Sht. 51a. 1/40000				
VENDEGIES	26th	10.00	Received message from G. (G.S. 621), 184 Bde is to co-operate with Right Bde of Left Division and work round side of ARTRES.	
		12.10	R.E. Rear Headquarters moved up to VENDEGIES. Received message from G (G.218), 183 Bde to relieve 184 Bde as Advance Guard Brigade and active touch to be maintained.	
		18.00	Received message from Div G. (G.S.627) 4th. Division forced withdraw to river. 184 Bde ordered to support operation of 4th. Division at bridgehead and to exploit eastwards. Advised all concerned of information from reconnaissances during the day. Issued work orders for tomorrow. C.R.E. met Corps Commander inspecting enemy defences round ECAILLON River. Ordered 476 Field Co to clear dams from the ECAILLON and inspected the work.	Appx 3
	27th	15.00	C.R.E. and Adjutant inspected forward roads up to SEMERIES. C.R.E. attended Divisional Conference. Advised all concerned of information obtained from reconnaissances during the day. Received from Major H.S. DAVIS, 476 Field Co suggestions and conclusions drawn from recent operations Received 184 Inf. Bde Order (Defence Scheme) Received from Major H.S. DAVIS, report on footbridge operations in connection with attack on SOMMAING and VENDEGIES. Sent C.R.E. 24th. Division information obtained from reconnaissances up to date. Sent all concerned information obtained from reconnaissances today. Issued work orders for 28th.	Appx 3 Appx 3 Appx 3 Appx 3

Army Form C. 2118.

WAR DIARY
of
~~INTELLIGENCE SUMMARY~~

(Erase heading not required.)

HEADQUARTERS
61st. DIV. ROYAL ENGINEERS.
Vol. XXI
Page 9.

Instructions regarding War Diaries and Intelligence Summaries are contained in F. S. Regs., Part II. and the Staff Manual respectively. Title pages will be prepared in manuscript.

Place	Date	Hour	Summary of Events and Information	Remarks and references to Appendices
VENDEGIES	OCTOBER 1918.		FRANCE. Sht. 51a. 1/40000	
	28th		Issued R.E. Order 130:- 2 sections Field Co detailed as Advance Guard Engineers, now provided from 478 Field Co	Appx 2
			C.R.E. attended conference at D.H.Q reference operation for 30th, by which our front will be changed from facing N.N.E. to N.E.	
			C.R.E. visited 183 Bde. H.Q.,LA JUSTICE, reference providing extra accomodation for two Bde. H.Q. As this is impossible, suggested LARBLIN.	
		14.00	C.R.E. met Chief Engineer Corps and obtained his bridging policy for River RHONELLE.	
			Conference of Company Commanders and discussed operations for 30th.	
			Inspected ladder bridges prepared by 476 Field Co.	
			Sent box car to WOOD Dump and D.A.D.O.S. lorry to DUFOUR Dump for material.	Appx 3
			Sent all concerned information obtained from reconnaissances today.	
	29th	11.15	Received letter from C.E. XVII Corps (C.E. 342) detailing C.R.E. to place footbridges over River RHONELLE for infantry of the Division and to arrange for heavy bridge at L.31.c.2.5.	Appx 3
			C.R.E. inspected forward roads.	
			C.R.E. has interviews with Chief Engineer, O.C. 178 T. Co R.E., O.C. 177 T. Co R.E.? and C.R.E. Corps Troops.	
		18.00	Received 61 Div Order 228 re operation of Division on 31st. inst. in conjunction with 4th. Division on our left, but this was subsequently postponed until morning of 1st. November.	
		22.00	Issued R.E. Order 231 re operation by Division and work of Field Companies.	Appx 2
			Issued orders for work for tomorrow.	Appx 3
		23.59	Received 61 Div Order 229 re the operation on 31st. will entail moves of Brigades. VENDEGIES shelled during the night and issued orders for H.Q. personnel to sleep in cellars.	a

WAR DIARY
INTELLIGENCE SUMMARY

OCTOBER 1918

HEADQUARTERS
61st. DIV. R. ENGINEERS
Vol. XXX

Army Form C. 2118.
Page 10.

Place	Date	Hour	Summary of Events and Information	Remarks and references to Appendices
FRANCE. Sht. 51a. 1/40000				Appx 1
VENDEGIES	30th		Issued Routine Orders 131-134 Wrote C.E. Corps giving him particulars of bridges used in connection with crossing of ECAILLON advised Companies that postponement of operations and increased enemy activity may mean attack by the enemy and all units are warned to be in constant readiness.	Appx 3
		13.00	Received 184 Bde. Order re attack by the Division.	
		13.00	Received 61 Div Art Order re attack by the Division.	
		13.55	Received 183 Bde. Order re attack by the Division.	
		19.00	Received 182 Bde. Order re attack by the Division. Instructed 479 Field Co to detail party to reconnoitre River RHONELLE at LA JUSTICE and LARBLIN. Ordered deep dugouts to be commenced at LA JUSTICE and LARBLIN. Ordered 476 Field Co to make "hair pins" and sent these	
		20.30	Div G. require bridge-head wired; up to Brigade and told them where a few coils of wire could be found, as no other wiring stores are available. Lieut. R.F. BOARD. 479 Field Co. seriously wounded and died half an hour afterwards.	
	31st	09.30	Lieut. STONE (R.A.M.C) proceeded on leave.	
		11.30	C.R.E. and adjutant attended Lieut. BOARDS funereal. C.R.E. and adjutant went to LA JUSTICE and LARBLIN inspecting progress on dugouts. C.R.E. had interviews with C.R.E. Corps Troops, C.R.E's 19th. and 24th. Divisions.	
		22.00	Advised all concerned of further reconnaissance of bridge at L.31.c.2.5.	Appx 3
		22.30	Received 61 Div Order 230 re consolidation of ground gained. Received 4th. Div. order No. 78 re work of 4th. Div R.E. Received 183 Bde. Order re move of Brigade.	appx 3.

Statement of work done by the RE during October

[signature]
Capt. Adjutant.

For C.R.E. 61st. Div.

October 31st. 1918.

War Diary.
(Original.)
for October 1918.
C.R.E. 61st Divn.

Appendix 1

Routine Orders

By

C.R.E.

ROUTINE ORDERS
-by-
Major M. WHITWELL, D.S.O., M.C.
Commanding:- 61st. Divisional ROYAL ENGINEERS.

R.E.H.Q. 2.10.18.

127. **COMMAND**.

Major M. WHITWELL, D.S.O., M.C., having returned from leave, assumes Command of the 61st. Divisional R.E. from this date.

(Signed) M.E.FITZGERALD,
Capt.,
Adjutant.

ROUTINE ORDERS
-by-
Lieut.-Colonel G.E.J. DURNFORD, D.S.O., R.E.
Commanding:- 61st. (S.M.) Divisional ROYAL ENGINEERS.

R.E.H.Q. 11th.Oct.1918.

128. **COMMAND.**
Lieut.Colonel G.E.J.DURNFORD, D.S.O., R.E., having returned from leave, resumed Command of the Divisional R.E. as from the 8th.inst.

129. **POSTINGS.**
Approval has been given for the following postings:-

(a) Major H.HUMPHREYS, Commanding 479 Field Co. R.E. to Command 476 Field Co. R.E., vice T/Lt.Col. M.WHITWILL, D.S.O, M.C., appointed C.R.E. 73rd.Division.

(b) Capt. B.LOBO, M.C., second-in-Command 479 Field Co. R.E., to Command 479 Field Co. R.E.

(Authority:- A.G. No.AG/56/6214 (O) dated 7-10-18.)

(Signed) H.E.FITZGERALD,
Capt.
Adjutant.

ROUTINE ORDERS:-

Lieut.-Colonel G.E.J. DURNFORD, D.S.O., R.E.,
Commanding:- 61st. (South Midland) Divisional ROYAL ENGINEERS.

R.E.H.Q. 20th.Oct.1918.

---

130. ACTING RANK:

Authority has been given for the undermentioned Officer to wear the Badges of Rank for which he has been recommended:

Lieut. B. LONG to be Acting Major whilst Commanding 479th. Field Company, R.E.

(Authority:- 61st.Division No.A.R.13/2 dated 18/10/18)

(Signed) G.H.SIMMONS, Lieut.,
A/Adjutant.

ROUTINE ORDERS

Issued by Lieut-Colonel, G.E.J. DURNFORD, D.S.O. R.E.

Commanding:- 61st. (South Midland) Divisional Royal Engineers.

R.E.H.Qrs.   Oct. 30th. 1918.

---

131. **LEAVE**. The following officers have been granted leave of absence:-

    (i) 2nd. Lt. D.S. WOOD.   476 Field Co.   25th.Oct - 8th. Nov.
    (ii) Lieut. J.D. RAWLINS.   478 Field Co.   28th.Oct - 11th.Nov.

132. **STRENGTH**.

    (i) Lieut. (A/Capt.) M.E.W. FITZGERALD having proceeded to join C.E. V Corps, is struck off the strength of R.E.H.Q with effect from 17.10.1918.
        (Auth:- 61 Div A. Wire. A.88/84 dated 16.10.18)

    (ii) Capt. J.K. RENNIE, M.C. (R.A.M.C) having proceeded to join 2/3rd. Field Amb. is struck off the strength of R.E.H.Qrs with effect from 18.10.1918.

    (iii) Lieut. G.H. SIMMONS, M.C. is struck off strength of 479 Field Co R.E. with effect from 17.10.1918 inclusive and taken on strength of R.E.H.Q with effect from 18.10.1918.

    (iv) Lieut. G.K. STONE. (R.A.M.C) is taken on strength of R.E.H.Q with effect from 18.10.1918.

133. **APPOINTMENT**.   The following appointment is approved.

    Lieut. G.H. SIMMONS, M.C. to be Adjutant 61 Div R.E.
    (Auth:- XVII Corps A.25/117. dated 24.10.18).
    (Auth:- 61st. Div A. A 2/4. dated 25.10.18)

134. **ACTING RANK**.
    Authority has been given for the undermentioned officers to wear badges of rank for which they have been recommended.

    Lieut. G.H. SIMMONS, M.C. to be A/Captain whilst Adjutant, Divisional Engineers.
    (Auth:- 61 Div A.   A.R. 13/3. dated 28.10.18)

    Lieut. R.F. BOARD to be A/Captain whilst acting as second-in-Command of 479 Field Co. R.E.
    (Auth:- 61 Div A.   A.R. 13/4. dated 28.10.18)

Sd.   G.H. SIMMONS.

Capt.   Adjutant, R.E.
For C.R.E. 61 Division

WAR DIARY.
(ORIGINAL.)
for OCTOBER 1918.
C.R.E. 61st DIVn.

APPENDIX 2

MOVE, RELIEF
&
OPERATION ORDERS
BY
C.R.E

LIST OF DOCUMENTS AND MAPS HANDED OVER

TO C.R.E. 59th. DIVN.

****

PROGRESS MAP ON DRAINAGE................... Marked A

R.E. ORDER No 124 and Addendum............Marked B

Emergency Sites for Pontoon Bridges....... Marked C

C.E. letter (Programme of Work on Forward
    Communications) No 114/32........... Marked D

C.E. letter No 114/27   do   do ...... Marked E

C.E. letter No 114/22   do   do ...... Marked F

DESCRIPTION OF COUNTRY ABOUT AUBERS RIDGE
    and immediately East of it............. Marked G

****

1/20000	Map Showing Bridges	one copy
1/20000	Progress on Drainage Map	six copies
1/20000	ERQUINGHEM LYS Sheets	eleven copies
1/20000	BOIS GRENIER Sheets	Sixteen copies

****

SECRET. Copy No. 16.

61st. Divisional R.E. ORDER No. 123.

Ref. Maps:
FRANCE
Sheets 36a & 36.

1. The 61st. DIVISION is being relieved by the 59th. DIVISION and is being withdrawn into G.H.Q. Reserve.

2. Reliefs and moves of the 61st. Divisional R.E. will take place in accordance with Table "A" issued herewith.

3. The following distances will be maintained on the march:-
    100 yards between Field Companies.
    500 yards between other formations.
    25 yards between groups of 6 vehicles or 33 cyclists.

4. All documents, trench maps and instructions relating to the present area, or action to be taken during an advance on this front, will be handed over.

5. All tents, trench shelters and other area stores held on charge will be handed over, either to relieving units or Area Commandants, and receipts will be sent to this office.

6. All details will rejoin their units by tonight with the following exceptions:-

    (a) R.S.M. will retain 6 men (D.C.L.I.) on PIONEER and L.T.S dumps until 10 a.m. when they will rejoin their units under instruction of 1/5 D.C.L.I.

    (b) One man of 57 Sanitary Section attached to each 478 and 479 Field Companies will be handed over to relieving units.

    (c) 6 men of 351 E. & M. Coy. rationed by 476 Field Co. will be handed over to the relieving unit.

    (d) Two drivers of water tank lorries attached R.E.H.Q. for rations will be handed over.

    (e) Usual details at R.E.H.Q. remain attached.

7. Arrangements have been made for Field Companies and 25 K.R.R. (Pioneer Battn.) to send advance parties today. All other details of relief will be arranged by Unit Commanders concerned.

8. One lorry will be provided to assist each Field Coy. move surplus stores. Details will be notified later.

9. Field Companies and 1/5 D.C.L.I. to acknowledge.

Issued at 18.00.
2nd. Oct. 1918.

Capt. Adjutant,
for C.R.E. 61st.Divn.

Distribution:-

Copy No. 1 to 476 Field Co.   Copy No. 6 to 61st.Div.G.   Copy No. 11 - 183 Bde.
"   2 to 478 Field Co.   "   7 to 61st.Div.Q.   "   12 - 184 Bde.
"   3 to 479 Field Co.   "   8 to 61st.Signals. "   13 - Camp Cdt.
"   4 to 1/5 D.C.L.I.   "   9 to C.E.XI Corps. "   14 - CRE 59 Div.
"   5 to R.S.M.   "   10 to 182 Inf.Bde.   "   15 & 16 - War Dy.
                                                        "   16 - File.

TABLE "A" issued with 61st Div R.E. Order 126

Serial No	Date	Troops	From	To	Route	Relieved by	Remarks
1	Oct 3rd	476 Field Co (max. 120 men)	L.13.a.8.5.	182 Bde Group HOLLEBEKE area	Entrains at L.35.c.1.1 9.00 A.M.	467 Field Co	Starting time 8.30 A.M.
2	do	476 Field Co Transport (incld cyclists)	L.16.a.8.6.	do	HERVILLE - ST VENANT	do	
3	do	478 Field Co (max. 120 men)	G.8.c.3.2	183 Bde Group STEENBECQUE area	Entrains at L.35.a.1.1. 11 a.m.	470 Field Co	Starting time 9.06 hours
4	do	478 Field Co Transport (incld cyclists)	L.25.b.3.8	do	NEUF BERQUIN - RUE des FORTS - LE PARC	do	
5	do	479 Field Co (max. 120 men)	L.26.b.7.5	184 Bde Group THIENNES area	Entrains at L.35.a.1.1. NOON	469 Field Co	Starting time 9.00 A.M.
6	do	479 Field Co Transport (incld cyclists)	L.26.b.7.3	do	HERVILLE - TANNAY	do	
7	do	R.E. HdQrs less Transport	L.27.d.8.4	MORBECQUE FONTEIN	By lorry & car	R.E.Hd.Qrs 59th Div	Closing time at L.27.d.3.4 10.30 A.M.
8	do	R.E. Head Qtrs. Transport	L.27.d.8.4	do	CALONNE - BUSNES	do	Starting time 10.00 A.M.

Oct. 2nd 1918

Capt. Adjutant
For C.R.E.
61st Div

SECRET.

Ref Map 56 and 36a.

HANDING OVER REPORT
to C.R.E. 59 Divn
from C.R.E. 61 Divn
****

1. <u>DISPOSITIONS</u>. The Division is advancing today on a two Brigade front, and R.E. Order No 124 (handed over herewith) has come into operation.
    The Divisional objectives and the duties allotted to the Field Companies and Pioneers are given in detail in this order.

2. <u>LOCATIONS</u>

    476 Field Co   (Reserve)   L.16.a.8.5
    478 Field Co   (Left Bde Area)   G.8.c.3.2
    479 Field Co   (Right Bde Area)   L.26.b.7.3
    1/5 D.C.L.I.   (Pioneers)   Gas Works, ESTAIRES
                                       G.25.d.1.7

3. <u>WORK</u>.   In addition to the work detailed in R.E. Order No 124, the following is also in hand:-

    476 Field Co..... Erecting Nissen Huts for "Q" Camp.
                      Repairing billets for a Battalion at KENNET CROSS. L.11.d.5.1.
                      Maintenance of bridges over METEREN BECQUE.

    478 Field Co..... Maintenance of bridges across LYS River from SAILLY PONT TOURNANT (incl) to N Div Boundary
                      Construction of forward Infantry Bde and Art. Bde Headquarters, at G.23.c.7.7

    479 Field Co..... Maintenance of bridges from LYS Bridge (excl) to SAILLY PONT TOURNANT (exclusive).
                      Construction of forward Infantry and Artillery Bde Headquarters at G.29.a.8.6

    All details of work to be handed over by respective Company Commanders.

    1/5 D.C.L.I...... Drainage in accordance with progress map handed over herewith.
                      Maintenance of roads and towpath shown on road map to be kept open for first line transport.

4. <u>SITES for PONTOON BRIDGES</u>.   Emergency sites have been selected and prepared for Pontoon Bridges.
    "A" and "B" sites can be bridged with a Field Company equipment. "C" requires one additional bay and the equipment for this is at my dump and is handed over herewith.

5. Two 150 gallon tank lorries have been attached to me by Army for use in advance.   The drivers are rationed and billeted by me.

H. Stratton Davis

2.10.1918   Major A/C.R.E. 61 Div.

Orders for move of RE HQ

(1) RE HQ will move tomorrow 9th Oct from DOULLENS to forward area as under

(2) The following will proceed by box car

    CRE
    Adjutant
    MO
    Lt. Simmons
    Sgt Featherstone
    Dr Lavington

Officers kits, officers mess, current office papers and telephone will be carried in box car.

(3) Lorry will report at RE HQ at 12.30 hrs to take all remaining baggage to No 9 train leaving DOULLENS 16.26 hours. Cpl PENNY will be in charge.

Following will travel with above

    Cpl Penny
    L/C Skinner
    L/C Angell
    L/C Mott
    Spr Newton
    Spr Collins
    Spr Ford
    Spr Gregory
    Spr Smith
    L/C Haycraft
    Interpreter.

RE HQ
8.10.1918

M A Snow
Capt. Ady
61 Div RE

Copies to CRE
         Cpl Penny

SECRET   Copy No. 7

Ref Maps
LENS 11 }
VALENCIENNES 12 } 1/100000
FRANCE 57c 1/40000

R.E. ORDER No 127.

1. It appears that the enemy is carrying out a retirement on a large scale. The Corps policy is to pursue the enemy vigorously, to force in his rear guards and give battle to his main troops.

2. The 61st Division is at present in the Reserve Group of the XVII Corps, which has the 24th Division in the Leading Group and 19th Division in the Support Group.

3. The XVII Corps boundaries are:-

NORTHERN. MOEUVRES (incl) to BOIS DE BOURLON (excl), FONTAINE NOTRE DAME (incl), FONTAINE - CAMBRAI ROAD (incl), CAMBRAI - ~~VENDEGIES~~ ROAD (excl).
    VENDEGIES

SOUTHERN. GRAINCOURT (incl) LA JUSTICE (incl), CANTAING (incl), NOYELLES (excl) NIERGNIES (excl) LA BELLE ETOILE, AWOINGT (incl), CARNIERES (excl) Point 74, ST AUBERT (incl) MAUSSY (incl), MAISON BLANCHE.

4. The Leading Group is accompanied by one section of Tunnellers whose duty it is to search for and remove mines and booby traps. The marking of buildings etc is to be as laid down in my 12/5 dated 7th inst. viz

    WHITE CHALK   O.K. SAFE
    GREEN CHALK   ⊗   SUSPICIOUS
    RED CHALK   ⊗   DANGER

with date and name of unit making the examination.

5. The 61st. Division is to be prepared to move forward at short notice. The strictest march discipline is to be enforced and troops are to move off roads to halt whenever possible.

6. Field Coys are still under the orders of ~~the~~ Group Commanders for purposes of moves.

7. In the event of the 61st Division moving forward through the Support and Leading Groups:-

(a) 183 Bde is to become the Divisional Advance Guard.

(b) 476 Field Co will become the Advanced Guard Engineers and will come under the orders of G.O.C. 183 Inf Bde.

8. Field Coys to ACKNOWLEDGE.

Issued at 17.45
R.E.H.Qrs,
October 10th 1918

Capt Adjutant
For C.R.E. 61st Divn

Distribution
Copy No 1 476 Field Co   Copy No 5 183 Inf Bde
       2 478 Field Co   6. G.O.C. 17th Corps
       3 479 Field Co   7.& 8 War Diary
       4 61 Div G.   9 File

SECRET.

Copy No. 12

Ref. Map 57B. 1/40,000.
"   "   51B. 1/40,000.

R.E. ORDER No. 128.

1.   The Division is moving forward on the 23rd.inst., preparatory to operations to take place on 24th.inst., and Field Companies will move in accordance with attached movement table.

2.   The usual distances will be maintained by units and transport on the line of march.

3.   All dismounted troops will march off the roads wherever possible, and in view of the congested and bad state of the roads, the most strict march discipline must be maintained.

4.   Accommodation forward will be extremely limited.

5.   R.E.H.Q. will close at RIEUX at 14.30 hrs. and open at 15.30 hrs. at ST. AUBERT.

6.   Completion of moves and locations will be reported as usual.

7.   Field Companies to ACKNOWLEDGE.

Issued at 21.00 hours,
22nd.October 1918.

Lieut. - Adjutant,
for C.R.E. 61st.Divn.

DISTRIBUTION:

Copy No. 1 to 475 Field Co.
"   "   2 to 476 Field Co.
"   "   3 to 479 Field Co.
"   "   4 to 61st.Div. "G".
"   "   5 to 61st.Div. "Q".
"   "   6 to 182 Inf. Bde.
"   "   7 to 183 Inf. Bde.
"   "   8 to 184 Inf. Bde.
"   "   9 to C.E. XVII Corps.
"   "   10 to C.R.E. 19th.Div.
"   "   11 to War Diary.
"   "   12 to "   "
"   "   13 to File.

Copy No............

MOVEMENT TABLE to accompany

R.E. ORDER No. 125 dated 22nd.October 1918.

Serial No.	Date	Unit	From	To	Route	Remarks
1.	25/10/18.	470 Field Co.	GARNONCHES.	ST. AUBERT.	-	To march under orders of C.O.C. 164 Bde. and come under orders of C.R.E. on arrival. Take over billets from 81st.Field Co. 19th. Division at U.34.b.4.5.
2.	25/10/18.	470 Field Co.	AVESNES.	ST. AUBERT.	-	To march under orders of C.O.C. 185 Bde. and come under orders of C.R.E. on arrival. Take over billets from 82nd.Field Co., 19th.Div. at U.13.b.30.25.
3.	25/10/18.	476 Field Co.	RIEUX.	ST. AUBERT.	AVESNES.	To march at 14.30 hours. Take over billets from 94th.Field Co., 19th. Division at U.19.a.4.9.

22/10/18.

Lieut. - A/Adjutant,
for C.R.E. 61st.Division.

SECRET.   Copy No. 11

                              R.E. ORDER No. 129.

Ref. Map 51.A.   23/10/18.
1/40,000.

                1.   The 61st Division is attacking and capturing the high
                        ground East of the River ECAILLON on the 24th October at
                        a Zero hour which has been notified to all concerned.

Dispositions.   2.   The attack is being carried out by the 183 Inf. Bde.
                        on the right and the 182 Inf. Bde. on the left.
                        184 Inf. Bde. is in Divisional Reserve.
                        At Zero hour, the attacking troops are advancing in
                        conformity with a creeping barrage, the general
                        direction of the advance being a magnetic compass bearing
                        of 58°.

Orders.   3.   The Divisional Engineers and 1/5 D.C.L.I. (Pioneers)
                        will work under orders of the C.R.E.

Detail of   4.   Detail of work and troops allotted are given in Table
Work.   "A" attached.

Reserve.   5.   Troops not allotted in Table "A" will be in general
                        Reserve and prepared to undertake any work required.

Pioneers   6.   The 6 Platoons of Pioneers allotted to 476 and 478
rendezvous   Field Companies for Serial Nos. 1, 2, 3, 4, & 5 will
& strength.   report to their respective Field Companies at 16.00 hrs.
                        23rd.; each Platoon to contain a minimum of 40 o.r.

Assembly   7.   Troops in general reserve will be assembled in
place for   MONTRECOURT Wood by 07.00 hours 24th.: 479 Field Co.
Reserve.   with tool carts and limbers; 1/5 D.C.L.I. with picks,
                        shovels and cutting tools.
                        Units concerned will reconnoitre the position today.

Runners &   8.   1/5 D.C.L.I. and each Field Company will detail 2
Liaison.   runners to report to C.R.E's office at 16.00 hours on
                        23rd.
                        D.C.L.I. and 479 Field Co., on arrival at MONTRECOURT
                        Wood, will each send one Officer and 4 runners to Advd.
                        D.H.Q.

Transport.   9.   476 and 478 Field Companies will utilize the Pontoon
                        or Trestle wagons they require for carrying stores for
                        Serial Nos. 3, 4 & 5.   All other bridging equipment
                        will be kept loaded at ST. AUBERT.

Signs and   10.   All Bridges and fords will be marked by the usual
Notice boards.   sign ✕ and the necessary notice boards will be
                        erected.

A.A.   11.   A.A. Lewis Guns will be mounted near Field Coy. H.Q.
Lewis Guns.

(2)

Section Lewis Guns.	12.	Section Lewis Guns will not be taken forward by Field Company working parties.
Dress.	13.	Dress for R.E. working parties: Battle Order, 100 rounds Ammunition.
Locations.	14.	D.H.Q. - U.24.b.6.3. - Adv.D.H.Q. - MONTRECOURT.
		R.E.H.Q. - U.24.b.6.1. - and at Advanced D.H.Q.
		476 Field Co. - " - V.19.a.4.9.
		478 Field Co. - " - U.18.b.30.25.
		479 Field Co. - " - U.24.b.4.5.
		1/5 D.C.L.I. - " - U.24.b.4.7.
		Right Bde. H.Q. - " - V.5.c.5.1.
		Left Bde. H.Q. - " - V.5.a. (Sandpits).
		Reserve Bde. H.Q. - " - V.5.a. (Sandpits).
Reports, etc.	15.	Copies of all reports and reconnaissances will be forwarded to R.E.H.Q. with as little delay as possible.
	16.	R.E.H.Q. will close at ST. AUBERT at Zero hour on 24th. and open at MONTRECOURT at the same hour.
	17.	Field Companies and 1/5 D.C.L.I. to acknowledge.

Issued at R.E.H.Q.
   at 11.15 hours.
23rd.October 1918.

Geo H Simmons Lt
a/ad
p Lieut.-Colonel, R.E.,
C.R.E. 61st.Division.

Distribution:

Copy No. 1 to 476 Field Co.
" 2 to 478 Field Co.
" 3 to 479 Field Co.
" 4 to 1/5 D.C.L.I.
" 5 to 61st.Div. "G".
" 6 to 182 Inf. Bde.
" 7 to 183 Inf. Bde.
" 8 to 184 Inf. Bde.
" 9 to C.E. XVII Corps.
" 10 to War Diary.
" 11 to " "
" 12 to File.

SECRET.

1. Reference R.E. Order No 129 dated 23/10/1918.
   Zero hour will be at __04.00__ hours (i.e. on the early morning of the __24th__ inst)

2. ACKNOWLEDGE.

23/10/1918.

Lieut   A/Adjutant
For C.R.E.   61st Divn.

Addressed three Field Coys and 1/5 D.C.L.I.

SECRET.

Copy No..... 6

R.E. Order No. 130.

1. Two sections Field Company are now detailed as Advance Guard Engineers. These will be found by 478 Field Co.

2. The O.C. Advance Guard Engineers, in addition to work required by Advance Guard Commander is responsible for detailing parties for Engineer Reconnaissance and sending back such information as is gained to R.E.Headquarters as soon as possible.

3. The O.C. Advance Guard Engineers will also act as R.E. Liaison officer between his Commander and the O.R.E.

Issued at 12.15 hours.
October 25th.1918.

Distribution.

Copy No.- 1.   476 Field Co.
        2.   478 Field Co.
        3.   479 Field Co.
        4.   Lieut. Best.
        5.   183 Inf. Bde.
        6 & 7 War Diary.
        8.   File.

J.H.Simmons
Lieut-Adjutant, R.E
For O.R.E. 61st. Division

SECRET.   Copy No...14..

                          R.E. ORDER NO. 131.

Ref. Map 51A. N.E.   29.10.1918.
    1/20,000.

                1.   61st. Division, in conjunction with 4th. Division
                     (XXII Corps), is attacking and capturing the high
                     ground east and North of the River RHONELLE and the
                     village of MARESCHES, at an hour to be notified
                     separately.

Dispositions.   2.   182 Inf. Bde. is attacking in an easterly direction,
                     North of the River RHONELLE, from the bridge-head at
                     Fme. de l'HOTEL DIEU.   183 Inf. Bde. is making good
                     that portion of the objective South of the River, until
                     relieved by 182 Inf. Bde., and is sending fighting
                     patrols across the River.

Artillery.   3.   One Brigade R.F.A. will commence to advance by
                     batteries at Zero plus 120 mins. and will cross the
                     River RHONELLE by medium bridge to be constructed at
                     Fme. de l'HOTEL DIEU (Serial No.2, Table "A").

Objectives   4.   As already explained verbally.
& Boundaries.

                5.   The Divisional Engineers and 1/5 D.C.L.I. (Pioneers)
                     will work under orders of the C.R.E.

Detail of   6.   Detail of work and troops allotted are given in
WORK.   Table "A" attached.

Liaison.   7.   Officers Commanding 476 and 478 Field Companies
                     will arrange for an Officer to be present at 182 and
                     183 Inf. Bde. H.Q. respectively from Zero hour onwards.

Transport.   8.   Trestle wagons will be kept loaded; pontoon wagons
                     off-loaded and ready to take material forward.
                     O.C. 479 Field Co. will place his trestle wagon,
                     with equipment, at disposal of O.C. 478 Field Co.
                     should he require it.

Lewis Guns.   9.   Section Lewis Guns will not be carried by parties
                     detailed in Table "A".

  Dress.   10.   Battle order; 100 rounds ammunition.

Reports, etc. 11.   All reports and reconnaissances to be sent to
                     R.E.H.Q. by telephone, cyclist, or mounted orderly,
                     with as little delay as possible.

Locations.   12.   Div. and R.E. H.Q. remain at VENDEGIES.
                     Advanced H.Q. 182 Inf. Bde. - Sunken road Q.4.c.6.5.
                         "   " 183 Inf. Bde. - LARBLIE.
                         "   " 184 Inf. Bde. - K.34.c.

13. Field Companies and 1/5 D.C.L.I. to acknowledge.

[signature] Lt
Adj.

Issued at 22.0 Hours.   for Lieut.-Colonel, R.E.
29.10.18.   C.R.E. 61st. Division.

Distribution:-

Copy No. 1 to 476 Field Co.
"   2 to 478 Field Co.
"   3 to 479 Field Co.
"   4 to 1/5 D.C.L.I.
"   5 to 61st. Div. "G".
"   6 to 182 Inf. Bde.
"   7 to 183 Inf. Bde.
"   8 to 184 Inf. Bde.
"   9 to 61st. Div. Art.
"   10 to O.C. Det. 178 (T) Co. R.E.
"   11 to C.E. XVII Corps.
"   12 to C.R.E. 4th. Division.
"   13 to War Diary.
"   14 to War Diary.
"   15 to File.

SECRET.   COPY NO. 114

TABLE "A" issued with R.E. Order No. 131.

Serial No.	Description of work	Troops allotted.	Remarks.
1.	Footbridges across R. RHONELLE and approaches.	476 Field Coy.	Night 30/31st. To be completed before zero hour.
2.	Bridge for field artillery across RHONELLE at Rue de L'HOTEL DIEU.	A. Coy. 1/5 D.C.L.I.	Night 30/31st. To be completed for Field Art. by zero plus 2 hours. Any work undertaken before zero hour to be as noiseless as possible. Repair party to remain near bridge.
3.	Clearing roads through AULNES and approaches to Bridge 2. above		
4.	Reconnaissance of roads N. of R. RHONELLE.	parties from 479 Field Co.	To report to O.C. 476 Field Co at 182 Bde. H.Qrs LA JUSTICE at 6 a.m. 31st.
5.	Water reconnaissance in ARTRES & Rue de L'HOTEL DIEU		
6.	Provide extemporised bridges for patrols of 183 Inf. Bde for crossing R. RHONELLE on 31st.		
7.	Additional footbridges across R. RHONELLE east of H.29.C.	476 Field Coy.	Night 31st. Oct/1st. Nov.
8.	Medium bridge over stream at L.21.c.2.5.	B. Coy. 1/5 D.C.L.I.	As soon as situation permits. Heavy bridge to be put in if practicable.
9.	Medium bridge at K.30.d.central		As soon as situation permits. Troops in Reserve to assist if necessary.
10.	Clearing roads in SEPMERIES area and approaches to Bridge 9. above.		
11.	Road reconnaissance S. of River RHONELLE		
12.	Water reconnaissance in SEPMERIES, FAMOUTIAUX and MARESCHES.	party from 479 Fld Co.	To report to O.C. 479 Fld Co at 183 Bde. H.Q. LARRIEU at 09.00 as hours on 31st.
	RESERVE.	479 Fld Co less parties 5 and 12. C.Coy 1/5 DCLI	In billets. Readiness 2 after zero plus 2 hours.

October 29th. 1918.

J.H.Hyrenius Lt.Col.
for Lieut-Colonel, R.S.
C.R.E. 61st Div.

S E C R E T.

470 Field Co: 1/5 D.C.L.I.
478 Field Co: 1/6 (W) Co. Detachment.
479 Field Co:

1. Reference R.E. Order No. 131 dated 29.10.18.

2. Zero hour will be 0515 hrs on 31.10.18.

ACKNOWLEDGE.

Geo. H. Simmons Lt
for Lieut-Colonel.
C.R.E.
61st (S. MIDLAND) Division.

29.10.18.

SECRET.

476 Field Co.
476 Field Co.
479 Field Co.
Copy to 61 Div C.
      O.C. Detachment 178 T. Co. R.E.

1.   The postponement of the operations referred to in R.E. Order 121 and the increased activity shown by the enemy yesterday, necessitate the constant readiness of units at all times to meet an enemy attack.

2.   The two Infantry Brigades responsible for the defence of the Corps line of Resistance have one battalion each in that line, one battalion ready to counter-attack should the enemy succeed in effecting a break in our line and one battalion in Reserve.

3.   The 1/5 D.C.L.I. is occupying the village line of BERMERAIN - VENDEGIES - SOMMAING.

4.   On the Alarm being given by the order "MAN BATTLE STATIONS", Field Coys. less sections detailed to the Advance Guard Brigade will concentrate at or near their H.Qrs in Readiness "A".
     Pontoon equipment will be loaded immediately and an officer and 2 men sent by each company to R.E.H.Q. They must know the fresh location of the company should it be intended to move.

5.   Till further orders, pontoon and trestle wagons will be kept loaded except when being sent forward with stores.

6.   Field Coys to ACKNOWLEDGE.

                                              Lieut-Colonel, R.E.
October 30th. 1918.   C.R.E. 61st. Division.

WAR DIARY.
(ORIGINAL.)
for OCTOBER 1918.
C.R.E. 61st DIVn.

APPENDIX 3

WORK ORDERS & INSTRUCTIONS BY CRE

RECONNAISSANCE REPORTS

C.E. XI Corps,

Reference your 1/322 dated 11th inst. the following bridges were erected by 61st Division between Sept 3rd and Sept 29th. over the LYS CANAL System.

    5   Heavy Bridges.
    6   First Line Transport Bridges
    5   Medium Pontoon Bridges.
    12   Pack Animal Bridges.
    6   Footbridges.

During the period advance in the MERVILLE sector up to and including October 3rd the 61st Division repaired and made fit for transport - 57 miles of road.

Lieut-Colonel
C.R.E. 61st Divn

Oct. 14th 1918

476 Field Co
478 Field Co
479 Field Co

NOTES ON CONFERENCE HELD AT R.E.H.Q.
16.10.1918.

LEWIS GUNS.   Each section to form Lewis Gun teams of one N.C.O. and 5 sappers and in addition to train 5 men per section.   As far as possible these men not to be cyclists. On the march the section guns to be carried in section limbers. The A.A. Gun to be carried in the Company G.S. Wagon.

BRIDGING EQUIPMENT DURING AN ADVANCE. In the event of an advance by the Division with one Brigade as Advance Guard Brigade and with one Field Company affiliated to each Infantry Brigade, the arrangement will be for the bridging equipment of Advance Guard Field Co to be attached and move with "Support Field Company". It is also probable that the bridging equipment of the "Reserve Field Co" will be attached to the "Support Field Company" in which case the middle Field Company will have the three bridging sets with it.   The remaining transport of the Advance Guard Company will be with it and the Quartermaster Sergeant with his wagon will probably have to remain with the Brigade Group Transport.

Oct 17th 1918

Capt Adjutant
For C.R.E. 61st Division

476 Field Co
478 Field Co
479 Field Co

NOTES ON CONFERENCE HELD AT R.E.H.Q.
16.10.1918.

    LEWIS GUNS.   Each section to form Lewis Gun teams of one N.C.O. and 5 sappers and in addition to train 5 men per section.   As far as possible these men not to be cyclists. On the march the section guns to be carried in section limbers. The A.A. Gun to be carried in the Company G.S. Wagon.

    BRIDGING EQUIPMENT DURING AN ADVANCE. In the event of an advance by the Division with one Brigade as Advance Guard Brigade and with one Field Company affiliated to each Infantry Brigade, the arrangement will be for the bridging equipment of Advance Guard Field Co to be attached and move with "Support Field Company". It is also probable that the bridging equipment of the "Reserve Field Co" will be attached to the "Support Field Company" in which case the middle Field Company will have the three bridging sets with it.   The remaining transport of the Advance Guard Company will be with it and the Quartermaster Sergeant with his wagon will probably have to remain with the Brigade Group Transport.

                                        Capt Adjutant
Oct 17th 1918   For C.R.E. 61st Division

C.R.E. 24th. Division.

Herewith copies of information obtained from Reconnaissances up to date.

ROADS. All first and second class roads in the Divisional area are passable as far east as a line drawn through Q.23.b.8.8 and L'EPINE Q.2.b.7.6. Roads on the whole little damaged.

WATER.
(1) Pumps yielding clear water at:
    Fm. a RIEUX. (W.2.b.7.7).
    House near MILL (Q.20.d.2.4)
    Fm. d'ORCHIVAL (Q.26.b.1.4).

(2)   Q.14.a.8.8.
    Q.14.a.9.2.
    Q.14.c.2.7.
    Q.14.c.3.8.
    Q.13.d.2.7.
    Q.13.c.9.9.
    Q.14.d.8.2.
    Q.14.d.5.5.
    Q.14.d.5.8.
    Q.14.d.2.9.
    Q.14.b.2.2. (In roadway)   } Pumps- good water.
    Q.14.c.2.4.
    Q.14.c.3.9.
    Q.14.a.4.8.
    Q.7.d.4.1.
    Q.8.c.7.1.

    Q.14.c.3.2. Well 15' deep; no pump.
    Q.14.c.4.8. Well & windlass; good water.
    Q.8.c.8.3. Well 15' deep.
    Q.8.c.3.0. Well 20' deep.
    Q.8.c.1.2.   "   "   "

(3) ST. MARTIN.

Name of Street.	Pumps at billets numbered.	Wells & windlasses at billets numbered.
Rue D'ENBAC.	4/4. 83/16. 11/11.	
Rue de L'EGLISE.	27/1. 117/5. 109/9.	105/13.
Rue d'ENBAC.	173/18. 169/15. 163/7.	181/29.
Rue BAUDET.	99	98/8. 96/92. 95/10. 90a/9.
Rue VALENCIENNES.	67/74.	90/25.
SHELDWACKER STR.		105/16. 109/20. 117/29. 119c/58.
VON DEUTCHSTER STR.	121/9. 182/13.	126/10. 131a/15. 49.
DUESNES STR.	187/12.	63/7. 194/7.

(2)

L.25.d.8.1 - width reported 10' to 15') flow sluggish.
L.25.d.7.1 -   "   "   20'   ) 30' footbridges would be
)   suitable for crossing.

K.30.d.5.5 - Bosche vehicle, possibly minenwerfer, crossed bridge at this point last night. Bridge could not be reached owing to M.G. fire. A weir is reported at this point.

K.30.d.4.7 - Width reported 20'.

It would appear that stream generally in this neighbourhood is 20' wide and sluggish, but the sound of running water in places may indicate the possibility of fording.

Ground S. of the river is open, with scattered wire fences.

Detailed reconnaissance not practicable as N. bank of river was held by enemy.

10 trees reported cut down across the river in K.29.c.

27/10/18.

Lieut.-Colonel, R.E.,
C.R.E. 61st.Division.

(Copy)

C.R.E. 61st.Div. No.23/2/1.

476 Field Co.	61st.Div.Art.
478 Field Co.	61st.Div."G".
479 Field Co.	61st.Div."Q".
182 Inf.Bde.	C.E.XVII Corps.
183 Inf.Bde.	C.R.E. 24th.Div.
184 Inf.Bde.	

INFORMATION OBTAINED FROM RECONNAISSANCES
27.10.1918.

ROADS.

From Crucifix Q.16.a to Le TAPAGE (K.33.b.) good metalled road for two way traffic. North of this through K.27.d. the road peters out.

From road junction Q.4.c.5.7 to Q.5.b.7.6 metalled, second class, 12 to 15ft. wide, fair condition. Will probably cut up in wet weather. No material on site for repairs.

From Q.11.d.0.2 to Railway Arch Q.6.b. metalled second class road, 12 to 15-ft. wide, fair condition, but will cut up in wet weather. Through the cutting in Q.6.a. road is wide enough for two way traffic and is being cleared.

From Railway arch Q.6.b.1.5 to cross roads R.7.a.5.2, first class two way road, pave 12ft. wide.

CHAUSSEE BRUNHAUT East of Q.11.d.0.2 is only a dry weather track.

BRIDGES.

Tunnelling Co. reports bridges N.E. of ARTRES at K.29.a.15. and K.29.a.4.6 destroyed. Bridges at L.25.a.9.3 and K.30.d.6.5 destroyed. Diversion bridge at Q.7.d.2.3 has been dismantled.

Trestle bridge at Fm. de RIEUX has now been taken out and replaced by an improvised bridge capable of taking first line transport.

ECAILLON RIVER.

The work of clearing the dams in ECAILLON River is nearing completion.

Oct. 27th. 1918.

(Sd.) G.H.SIMMONS,
Lieut. - Adjutant R.E.
for C.R.E. 61st.Division.

Ref. Map 51A.
1/20,000.

SUMMARY OF INFORMATION
obtained from Reconnaissances 28.10.18.

ROADS. Road from Chateau (K.35.a.9.8) through ARTRES K.28.d.7.9 – K.29.a.2.1 – K.28.b.8.7 to Bridge K.29.a.35.85 is good, 2 way, metalled, pave through village. Two large shell holes mear K.28.d.5.6 and debris near church. This is being cleared tomorrow.

FOOTBRIDGES. Three footbridges were placed over RHONELLE River during the night 27th./28th. between K.29.a.6.1 and K.29.d.0.5
Duckboard bridges are reported at K.29.a.4.6 (FERME de l'HOTEL DIEU) and at K.29.a.35.85.

RHONELLE RIVER. Reported 30ft. wide and 6ft. deep in the neighbourhood of K.29.c.
At the destroyed bridge K.29.a.35.85 water is only about 12 inches deep.

MINES (Delay action).
Two charges removed from Railway Bridge at K.34.b.8.3, each consisting of a 5.9 shell and 50-lbs. of perdite.
Sixteen light charges of about 3-lbs. of perdite have been removed from the railway between K.27.d.8.4 and K.35.c.6.8.

J.H. Simmons Lt
a/q
Lieut.-Colonel, R.E.
C.R.E. 61st.Division.

28.10.18.

Distribution:-

476 Field Co.
478 Field Co.
479 Field Co.
182 Inf. Bde.
183 Inf. Bde.
184 Inf. Bde.
61st.Div.Art.
61st.Div. "G".
61st.Div. "Q".
1/5 D.C.L.I.
C.E. XVII Corps.
C.R.E. 24th.Div.

476 Field Co.
478 Field Co.
479 Field Co.
1/5 D.C.L.I.

WORK ORDERS for 29th. Oct.

Work to be carried out tomorrow as arranged at Conference today.

479 Field Co will improve accomodation at LARBLIN 8 sheets of C.I. may be drawn from C.R.E.

478 Field Co will continue improvement of accomodation in the cutting at LA JUSTICE. 8 sheets of C.I. may be drawn from C.R.E.

1/5 D.C.L.I. will clear the road near the church in ARTRES and fill in adjoining shell holes at K.28.d.4.5., also continue work of clearing roads now in hand.

Orders for work on the night 29th/30th. and 30th. inst will be issued later.

October 28th. 1918.

Lieut. Adjutant, R.E.
For C.R.E. 61st. Division

C.E. XVII Corps.

Reference C.E. 321 dated 27.10.18;

1. I attach a sketch of the light bridges thrown over the ECAILLON in the attack on the 24th.inst.

2. It was decided to adopt a lighter type than was successfully used by the 19th.Division for crossing the SELLE, because it was considered improbable that the Bridges could be taken up to the River on wheels owing to obstacles and strong enemy opposition.   This proved to be the case.

3. On the whole, the bridges were fairly satisfactory.   8 men carried the skeleton bridge and 5 men each carried two 3-ft. duckboards, which were dropped in position as soon as the bridge was in place.

4. Each bridge party consisted of 5 R.E. and 10 pioneers. This party was able to keep up with the infantry so long as it was not seriously reduced by casualties.

5. The strength of the party was not sufficient however to replace casualties, especially when the duckboard decking was made of heavy wood and a man could not carry more than one. This could not be avoided as suitable material was not available for all of the bridges

6. From experience gained in getting assaulting infantry over the ECAILLON and similar obstacles, I am convinced that it would be much better if footbridges, improvised from ladders, were used by the first wave, the heavier bridges being brought down by the second and third wave, or even the supporting troops.   These can be easily carried by 2 to 4 men according to the length and can be much more easily taken through entanglements and thick undergrowth, and launched.

7. A 20ft. to 30ft. ladder, strengthened as shown below, will carry three men in the centre.

A ladder in fair condition and not strengthened will carry two men over about 25ft.
Ladders might also be used for longer spans as shown below:-

8. I attach a copy of a minute written to 61st.Division, "G", on the subject.

30th.October 1918.

Lieut.-Colonel, R.E.
C.R.E. 61st.Division.

61 Div G.   476 Field Co.
182 Inf. Bde   478 Field Co.
183 Inf. Bde.   479 Field Co.
184 Inf. Bde   C.R.E.   Divn. 19 & 74
61 Div Art.   68 Bde. R.G.A
                 1/5 Devon
                 or Det. 178 Co.

1. Further reconnaissance of the destroyed road bridge at L.31.c.2.5. today shows that there is an existing bridge over the stream at about L.31.c.5.5. which is fit for First Line Transport and Field Artillery.

2. A track to this bridge will be marked out from the road at R.1.a.y.6.

3. A heavy bridge capable of taking all loads will be constructed at L.31.c.2.5. during night 1st/2nd Nov.

J.H. Simmons Capt
RE

for Lieut-Colonel, R.E.
22.00 hours.   C.R.E. 61st. Division.
31.10.1918.

WORK CARRIED OUT BY
61st. DIVISION ROYAL ENGINEERS.

in connection with operations on 24th. October & 1st. Novby. 1918

Preparation.   Constructed at R.E. Dump and at Transport Lines

    20 footbridges   30 ft long
    10 footbridges   10 ft long
    10 ladder footbridges.

During the operation.   Placed over ECAILLON River and HARPIES River

    13 infantry assault bridges.
    5 pack animal bridges
    3 first line transport bridges.

and over the RHONELLE River & PRECHELLES STREAM

    15 infantry assault bridges
    3 first line transport bridges.
    1 heavy bridge.

Roads repaired and cleared through 5 villages.

27½ miles of road reconnoitred and reported upon to all concerned.

Water supplies reconnoitred in 6 villages and outlying farms and reported to all concerned.

9000 yards of river reconnoitred. Bridge gaps measured. Dams removed.

6 dugout shafts put down for Advance Brigade H.Q with 15' of cover excavated.

Several of the footbridges used in the first action were salved and repaired and replaced by improvised bridges, and used again in the second action.

Two first line transport bridges were taken out and one replaced by a Corps Heavy bridge and another was replaced by salved material in order to have the Weldon Trestle equipment available again in the second action.

Lt-Col
CRE. 61 Div.

War Diary.
(Original.)
for OCTOBER 1918.
C.R.E. 61st DIVn.

APPENDIX 4

NOMINAL ROLLS

NOMINAL ROLL OF UNIT.

1st. October 1918.

Officers.

Lieut Colonel	G.E.J. DURNFORD, D.S.O.	C.R.E. (on leave)
Captain	H.E.W. FITZGERALD.	Adjutant
Captain	J.K. RENNIE (R.A.M.C)	M.O. attached 479 Field Co, R.E

Other Ranks.

52959	R.S.M. H. DEYERMOND. D.C.M.
500121	Sergt. W.A. FEATHERSTONE.
500336	L/Cpl A. SKINNER
468197	L/Cpl F. HAYCRAFT
99315	Sapper G. BOLLAND (on leave)
500171	Driver L. WATTS
500303	Driver J. GREGORY
56185	Driver A. DAVIES (on leave)
61497	Driver G. PATTEN.
494779	Driver G. DOLLING.
T4/248151	Driver E. LORTON (A.S.C)

Attached.

Officers.

Major	H.S. DAVIS M.C.	476 Field Co	A/C.R.E.
Lieut.	G.H. SIMMONS, M.C.	479 Field Co.	

Other Ranks.

476 Field Co.

498134	L/Cpl A.L. MOTT
498223	Sapper J. COLLINS
84338	Driver G. KING

478 Field Co

496773	Corpl. F.L. PENNY

479 Field Co

494375	Sapper H. TALBOT
488601	Sapper E.S. NEWTON

French Mission

Interpreter GUEUX

WAR DIARY.
(ORIGINAL.)
for OCTOBER 1918.
C.R.E. 61ST DIVN.

APPENDIX 4

NOMINAL ROLLS

NOMINAL ROLL OF UNIT.

1st. Setober 1918.

Officers.

Lieut Colonel	G.E.J. DURNFORD, D.S.O.	C.R.E. (on leave)
Captain	M.E.W. FITZGERALD.	Adjutant
Captain	J. K. RENNIE (R.A.M.C)	M.O. attached 479 Field Co, R.E.

Other Ranks.

52959	R.S.M. H. DEYERMOND. D.C.M.
500121	Sergt, W.A. FEATHERSTONE.
500336	L/Cpl A. SKINNER
408197	L/Cpl F. HAYCRAFT
99315	Sapper G. BOLLAND (on leave)
500171	Driver L. WATTS
500303	Driver J. GREGORY
56185	Driver A. DAVIES (on leave)
61497	Driver G. PATTEN.
494779	Driver G. DOLLING.
T4/248151	Driver E. LORTON (A.S.C)

Attached.

Officers.

Major	H.S. DAVIS M.C.	476 Field Co	A/C.R.E.
Lieut.	G.H. SIMMONS, M.C.	479 Field Co.	

Other Ranks.

476 Field Co.

498134	L/Cpl A.L. MOTT
498223	Sapper J. COLLINS
84336	Driver G. KING

478 Field Co

496773	Corpl. F.L. PENNY

479 Field Co

494275	Sapper H. TALBOT
488601	Sapper E.S. NEWTON

French Mission

Interpreter GUEUX

SPECIAL ORDER OF THE DAY,

by

Major-General F.J. DUNCAN, C.M.G., D.S.O.,
Commanding 61st Division.
----------oOo----------

Headquarters, 7th October, 1918.

The following letter has been received from General Sir W.R. BIRDWOOD, K.C.B., K.C.S.I., K.C.M.G., C.I.E., D.S.O., Commanding Fifth Army.

"This is just a line to wish you and all the 61st goodbye, and to thank you so much for all the good work you have done while serving with the Fifth Army, from which we are so sorry to lose you. However, I can only hope that you are going to more important work elsewhere, and I am sure you know how heartily I wish you, your Brigadiers, and all your officers and men the very best of good fortune in all that may be before you."

F.J. Duncan
Major-General.
Commanding 61st Division.

APX C

1/20,000

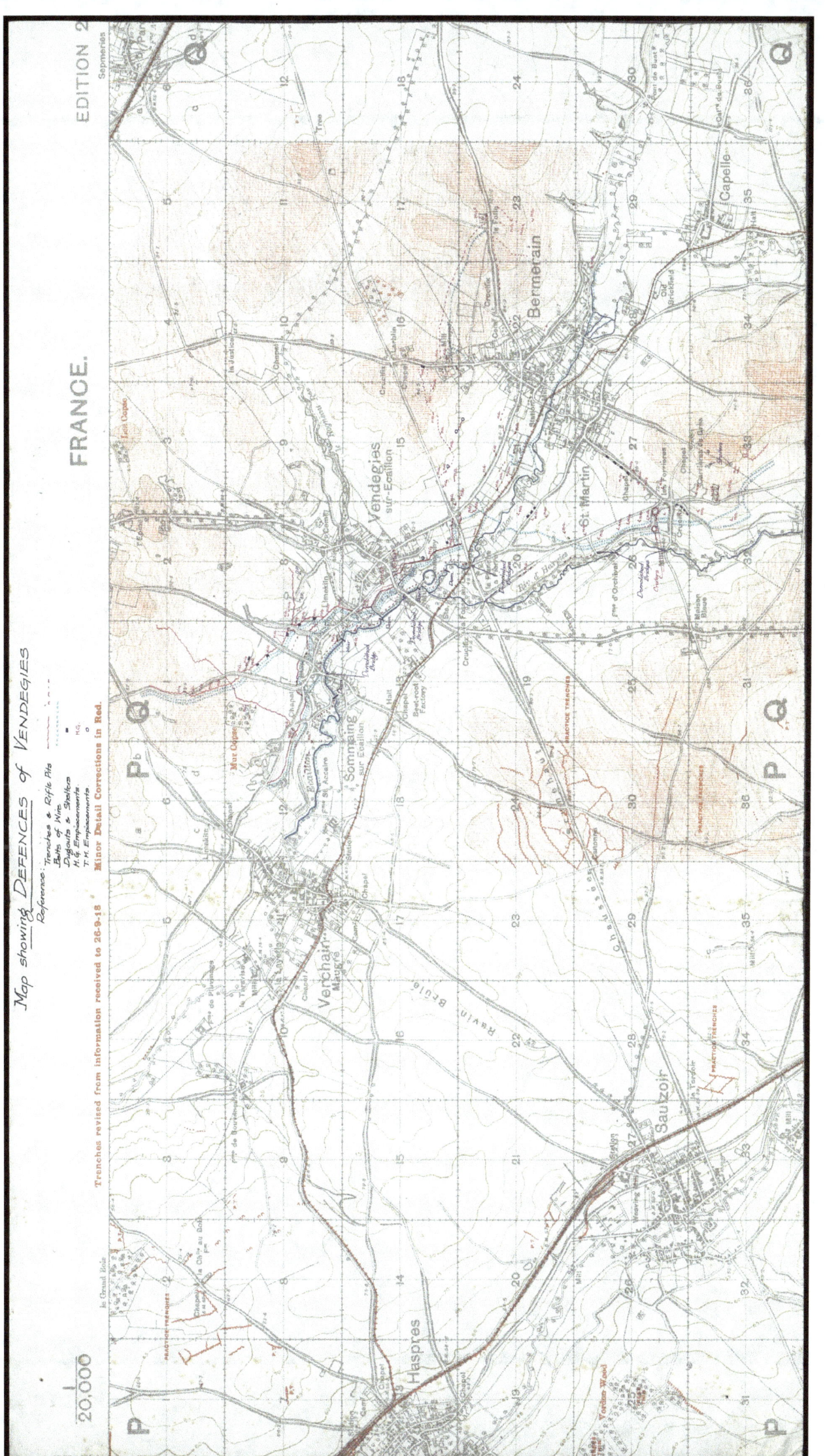

Confidential
ORIGINAL

WP 31

War Diary

of

HQ 61st (SM) Div RE

for the month of

November 1918

Vol XXXI

Army Form C. 2118.

WAR DIARY
of
HEADQUARTERS 61st. DIV. ROYAL ENGINEERS

(Erase heading not required.)

VOL. XXXI page 1.

Instructions regarding War Diaries and Intelligence Summaries are contained in F. S. Regs., Part II. and the Staff Manual respectively. Title pages will be prepared in manuscript.

Place	Date	Hour	Summary of Events and Information	Remarks and references to Appendices
VENDEGIES	NOVEMBER 1918.		FRANCE. 51.a. 1/40000	
	1st.	04.15	Advised all concerned that bridge for first Line Transport at K.29.a.4.6. completed at 02.30 hrs. Zero Hour.	
		05.15	Advised all concerned that bridge at K.29.a.4.6. still O.K. at 07.00 hours.	
		08.00	Received 61 Div Order 231 re relief of Divn by 19th. and 24th. Divns on 2/3rd. inst.	
		12.15	Received 183 Bde. Order 266 re relief of Division.	
		16.30	Issued R.E. Order 132 re relief of Divisional R.E on 2/3rd.	Appx 2
		20.00	Advised all concerned of information obtained from reconnaissances of water supplies. Advised G. and Div art that dry weather track to culvert across stream at L.31.a.5.5. open. Instructed 476 Field Co to put trestle bridge across River RHONELLE at K.29.a.5.3. tonight. Attack in the first instance successful, but counter attack supported by 5 tanks pushed 4th. Division out of PRESEAU and pushed our line back to about MARESCHES. 184 Bde counter-attacked at 19.30 hours and established our line beyond original objective.	Appx 3
	2nd	01.45	Instructed 1/5 D.C.L.I. (Pioneers) to place one platoon at disposal of 479 Field Co to assist in bridging at L.31.c.2.5.	
		01.45	Instructed 479 Field Co to continue bridge at L.31.c.2.5.	
		03.00	Advised G, Div Art, and C.E. that medium bridge for Field art and First Line Transport at K.29.a.65.20 open for traffic at 02.00 hours.	
		04.30	Advised G, of 6 footbridges placed across River as follows:- Two between K.29.d.8.4. and K.30.d.5.6. Two between K.30.d.5.7. and L.25.c.9.2. and two between L.25.c.9.2. and L.26.c.0.1. completed at 03.00 hours.	
		12.15	Advised all concerned that heavy bridge to take all loads except tanks at L.31.c.2.5. completed at 11.00 hours. Captures by the Division since zero 1st. inst. approximately 40 officers, 1400 prisoners, 2 tanks, two field guns and many M.G's. Received instructions for Capt. HOLBROW to report 16th. Div R.E to command 155 Field Co. C.R.E. and Capt. HOLBROW inspected work along the RHONELLE. C.R.E. had interviews with C.R.E's 19th. and 24th. Divns and handed over maps of the RHONELLE giving all information about crossings, roads, etc.	

Army Form C. 2118.

WAR DIARY
INTELLIGENCE SUMMARY
(Erase heading not required.)

HEADQUARTERS
61st. DIV. ROYAL ENGINEERS.

Vol. XXXI Page. 2

Place	Date	Hour	Summary of Events and Information	Remarks and references to Appendices
ST AUBERT.			FRANCE. 51a. 1/40000. NOVEMBER 1918.	
	3rd	10.00	R.E. Headquarters moved to ST AUBERT. Sent Field Companies message received from Divisional Commander congratulating them R.E. on their "wonderful" work	Appx 4
		19.00	Received 61 Div Order 232. Enemy retiring and Division will prepare to move forward C.E. Corps. wired "why wont bridge at L.31.c.2.5. take tanks", and replied that bridge was built in accordance with Class A loads and will carry Class A Loads. Box car returned to M.T. Column by orders of 61st. Div Q.	
	4th		Recd. 184 Brigade Order 247 re forward move of Brigade C.R.E. visited 478 and 479 Field Companies.	
	5th		C.R.E. visited 476 Field Co at HAUSSY.	
	6th		Lce.Cpl. A. SKINNER proceeded on leave.	
	7th	16.30	Recd. 61 Div Order 233 re move forward of Division tomorrow	
		22.50	Recd. 183 Bde Order 267 re move to BERMERAIN area. Lce.Cpl. MOTT rejoined R.E.H.Qrs from leave.	
VENDEGIES	8th		R.E.H.Qrs moved to VENDEGIES. Lieut. MEADOWCROFT, 476 Field Co. died in C.C.S. from influenza.	
	9th		Issued Routine Orders 135 - 137. C.R.E. visited 479 Field Co at SEPMERIES. C.R.E. attended conference at D.H.Q. Lent 479 Field Co one rider, owing to their being so short in animals.	Appx 1
	10th.	14.30	C.R.E. attended church parade service at 476 Field Co. C.R.E. visited 478 Field Company.	

Army Form C. 2118.

WAR DIARY
or
INTELLIGENCE SUMMARY

(Erase heading not required.)

HEADQUARTERS.
61st. DIVN. ROYAL ENGINEERS
vol.XXXI.
Page 3

Place	Date	Hour	Summary of Events and Information	Remarks and references to Appendices
			FRANCE. Sht. 51a. 1/40000. NOVEMBER 1918.	
VENDEGIES.	11th.		C.R.E. and Adjutant visited 479 Field Co. Armistice signed to take effect from 11.00 hours today.	
	12th.	15.30	C.R.E. visited 478 Field Co. C.R.E. attended conference at Corps Headquarters BAVAI to meet C.E. 3rd Army.	Appx 1
	13th.	22.55 23.00	Issued Routine Order 138 - 140. Recd. 61 Div Order 234 re move of Division Recd. 183 Bde. Order 268 :- Brigade to move to St AUBERT area. C:R.E. visited 476 Field Co, 479 Field Co and 1/5 D.C.L.I. (P)	
RIEUX.	14th.	19.00	Recd. 61 Div Order 235. Division to move to CAMBRAI. R.E. Headquarters moved to RIEUX.	
CAMBRAI.	15th.		R.E.Headquarters moved to CAMBRAI.	
	16th.		Issued Routine Orders 141 - 142. C.R.E. visited 476 and 478 Field Co and 1/5 D.C.L.I. (P) C.R.E. and Adjutant attended Thanksgiving Service.	Appx 1
	17th.		Driver DOLLING reported back from leave.	
	18th.		C.R.E. visited Companies.	
	19th.		-	
	20th.	17.00	Conference of Company Commanders. Made arrangements for general inspection on 22nd. and 23rd. inst.	

WAR DIARY

INTELLIGENCE SUMMARY.

HEADQUARTERS 61st. DIV. ROYAL ENGINEERS.

Vol XXXI   Page 4

Army Form C. 2118.

NOVEMBER 1918.

Place	Date	Hour	Summary of Events and Information	Remarks and references to Appendices
CAMBRAI	21st		FRANCE VALENCIENNES. 1/100000. Received order that all training will cease on 22nd and 23rd, and Division will be employed on salvage, but this was cancelled later as far as the R.E. were concerned, and upset arrangements for inspection.	
		19.00	Received 61st. Div Warning Order 236. re move to BERNAVILLE area 23/24th	
	22nd.		Received 183 Bde. Order 270 re move to BERNAVILLE area. Received A.D.M.S. Order No. 79. re medical arrangements.	
		18.45	Received 61 Div Order 237, giving details of move to BERNAVILLE area. Received 183 Bde. Order 271 giving further details of move to BERNAVILLE area. Received A.D.M.S. letter No. 913 re medical arrangements in connection with move.	
	23rd.		R.E.H.Qrs transport moved to staging area en route for BERNAVILLE.	
	24th.		Received Camp Commendants Order re move of D.H.Q tomorrow to BERNAVILLE.	
BERNAVILLE.	25th	11.45.	R.E.H.Q moved to BERNAVILLE by lorry, via ARRAS - DOULLENS.	
		22.00	Transport of R.E.H.Q arrived complete.	
	26th.		Issued Routine Orders 143 - 144 Adjutant went to AUXI le CHATEAU endeavouring to locate R.E. dumps for use in this area.	Appx 1.
	27th.		C.R.E. and Adjutant visited Army Parks at WARLINCOURT, ROSEL and POULAINVILLE endeavouring to obtain material to repair billets which are very bad in the Divisional area. C.R.E. visited 479 Field Co at St HILAIRE.	
	28th.		C.R.E. saw G.O.C. and Q. with reference to billet repairs and explained situation of stores and transport. Instructed 476 Field Co to attach one section to the R.A. to administer R.E. stores.	

Army Form C. 2118.

WAR DIARY
or
INTELLIGENCE SUMMARY
(Erase heading not required.)

HEADQUARTERS.
61st. DIV. ROYAL ENGINEERS
Vol XXXI

NOVEMBER 1918.

Page 5.

Place	Date	Hour	Summary of Events and Information	Remarks and references to Appendices
BERNAVILLE	29th.		LENS 11. 1/100000. Issued Routine Order 148.	Appx 1
	30th.	17.00	C.E. called. Discussed situation as regards stores.	

[signature]
Capt. Adjutant.
For C.R.E. 61st. Divn.

War Diary.
(Original.)
for Novbr 1918.
C.R.E. 61st Divn.

Appendix 1

Routine Orders issued by C.R.E.

War Diary.
(ORIGINAL.)
for NOVBR 1918.
C.R.E. 61st DIVN.

APPENDIX 1

Routine Orders issued by C.R.E.

ROUTINE ORDERS.

Issued by:- Lieut-Col. G. E. P. DURNFORD. D.S.O. R.E.

Commanding:- 61st. (South Midland) Divisional Royal Engineers

R.E. H.Qrs. November 9th. 1918.

---

135. HONOURS and AWARDS.

The following awards for gallantry and devotion to duty have been made.

<u>BAR TO MILITARY MEDAL</u>

498233. Spr (A/Lce-Cpl) S.G. PARSONS. MM.   476 Field Co. R.E.

<u>MILITARY MEDAL.</u>

498312	Corpl. H. BRAGG.	476 Field Co. R.E
160278	Sapper F. STAGG	476 Field Co. R.E
224006	Sapper J. BROWN	476 Field Co. R.E

136. PROTECTION OF CIVILIAN PROPERTY.

A.R.O. 1838 is republished.

"As a consequence of the present operations, many French people have been forced to leave their homes and abandon the whole of their possessions. Many of these homes lie in the area occupied by British Troops, who therefore become trustees to the French people for their abandoned property.

The Army Commander exhorts every officer, warrant officer, non-commissioned officer and man in the Third Army to do all in his power to protect the homes and property of our Allies, who are fighting our common enemy.

This order will be constantly brought to the notice of all troops in the Third Army"

The above will be published in Orders of all units.

137. DAMAGE to TREES.

A.R.O. 1848 is republished.

"As the country in advance of the present area in which horse lines are situated has many valuable orchards, the following order is republished. Great care is to be exercised to prevent any unnecessary damage to trees, and to ensure that this order is complied with:-

When the occupation of orchards etc by mounted troops is necessary, horses will on no account be tied to trees; and care must be taken to tether them, whenever possible, out of reach of any trees.

Cases have occurred where the trunks of trees have been barked all round by horses being tied to them or by the horses themselves eating the bark, with the result that the trees perish.

To protect them from such injury, sacking or some similar material will invariably be wrapped round the trunks."

(Sd) G.H. SIMMONS, Capt.
Adjutant. 61 Div R.E.

ROUTINE ORDERS

Issued by Lieut-Colonel, G.E.J. DURNFORD, D.S.O. R.E.

Commanding:- 61st. (South Midland) Divisional Royal Engineers.

R.E.H.Q. 13th. November 1918.

---

138. **HONOURS AND AWARDS.** The following Awards for gallantry and devotion to duty have been made.

MILITARY MEDAL.

498042.	2nd. Cpl. F. SHEPHERD.	476 Field Co. R.E.
496242.	Lce. Cpl. H. PEDWELL.	479 Field Co. R.E.

MERITORIOUS SERVICE MEDAL.

387930.	Sapper. W. RICHARDSON	479 Field Co. R.E.
354486.	Sapper. R. HOLYWELL.	479 Field Co. R.E.

139. **STRENGTH.** Lieut. A/Captain H. HOLBROW having proceeded to join 16th. Div. R.E. (155 Field Co) is struck off the strength of 476 Field Co with effect from 5th. November 1918.
(Auth:- G.H.Q No. AG/55/5571 (O) dated 28.10.1918.

2nd. Lieut. E.J. NAYLOR having reported for duty 7th. inst. is taken on strength of 476 Field Co. R.E.

2nd. Lieut. MEADOWCROFT having arrived Div. Reception Camp is taken on strength of 476 Field Co. R.E.

2nd. Lieut. W. MACKINTOSH having reported for duty 11th. inst. is taken on strength of 479 Field Co. R.E.

140. **REPRESENTATION OF THE PEOPLE ACT.** Attention is directed to G.R.O. 5528. Officers desiring to vote at coming election should communicate at once at once with the Registration Officers of the constituencies in which they believe themselves qualified to vote.

(Sd) G.H. SIMMONS.

Capt. Adjutant.
61 Div R.E.

ROUTINE ORDERS.

Issued by:- Lieut-Colonel G.E.J. DURNFORD, D.S.O. R.E.

Commanding:- 61st. (South Midland) Divisional Royal Engineers.

R.E.H.Q.   16th. Nov. 1918

---

141. POSTING.

Lieut. J.D. RAWLINS is ~~posted~~ *attached* to 479 Field Co and will assume temporary duties as Second in Command.

142. LEAVE.

The undermentioned officers have been granted leave of absence on dates shown.

2nd. Lieut. D. ROBINSON.	4th. to 18th. Nov. 1918.
Lieut. W.H. HAMES.	17th. Nov. to 1 Dec. 1918.

(Sd)   G.H. SIMMONS.

Capt.

Adjutant, 61 Div R.E.

ROUTINE ORDERS.2

Issued by Lieut-Colonel. G.R.J. DUNSFORD,D.S.O. (R.E)

Comprising:- 61st. (South Midland) Divisional Royal Engineers.

R.E.H.Q.   26th. November 1918.

---

143. HONOURS AND AWARDS.   The following Awards for gallantry and devotion to duty have been made:-

BAR TO MILITARY CROSS.

T/Lieut. R.E. ROSE, M.C.   476 Field Co. R.E.
2nd.Lieut. H.W. KING, M.C.   476 Field Co. R.E.

DISTINGUISHED CONDUCT MEDAL.

158948 Spr. (A/Lce.Cpl) G.FOX.   476 Field Co. R.E.

MILITARY MEDAL.

494710. Lce.Cpl. W.H.HOLLIWEY.   479 Field Co. R.E.

---

144. LEAVE. The undermentioned Officer has been granted leave on absence on dates shown.

Major. B. LONG, M.C.   28th. Nov. to 12th. Dec. 1918.

(Sd) G.H. 31 MONS.
Capt. Adj.

ROUTINE ORDERS.

Issued by:- Lieut-Colonel G.E.J. DURNFORD, D.S.O., R.E.

Commanding:- 61st. (South Midland) Divisional Royal Engineers.

R.E.H.Qrs. 29th. Nov. 1918.

---

145. ABSENCE WITHOUT LEAVE. The crime of "absence without leave", i.e. overstaying leave to the U.K. has become prevalent.
In future, such cases will not be disposed of summarily by O's.C. Companies but will be sent mx for Court Martial. This order will be read out on three consecutive parades and will be repeated periodically in Company Orders.

(sd) G.E.SI MOSS.
Capt.
Adjutant. 61 Div R.E.

War Diary.
(ORIGINAL.)
for NOVBR 1918.
C.R.E. 61st DIVN.

APPENDIX 2

MOVE, RELIEF
&
OPERATION ORDERS
BY
C.R.E

SECRET.   Copy No. 9.

Ref. Map Sh.
1/40000   R.E. ORDER NO. 132.

1. The Division (less Art. R.E and Nos. 1 and 2
Section D.A.C. and No.1 Coy (Train) is being relieved on
the 2nd. and 3rd. inst. by 19th. and 24th. Divisions, and
is marching to the AVESNES - ST AUBERT area. 476 Field Co
will march in accordance with march table attached, remaining
Field Coys with their Brigade groups.

2. The 24th. Division will be the right Division
and the 19th. Division will be the left Division.

3. In order to avoid congestion, dismounted troops
will march across country or on the side of the road whenever
possible.
        The usual distances will be maintained.
        Accommodation for troops and transport must be arranged
before either enters villages, so that there is no delay in
clearing roads.
        If necessary, troops must halt, and transport park
off the road clear of the villages until arrangements can be
made to receive them.
        Transport will not halt in any village.

4. Command of the Divisional Front passes at 10.40
hours on the 3rd. inst. to G.O's C. 19th. and 24th. Divisions.

5. Completion of above will be reported to R.E.H.qrs
as soon as possible.

6. R.E.H.qrs will close at VENDHUILE at 10.40 hours
on the 3rd. inst. and open at ST AUBERT at that hour.

7. Field Companies to acknowledge.

                                    J H Simmons
Issued at 61 R.E.H.Q.
    16.20 Hours   Capt. Adjutant, R.E.
November 1st. 1918.   for C.R.E. 61st. Division.

Distribution.

Copy No. 1.   475 Field Co.
        2.   476 Field Co.
        3.   479 Field Co.
        4.   61 Div G.
        5.   61 Div Q.
        6.   C.E. XVII Corps.
        7.   C.R.E. 19th. Div.
        8.   C.R.E. 24th. Div.
        9.   War Diary.
        10.   War Diary.
        11.   File.

Copy No......

MARCH TABLE ISSUED WITH W.W.O. ORDER 150.

Serial No.	Date	Unit	From	To	Camp	Remarks
1.	2.11.15.	476 Field Co.	RUMIGNY	AVESNES LE SEC	CHATEAU BEHAGNIES	Trains in camp at CROIX not until 12-10 hours.
2.	2.11.15.	475 Field Co.	ELINCOURT	TWENTY LES USAGES	CHATEAU SOMERANS ECOURT	March via BAPAUME not the day.
3.	3.11.15.	R.E.H.Q.	TRESCAUT	ST QUENTIN	CHATEAU EVENTAIL ARBONCOURT	Arrive at F.M.O.
4.	3.11.15.	476 Field Co.	LEDEGEM	ST AUBERT	CHATEAU DU BOIS MORBRONNE	March via PROVEN to the camp.

J.M........
Capt. Adjutant, R.E.
for O.C., 61st. Division.

1.11.1915.

War Diary (Original)
for November 1918
C.R.E. 61st Divⁿ

Appendix 3

Work Orders & Instructions by CRE

Reconnaissance Reports

182 Inf. Bde.
183 Inf. Bde.
184 Inf. Bde.
61 Div G.
61 Div Q.
A.D.M.S. 61st. Div.

(Ref. Map. 1/20000)

SUMMARY OF INFORMATION OBTAINED FROM RECONNAISSANCE REPORTS ON WATER SUPPLIES.

ARTRES. Pumps etc in working order at:-

FABRIK STRASSE	well and windlass.
do	4 wells & pumps require repair.
do No. 35.	1 hand pump.
REGENT WASSER	2 pumps) several others broken
	) but can easily be
do No. 88.	1 pump.) repaired.
Rue de l'HOTEL DIEU.	1 pump
do	good watering for horses at river.
BRIDGE STRASSE	1 pump.

MARCOING and SEPMERIES. There are pumps at Q.6.b.1.6 -
b.7.7. (six) c.3.6. b.30.95. K.36.c.6.2. (three) c.6.1. (horse
troughs) c.7.3. (two). K.36.d.10.15 (two) d.1.4.,
d.4.3. (three) and d.5.8.

MARESCHES. Several pumps in L.25.c. not actually located
yet.

20.30 hours.
November 1st. 1918.

Capt. Adjutant, R.E.
For C.R.E. 61st. Division.

476 Field Co.
478 Field Co.
479 Field Co.

The following message received from the Divisional Commander is to be made known to all ranks:-

"The R.E. of the Division already know my feelings of admiration for them, which I have often expressed. By their wonderful work since the Division has been in the line they have once more given proof of their high moral and great efficiency. Please convey to all ranks my heartiest congratulations.

General DUNCAN."

The C.R.E., in congratulating the Field Companies on their splendid work, which has earned this further mark of their Divisional Commander's approbation, particularly wishes to thank the drivers for the gallant manner in which they have worked the transport forward, thereby supplying the materials, without which the operations could not have been made a success.

Simmons
Captain,
Adjutant R.E., 61st. Division.

3rd. Nov.1918.

CONFIDENTIAL

WAR DIARY OF

C.R.E. 61st DIVISION.

From Dec. 1st to Dec. 31st 1918.

Vol. XXXII

WAR DIARY or INTELLIGENCE SUMMARY

HEADQUARTERS. 61st. Div. ROYAL ENGINEERS.

Army Form C. 2118.
Vol. XXXII.
Page. 1

DECEMBER. 1918. Sht. LENS. 11. 1/100000.

Place	Date	Hour	Summary of Events and Information	Remarks and references to Appendices
BERNAVILLE	1st.		C.R.E. visited 184 Brigade and 479 Field Company.	
	2nd to 5th.		Usual routine.	
	6th.		C.R.E. and Adjutant went to DOMLEGER, CONTEVILLE and ST RIQUIER re site for C.R.E. Dump, and finally selected site at "T" Road sidings at DOMLEGER.	
		10.25	Corpl. PENNY (Stores Corporal) attached R.E.H.Qrs admitted to hospital. Received 61 Div Order 238; readjustment of Divisional Area Received 183 Bde. Order 272 readjustment of Brigade area	
	7th.		Received Camp Commandants Order re move to ST. RIQUIER tomorrow.	
ST RIQUIER	8th.		R.E.H.Qrs moved to St. RIQUIER.	
	9th.		C.R.E. and Adjutant went to ABBEVILLE and visited C.R.E. ABBEVILLE'S DUMP re issue of stores. Visited 476 Field Co at DOMLEGER and handed over to 2nd. Lieut. DICKINSON, 476 Field Co duties of work as Stores Officer at the Dump. C.R.E. attended conference at Army Headquarters FLEXICOURT and discussed question of stores and transport. Issued Routine Orders 146 - 151.	Apppx 1
	10th.		Visited Canadian Forestry Co at MEZEROLLES with Stores Officer.	
	11th.		Daily Routine.	

Army Form C. 2118.

WAR DIARY
or
INTELLIGENCE SUMMARY

(Erase heading not required.)

HEADQUARTERS.
61st. DIV. ROYAL ENGINEERS.
VOL. XXXII.   Page 2

DECEMBER 1918.   XABBEVILLE. Sht. 14. 1/100000.

Place	Date	Hour	Summary of Events and Information	Remarks and references to Appendices
ST RIQUIER.	12th.		Advised by Corps that a pack train is being sent to DOMLEGER from BASE. Rode over and arranged with Stores Officer for off-loading parties.	
	13th.		C.R.E. and Adjutant went locating brickyards in the area at FORTEL, FREVENT and DOULLENS.	
	14th.		Informed by Corps that Corps Ambulance Car was being placed at disposal of C.R.E.	
	15th.		A/Chief Engineer Corps and S.O.R.E. called and discussed situation as regards stores and transport. C.R.E. and Adjutant inspected NEUF MOULIN and CAOURS as likely villages for concentration of Field Companies. Located Brickyard at L'HEURE.	
	16th.		Pack train arrived and off-loaded at DOMLEGER. Capt. ROBINSON, 478 Field Co joined R.E.H.Q to take over duties as Acting Adjutant, during absence of Adjutant on leave. C.R.E. visited all units of 182 Brigade.	
	17th.		Met Ordnance Officer at DOMLEGER sidings by appointment reference moving site of C.R.E dump as present site is required for an ordnance depot. C.R.E. visited units in the Divisional Artillery area with Staff Capt. R.A.	
	18th.		C.R.E. visited units in the 183 Brigade area.	

Army Form C. 2118.

Page 3.

WAR DIARY
INTELLIGENCE SUMMARY

HEADQUARTERS 61st.DIV. ROYAL ENGINEERS.

DECEMBER 1918. VOL. XXII.

Place	Date	Hour	Summary of Events and Information	Remarks and references to Appendices
ST.RIQUIER	19.		ABBEVILLE. Sht. 14. 1/100,000. C.R.E. visited Battalions, 184 Bde. with O.C. 479 Field Coy., also M.G. Bn. and D.C.L.I. Capt. SIMMONS, Adjutant, goes on leave. Capt. ROBINSON, 478 Field Coy. takes over. No. 2 Pack Train in and unloaded.	m
	20.		C.R.E. and Adjutant visited 476 Field Coy. and Dump; Army H.Q. and saw C.R.E. ABBEVILLE.	m
	21.		Looked round CAOURS with a view to concentrating Field Companies there.	m
	22.		Visited DOMLEGER Dump and 2/8th. Worcesters.	m
	23.		Visited PROUVILLE, BERNAVILLE, 5th. Army Park, & Forestry Coy. at MEZEROLLES and C.R.A.	m
	24.		Visited Forestry Coy. LABROYE, where XVII Corps have allotted timber. 10 G.H.Q. lorries arrived warning at DOMLEGER DUMP at 3 p.m. and had to be sent back as there was no Nloading party available.	m
	25.		Visited all Field Companies and D.C.L.I.	m
	26.		Visited HESDIN and saw Cinema Hut erected.	m
	27.		Visited 478 Field Coy., 184 Brigade, 479 Field Coy, D.C.L.I., DOMLEGER DUMP and 476 Field Co. Train from WARLINCOURT arrived but without slabs for roadway.	m
	28.		Settled sites for cinema hut with D.C.L.I. Routine Order 152 issued.	m
	29.		Usual Routine.	m
	30.		10 Trucks sausage hutting arrived DOMLEGER.	aff.1.
	31.		Routine office work.	m

W.G. Robinson
Capt.-A/Adjt.
for C.R.E. 61 Div.

WAR DIARY.
(ORIGINAL.)
for DECEMBER 1918.
C.R.E. 61st DIVn.

APPENDIX 1

ROUTINE

ORDERS

BY

CRE

ROUTINE ORDERS.

Issued by:- Lieut-Colonel G.E.J. DURNFORD, D.S.O., R.E.

Commanding:- 61st. (South Midland) Divisional Royal Engineers.

R.E.H.Q. December 9th.1918.

---

146. BOX RESPIRATORS.   Box Respirators will be withdrawn and stored in Q.M. Stores.

147. AMMUNITION - LEWIS GUN.   Ammunition held for Lewis guns should be expended as opportunity offers and not replaced.

148. WORK.   As far as possible only work of an urgent nature should be undertaken on Sundays in future. This applies equally to transport. O's. C. Field Companies will, however, ascertain the wishes of Brigade Commanders.

149. CASUALTIES - REPORTING OF.
       Attention is directed to the instructions laid down in G.R.O. 3867, para 7 with regard to the reporting of all casualties other than battle casualties, in the daily casualty wire due this office 3 p.m. daily. *see also GRO 5757.*

150. STRENGTH.
       Lieut. E. MALLINSON having reported for duty is taken on the strength of 476 Field Co R.E. with effect from 8th. inst.

151. RETURNS.   The following returns are cancelled:-

       Return No.16.
       Return No.20.

Return No. 15. should be amended to read:- "Two copies to be sent to C.R.E. office by 9 a.m. last day."

(Sd) G.H. SIMMONS.
Capt.
Adjutant 61 Div R.E

ROUTINE ORDERS

Issued by:- Lieut-Colonel C.E.J. BURNFORD, D.S.O., R.E.

Commanding:- 61st. (South Midland) Divisional Royal Engineers.

M. E. & Q. December 29th, 1918.

152. EQUIPMENT. Ammunition and Steel Helmets will be withdrawn from the troops and returned to Company Quarter-Master's store.

(sd) H.G. ROBINSON.
Capt. A/Adjutant.
61 Div R.E.

CONFIDENTIAL

WAR DIARY OF

C.R.E. 61st. DIVN.

JANUARY, 1919

VOL. XXXIII

Army Form C. 2118.

WAR DIARY
or
INTELLIGENCE SUMMARY.
(Erase heading not required.)

HEADQUARTERS, 61ST DIV ROYAL ENGINEERS

VOL XXXIII

PAGE 1.

Instructions regarding War Diaries and Intelligence Summaries are contained in F. S. Regs., Part II. and the Staff Manual respectively. Title pages will be prepared in manuscript.

Place	Date	Hour	Summary of Events and Information	Remarks and references to Appendices
ST RIQUIER	4th.		ABBEVILLE Sht 16. 1/100,000	
"	4th		Adjutant rejoined from leave	JWS.
"	5th		Interpreter GOEUX rejoined from leave	JWS.
"	8th		Major H. HUMPHREYS joined R.E. H.Q. to take over duties of CRE	JWS.
"	9th		CRE granted leave to U.K. from 10-1-19 to 24-1-19.	JWS
"	22nd	10am	at CRE attended Conference of CREs at XVII Corps H.Q.	
"	24th		Major H. STRATTON DAVIS, 476 Field Company, appointed R.E. member	JWS
			to sit on Military Advisory Committee.	
			Routine Order No 1 issued. (New Year Honours)	JWS Att. 1.
"	25th		CRE returned from leave.	
"	26th		Major M. HUMPHREYS rejoined 476 Field Coy.	
"	28th		T/RSM DEVERMOND Proceeded to Corps Concentration Camp, CANDAS for	JWS
			dispersal.	
"	30th		Interpreter GOEUX demobilized	JWS
"	31st		Total no. of 61 Div. R.E. demobilized during the month:-	
			4 Officers	
			3 Warrant Officers	
			101 NCOs & men	

[signature]
Lieut [signature]
Capt - Adjutant
L CRE 61st Div.

ROUTINE ORDERS

Issued by:- Major H. HUMPHREYS,

Commanding:- 61st. (South Midland) Divisional Royal Engineers.

R.E.H.Q. January 24th. 1919.

---

1. NEW YEAR HONOURS.

The following extracts from the LONDON GAZETTE are published for information:-

TO BE BREVET LIEUTENANT COLONEL.

Major (A/Lt.Col.) G.E.J. DURNFORD, D.S.O.   C.R.E.

O.B.E.

Lieut. (A/Capt.) H.E.W. FITZGERALD.   Late Adjutant.

MENTIONED.

Major H. HUMPHREYS   478 Field Company.

Capt. H. HOLBROW   late 476 Field Company.

DISTINGUISHED CONDUCT MEDAL.

494363, Sgt. DAVY, E.E.   479 Field Company.

MERITORIOUS SERVICE MEDAL.

500181, Sgt. FEATHERSTONE, D.A.   R.E. H.Q.
498277, Sgt. PITT, B.   478 Field Coy.

MENTIONED.

496819, Farr. Sgt. TAYLOR, C.I.   478 Field Coy.

                              (Signed)   C. H. SIMMONS,
                                           Capt. -Adjutant,
                                           61st. Divisional R.E.

CONFIDENTIAL

WAR DIARY OF

C.R.E. 61st. DIVISION

FEBRUARY 1919.

WAR DIARY
or
INTELLIGENCE SUMMARY

(Erase heading not required.)

HEADQUARTERS
61st Div. ROYAL ENGINEERS.
Vol. XXXIV

Army Form C. 2118.

February 1912

Page 1.

Place	Date	Hour	Summary of Events and Information	Remarks and references to Appendices
Ref. MAP. ABBEVILLE- Sheet 14, 1/100,000.				
ST. RIQUIER.	3rd	15.30	C.R?E. held conference of Company Commanders at 479 Field Co. H. Qrs St. HILAIRE.	
"	4th		Issued Routine Order NO.2.	AP 1(I)
"	12th		Received 61st Division Order No 239 Ref. concentrating remaining units of Division in the present 183 Brigade Area.	APP
"	"		Issued R.E. Order No 132 Ref. move of 476 and 479 Field Coys to AILLY-le-Haut-CLOCHER (163 Brigade Area.)	APPX / (2)
"	13th		Received A.D.M.S. order No 935/913 Ref. Medical arrangements in connection with 61 st. Division Order NO. 239.	
"	"	14.30	Royal Engineer Corps Band visited 61st Division and gave Concerts in the Theatre at AUXI-LE-CHATEAU at 14.30 hrs and 18.30 hrs.	

Army Form C. 2118.

WAR DIARY

HEADQUARTERS 61st Div. ROYAL ENGINEERS
VOL. XXXIV

Page 2.

February 1919.

Place: ABBEVILLE – S¹. RIQUIER.
Ref. Map: Sheet 14, 1/100.000.

Date	Hour	Summary of Events and Information	Remarks and references to Appendices
13th		61st Divisional R.E. came under the administration of L.ofC. ABBEVILLE Area instead of XVII Corps.	
17th		Issued Routine Orders Nos. 3 and 4.	App 1 (3)
23rd		No 500121 Sergt. FEATHERSTONE. W. A. proceeded to Concentration Camp ABBEVILLE for Demobilisation.	
"		No 234830 Sapper BRAND. S. 478 Field Co. attached to R.E.H.Qrs. vice Sergt. FEATHERSTONE pending transfer.	
28th		Issued Routine Order No. 5.	" 1 (4)
"		R.E. Personnel detached for Demobilisation during February	

	Off.	O.R.
previous to Feby.	4	125
" " "	4	164
Total to date —	8	289.

Geo.K.Simmons Capt.
Adj¹ for C R E 61 Div.

War Diary.
(ORIGINAL.)
for FEBY 1918.
C.R.E. 61st DIVN.

APPENDIX 1

Routine Orders by CRE

ROUTINE ORDERS

Issued by:- Lieut. Colonel G.E.J. DURNFORD, D.S.O.

Commanding:- 61st (South Midland) Divisional Royal Engineers.

R.E.H.Q. Feb. 4th.1919.

---

2. LEAVE.

Officers and soldiers proceeding on leave to the United Kingdom and Ireland, or via United Kingdom to places abroad must not be permitted to travel except by authorised leave trains.

The only exceptions allowed are those stated in G.R.O. 1645 and 3532 (Extracts Part 2).

(Signed)
Geo. H. SIMMONS,
Capt.-Adjutant,
61st Divl. R.E.

SECRET.   Copy No. 10

R.E. ORDER NO. 152.

Ref. Maps. Lens 11.
     ABBEVILLE. 14.

1. The Division (less Artillery) is being transferred to the L. of C. area on the 13th.

2. All units remaining in present Divisional area are closing up into the present 183 Inf. Bde area.

3. The following moves will take place on the 13th:-

   (a) 476 Field Co (less one section attached to Divisional Artillery. Lieut. COOB in charge) from DOMLEGER to AILLY le HAUT CLOCHER.

   (b) 479 Field Co from DOMART to AILLY le HAUT CLOCHER.

4. Advance parties from 476 and 479 Field Companies will report to O.C. 478 Field Co at FAMECHON on 12th. inst.

5. 476 and 479 Field Coys will leave guards with three days rations on their area stores. R.E. stores to be kept apart from Ordnance stores. These guards should have written instructions that all R.E. stores are to be sent to C.R.E's dump DOMLEGER and Ordnance stores to Corps Intermediate Collecting Station at the R.A.F. Hangars situated near the C in CANDAS. Sufficient lorries will probably be available on the 14th. and 15th. to clear these dumps.

6. 476 Field Co guard will also be in charge of the R.E dump at DOMLEGER until such time as it is taken over by the Corps,— possibly on the 15th.

7. In the event of animals being insufficient to move the whole transport on the 13th., teams must be sent back to complete the move on the 14th.

8. The section of 476 Field Co will remain with Divnl. Artillery and rejoin their unit on the 20th. inst.

9. Locations to be reported to this office on completion of the move on 13th.

R.E. Headquarters, 61. Div.
Issued at 14.00 hours
February 12th. 1919.

                                                 Capt. Adjutant.
                                              for C.R.E. 61st. Division.

Distribution.

    Copy No. 1.   476 Field Co.
            2.   478 Field Co.
            3.   479 Field Co.
            4.   61 Div G.
            5.   61 Div Q.
            6.   61 Div Train.
            7.   61 Div Art.
            8.   C.E. 17th. Corps.
         9 & 10 HQ R.E.

ROUTINE ORDERS

Issued by:- Lieut-Colonel G.E.J. BURNFORD, D.S.O. R.E

Commanding:- 61st. (South Midland) Divisional Royal Engineers.

R.E.H.Qrs. February 17th. 1919

3. **DEMOBILIZATION. CARE & PRESERVATION OF EQUIPMENT.** Attention is directed to Third Army Routine Order No. 1957.

4. **DISCIPLINE.** G.R.O. 6212 is republished herewith.

6212. DISCIPLINE. Any officer or men who, when due for demobilization, is guilty of any form of insubordination will, apart from any other punishment, be put back to the bottom of the list of those waiting for dispersal, and if he has left his unit he will be returned to his unit after his case has been disposed of.

For further detailed instructions see Chapter XVI, Army Demobilization Instructions, France dated January 1919.

No one will be detained under this order without the written approval of an officer not below the status of a Brigade Commander.

This order is to be republished in the order of all formations and units, and placed on the notice boards at all Concentration and Embarkation Camps.

(sd) G.H.SIMMONS.
Capt. Adjutant.
61st. Divnl. R.E.

ROUTINE ORDERS

Issued by:- Lieut:- Colonel G.E.J. DURMFORD. D.S.O. R.E.

Commanding:- 61st Divisional Royal Engineers (South Midland).

R.E.H.Qrs.   February 28th. 1919.

---

5. Entertainment Committee

A committee consisting of Maj:- LONG M.C. President, and one officer from 475 and 478 Field Coys as members will be formed to undertake and regulate the provisions of entertainments in the theatre at AILLY- le - haut- CLOCHER.

This committee will also be responsible for keeping the accounts of the theatre and will submit them to the C.R.E. for audit at the end of each month.

A balance sheet will then be sent to each unit for posting.

(Sd) G.H. SIMMONS
Capt:- Adjutant.
For C.R.E. 61st, Division.

CONFIDENTIAL

WAR DIARY OF

C.R.E. 61st DIVISION

MARCH 1919.

VOL XXXV

ORIGINAL

Army Form C. 2118.

WAR DIARY
or
INTELLIGENCE SUMMARY
(Erase heading not required.)

HEADQUARTERS
61st. DIVISION. ROYAL ENGINEERS.
Vol. XXXV
Page 1.

Instructions regarding War Diaries and Intelligence Summaries are contained in F. S. Regs., Part II. and the Staff Manual respectively. Title pages will be prepared in manuscript.

MARCH 1919   ABBEVILLE SHT. 14 1/100,000

Place	Date	Hour	Summary of Events and Information	Remarks and references to Appendices
ST. RIQUIER.	3rd		Issued Routine Order No.6. Reference Sapper BRAND attached to R.E. H.Qrs.	APP.1(1)
	4th	11.45	Conference of Coy Commanders at AILLY-LE-HAUT-CLOCHER.	
	14th		Issued Routine Orders Nos. 7. 8. 9. 10.	APP.1(2)
	15th		Received L of C. List of Officers posted to 476 Field Co for duty with the clearing up Army.	
			do do 478 Field Co do	
			do do 479 Field Co do	
	20th		Received from 61st Division D.A.C. Wire C.W. 794 "Field Coys in your Division to be reduced to Cadre "A"	
	21st		Received copy of L. of C Routine Order Reference vacated Hutments when Division moves to LE TREPORT.	

Army Form C. 2118.

WAR DIARY
or
INTELLIGENCE SUMMARY.
(Erase heading not required.)

HEADQUARTERS 61st DIVISION ROYAL ENGINEERS.
Page 2.
Vol. XXV

MARCH 1919

Instructions regarding War Diaries and Intelligence Summaries are contained in F.S. Regs., Part II. and the Staff Manual respectively. Title pages will be prepared in manuscript.

Summary of Events and Information

Place	Date	Hour	Summary of Events and Information	Remarks and references to Appendices
ST. RIQUIER.	21st		ABBEVILLE SHT. 14 1/100%000.	
	21st		Received 61st Division Order No. 240 Reference move of Division to LE TREPORT.	
	"		Received from 61st Division Q. Notification "There is accommodation at No 5 Veterinary hospital ABBEVILLE for the Field Coys.	
	22nd		C.R.E. and Adjutant went to ABBEVILLE. Saw Area Commandant reference above and learned same had been cancelled by A.A.Q.M.G.	
	"		Issued R.E.Order No. 133 reference move of Division. Divisional R.Es will come under orders of G.O.C. 183 Infantry Brigade from that date.	App 2(1)
	"		Received A.D.M.S. letter No 913 reference medical arrangements after move of Division.	
	24th	10.00	61st Division H.Qrs moved to LE TREPORT.	
	25th	10.00	Issued R.E.Order No. 134 reference move of R.E.H.Qrs from ST. RIQUIER to AILLY-LE-HAUT-CLOCHER.	App 2(2)
	26th	02.00	183 Infantry Brigade moved from AILLY-LE-HAUT-CLOCHER to ST RIQUIER.	

Army Form C. 2118.

WAR DIARY
or
INTELLIGENCE SUMMARY

(Erase heading not required.)

HEADQUARTERS 61st DIVISIONAL ROYAL ENGINEERS

VOL LXXV

MARCH 1919.

Page 3.

Place	Date	Hour	Summary of Events and Information	Remarks and references to Appendices
ST RIQUIER. ALLY-LE-HAUT-CLOCHER			ABBEVILLE Sheet 14 1/100,000.	
	27th	02.00	R.E. H.Qrs. moved from ST. RIQUIER to AILLY-LE-HAUT-CLOCHER by lorry. Transport by road.	
	27th.		Received Copy of C. no. Q.L. 514/W/191. Reference handing in animals.	APP 2/9.
	29th.		Issued R.E. Order No. 135 Reference Reducing Coys to Cadre	APP 1/3)
	"		Issued Routine Orders Nos. 11, 12,13,14,15,16 and 17.	
ABBEVILLE.	30th.		Being informed by 183 Infantry Brigade there was no likelyhood likelihood of being moved to ABBEVILLE. Informed then Divisional R.E. would reduce to Cadre at AILLY-LE-HAUT-CLOCHER. Forwarded to No.2 Remount Depot list of animals available for handing in at once.	
	31st.		R.E. Personnel detached for Demobilization during MARCH	

```
                                    Officers    N.C.O. R.
                Previous to MARCH.       8        3   286
                Total to Date......      8        3   291
```

Capt. Adjutant
For C.R.E. 61st Division

WAR DIARY.
(ORIGINAL.)
for MARCH 1919
C.R.E. 61st DIVN.

APPENDIX (2)

ORDERS

RECEIVED &

ISSUED

Copy No ... 5 ...

R.E. Order No. 133.

Ref. Map. ABBEVILLE
1/100,000.

1. 61st. Divisional Headquarters is moving from ST. RIQUIER to LE TREPORT on 24th and 25th of March.

2. The following Units are included in Div. H.Q. for this move.

    61st. Div. Signal Co.   )
    H.Q. 61st. Div. Train.   )   To move 24th inst.
    61st. M.T. Coy.   )

    2/1 Field Ambulance.   )
    2/3   do.   )   To move 25th inst.

3. The following Units will, on the move of Div H.Q., come under orders of G.O.C. 183 Inf. Bde. :-

    Divisional R.E.
    2/3 Field Amb.
    No. 2. Coy. Train
    No. 3.   do.
    61 Mob. Vet. Sect.

R.E. Headquarters, 61 Div.
  issued at 14.00 hours.
  March. 22nd. 1919.

                            Capt. Adjutant.
                        For C.R.E. 61st. Division.

Distribution

Copy No. 1. 476 Field Co.
       2. 478 Field Co.
       3. 479 Field Co.
       4. War Diary.
       5. War Diary.
       6. File.

R.O. Order No. 184.

Ref. Map. ABBEVILLE
1/100,000.

1. D. H. Q. Rs. will move from ST. RIQUIER to
    AILLY-LE-HAUT-CLOCHER on THURSDAY the 27th.inst.

2. D. H. Q.Rs. will close at ST. RIQUIER at 14.00 hrs.
    and re-open at AILLY-LE-HAUT-CLOCHER at 16.00 hrs.

D.H. Headquarters, 61st. Div.
Issued at 14.00 hrs.
March 25th.1919.

Capt. Adjutant.
for G.S.O. 61st. Division.

Distribution.

Copy No. 1.- Division "G"   Copy No. 9.- Area Commdt. AILLY.
         2.- Division "Q"   10.- O. H. S. ABBEVILLE.
         3.- 183 Bde.   11.- War Diary.
         4.- 475 Field Coy.   12.- War Diary.
         5.- 478 Field Coy.   13.- File.
         6.- 479 Field Coy.
         7.- No. 3 Coy. Train.
         8.- 7/8 Field Amb.

R.E. ORDER NO 135   Copy No— 5

2 (9)

REDUCTION TO CADRE

1.   The 61st Divisional R.E. will not move from Ailly at present.
   Reduction to Cadre "A" will consequently commence.
   Steps are being taken to withdraw X and Y animals forthwith.
   Z animals, with the exception of animals essential for the use of Cadres, will be withdrawn as soon as arrangements can be made to do so.

2.   The following action will be taken at once:-
   Returns to be furnished to this office showing
   (a) X.Y.Z. animals considered essential for retention for use of cadres.
   (b) X.Y.Z. animals available to be withdrawn (exclusive of X.Y. animals already returned as available for withdrawal).
   (c) Return of personnel selected for Cadres (Officers, S.Sergeants, Sergeants and Artificers to be named).
   (d) The checking and inspection of mobilization equipment as laid down in "Demobilisation Instructions FRANCE" Chapter XIX Part.1. paras 45 to 51. will be commenced at once.
   (e) The completion of the verification and conditioning of Equipment as laid down in paras 45 will be reported to this office.
   (f) Reference para 45 (iii) all bicycles except 2 per Coy Cadre will be handed in to Ordnance.

R.E. H.Quarters, 61st. Div.
29/3/1919.
Issued at 14.00 hrs.

Capt. Adjutant.
For C.R.E. 61st. Division.

Distribution.

Copy.1. 183 Inf. Bde. H.Q.
2. 476 Field Coy.
3. 478 Field Coy.
4. 479 Field Coy.

Copy.5. War Diary.
6. War Diary.
7. File.

War Diary.
(ORIGINAL.)
for MARCH 1918.
C.R.E. 61st DIVN.

APPENDIX (1)

ROUTINE

ORDERS

BY

C.R.E.

ROUTINE ORDERS

Issued by:- Lieut:- Colonel C.E.J. DURNFORD D.S.O. R.E.

Commanding:- 61st (South Midland) Divisional Royal Engineers.

R.E.H.Qrs. March 3rd 1919.

No. 6.

No.234830 Sapper BRAND S. 478 Field Co.

Attached to R.E.H.Qrs. pending transfer, to be L/Cpl unpaid as from 24. 2. 19.

Capt:- Adjutant.

for C.R.E. 61st Division.

ROUTINE ORDERS.

Issued by Lieut-Colonel G.E.J. DURNFORD. D.S.O. R.E.
Commanding 61st.(South Midland) Divisional Royal Engineers.

R.E.H.Qrs. March 14th.1919.

7. ESTABLISHMENT AT WHICH UNITS ARE TO BE MAINTAINED.

Attention is directed to G.R.O. 6341 para.(c).

8. INTERNAL TRANSFER.

Approval has been received for the following internal transfer:-

No. 234830 Spr. BRAND. S. from 476 Field Coy.R.E. to R.E.H.Qrs. dated 24/2/19.
(Authy. D.A.G. 3rd Echelon. G.R.4251/591 C. dated 5/3/1919.)

9. PROMOTION:

The following promotion is published for information:-

No. 234830. L/Cpl. BRAND. S. R.E.H.Qrs. (unpaid) to be acting Corporal on pay. Dated 24/2/1919.

10. LEAVE.

The following Officers have been granted leave to U.K. :-

(a) 2nd.Lt. HOWARD. S.B. 479 Fd.Co. From March 7th. to March 21st.
(b) Lt. MALLINSON. F. 476 Fd.Co. From March 8th. to March 22nd.
(c) Lt. DICKENSON. A.R. 476 Fd.Co. From March 9th. On Duty.
(d) 2nd.Lt. MACKINTOSH. W. 479 Fd.Co. From March 10th. On Duty.

(Signed) G.H. SIMMONS.
Capt. Adjutant.
61st. Divisional. R.E.

Page 1.

ROUTINE ORDERS

Issued by Lieut-Colonel G.E.J. DURNFORD. D.S.O. R.E.

Commanding 61st.(South Midland) Divisional Royal Engineers

R.E.H.Qrs. March 29th. 1919.

11. HONOURS AND AWARDS

The following Awards for Gallantry and Devotion to Duty have been made.

CHEVALIER CROWN OF ROUMANIA

Lt. A/Capt G.S. RIGDEN 476 (S.M.) Field Co.

12. STRENGTH

The following Officers have reported for duty.

Rank	Name	Company	Date
2nd Lt.	M.C. RAY.	478 Field Co.	20. 3. 1919.
Capt A/Major.	P. COCHRAN. M.C.	"	21. 3. 1919.
Lieut.	E.S.C. BETTERLEY.	476 Field Co.	23. 3. 1919.
Lieut.	P.H. WAKEFIELD.	"	23. 3. 1919.
Lieut.	S. RUBERY.	479 Field Co.	23. 3. 1919.
Capt A/major.	J.S. WILLIAMS.	"	23. 3. 1919.

Capt A/Major P. COCHRAN. M.C. 478 Field Co.

proceeded to LE TREPORT on 24. 3. 1919. attached to D.H.Q. for duty.

13. LEAVE

The following Officers have been granted leave to U.K.

Lieut W.M. HAMES 478 Field Co. from March 23rd to April 6th.
Capt A/Major COCHRAN M.C. " " " 26th " " 9th.

14. ARMY ACT

Attention is directed to Kings Regulations para 461.
The proceedure laid down therein will be taken once a month until further orders are issued from this office.

15. RELINQUISHMENT OF ACTING RANK

The undermentioned reliquish the acting rank of Captain on ceasing to be employed as 2nd in command of Field Coys.

Lieut H.G. ROBINSON. 478 Field Co. from 29. 1. 1919.
"   J.D. RAWLINS. 479 Field Co. " 13. 2. 1919.

Authority G.H.Q. List No. 230 9.2.1919.

Page 2.

ROUTINE ORDERS

Issued by Lieut.Colonel G.E.J. DURNFORD D.S.O. R.E.

Commanding 61st (South Midland) Divisional Royal Engineers

R.E.H.Qrs. March 29th 1919.

---

16. **D.R.L.S.**

  Mounted Orderlies will leave R.E.H.Qrs daily at 09.15 Hrs and 14.00 Hrs for 183 Inf. Bde. H.Q. ST RIQUIER.
  The Orderly in the morning will be detailed by the Companies, in cycles of 3 days as follows:-

   476 Field Co------------------------March 27th, 28. 29th.
   478 Field Co------------------------April 1. March 30 &31.
   479 Field Co------------------------   "   2. 3. & 4th.

  H.Qrs is detailing the orderly every afternoon.

17. **MAIL**

  Companys will deliver their Mail to R.E.H.Qrs by 08.30 hrs daily, where it will be picked up and taken to St. RIQUIER under the existing arrangements between the Companys.

       (Sd) G.H. SIMMONS.
        Capt. Adjutant.
       For C.R.E. 61st. Division.

Vol 36

CONFIDENTIAL

WAR DIARY of

C.R.E. 61st DIVISION

APRIL 1919.

VOL XXXVI

ORIGINAL

Army Form C. 2118.

WAR DIARY
or
~~INTELLIGENCE~~ SUMMARY.
(Erase heading not required.)

HEADQUARTERS 61st. DIVISIONAL ROYAL ENGINEERS Vol. XXXVI.

APRIL 1919.

Page 1.

Instructions regarding War Diaries and Intelligence Summaries are contained in F. S. Regs., Part II. and the Staff Manual respectively. Title pages will be prepared in manuscript.

ABBEVILLE SHEET 14 1/100,000

Place	Date	Hour	Summary of Events and Information	Remarks and references to Appendices
AILLY-LE-HAUT-CLOCHER.	2nd.		Received reposting order for Lt. S. RUBERY -- to NIVELLES Sub Area. H.Q. CHARLEROI.	APP.2 (2)
	3rd.		Issued R.E. ORDER No.136. Also amendment to same.	
	"		Received reposting order for :- Lt. B.C. DAVRY to 207 Field Coy. Lt. S.A.H. BATTEN to 237 Field Coy. Lt. P.H. WAKEFIELD to 552 Army Troops Coy. 2.Lt. M.C. RAY to be attached to C.E. No.3 Area. Lt. E.S.C. BETTELEY to 135 Army Troops Coy.	
	4th.		Received reposting order for Lt 2.Lt. J.F. WARREN) To be attached to C.E. No.1 Area. 2.Lt. W. MACKINTOSH)	
	5th.		167 Animals handed over to No.2 Remount Depot ABBEVILLE. Sent notification to 61st.Division "A" that R.E. Units will be ready to depart to U.K. on 21st.	
	7th.		Issued Special Order of the Day re Departure of C.R.E. to U.K.	APP. 2 (8)
	8th.		Lt-Col. G.E.J. DURNFORD departed for U.K. and relinquished the acting rank of Lt-Col on ceasing to Command 61st. Div. R.E.	
	9th.		Issued Routine Orders No. 18,19, and 20.	APP.1 (1)
	12th.		Issued Order convening Board of Officers on 16th.	APP.2 (9.)
	16th.		Board of Officers held in C.R.E. Office to enquire into deficiencies in Mob. Store ~~tanks~~ Equipment.	
			Received reposting order for :- Lt. N.W. KING) Lt. E. MALLINSON) - to 30th. Division. Lt. S.B. HOWARD)	

Army Form C. 2118.

WAR DIARY
of
INTELLIGENCE SUMMARY.
(Erase heading not required.)

HEADQUARTERS.
61st. DIVISIONAL ROYAL ENGINEERS.
Vol. XXXVI.
page 2.

Instructions regarding War Diaries and Intelligence Summaries are contained in F. S. Regs., Part II. and the Staff Manual respectively. Title pages will be prepared in manuscript.

APRIL 1919.

ABBEVILLE Sheet No.14. 1/100,000.

Place	Date	Hour	Summary of Events and Information	Remarks and references to Appendices
AILLY-LE-HAUT-CLOCHER.				
	19th.		Received D.A.G. wire A.D. 66. ordering Lt. W.M. HAMES to report to C.E. No. 5 Area.	
	22nd.		Unserviceable and Surplus Stores inspected by Ordnance Inspecting Officers.	
	24th.		Surplus Stores handed in to No.2. Ordnance Depot ABBEVILLE. Received wire from 61st.Division "A". Send Retainable personnel to C.R.E. 62nd Division Reinforcement Camp COLOGNE.	
	25th.		36 Retainable and Volunteer Personnel of 61st.Div.R.E. departed for RHINE ARMY. COLOGNE.	
	26th.		Court Martial held in Hotel-de-Ville, AILLY-LE-HAUT-CLOCHER. Received reposting order for 2nd Lt J.F. WARREN to 58th Artisan Works Co. Board of Officers held at No.14 Veterinary Hospital ABBEVILLE to examine and test Drivers to fill vacancies for Artificers.	
	29th.		Remainder of Retainable and Volunteers Personnel departed for RHINE ARMY. COLOGNE. Notified Command Paymaster Base, 61st.Div.R.E. finally reduced to Cadre "A".	
	30th.		R.E. Personnel detached for demobilization during APRIL	Officers. W.O. O.R.
	"		previous to APRIL.	8 - 47.
	"		Total to Date.	- 3 291.
				8 3 338

[signature] Capt.
Adjutant 61st.Div.R.E.

War Diary.
(ORIGINAL.)
for APRIL 1919
C.R.E. 61st DIVn.

APPENDIX 1

ROUTINE

ORDERS

BY

C.R.E.

ROUTINE ORDERS.

Issued by Major H. HUMPHREYS.

Commanding 61st. (South Midland) Divisional Engineers.

R.E. H.Q. April 9th. 1919.

---

18. POSTINGS.

Rank	Name		Unit	Posted to:-	Date of Leaving Coy.
Lt.	DICKINSON.	A.R.	476 Field Coy.	To TOURNAI.	5/4/1919.
2nd.Lt.	SANDEAU.	V.E.H.	" " "	To 218 Fd.Co. Rhine.	1/4/1919.
Lt.	BETTELEY.	E.S.C?	Attached to 476 Field Coy.	To 135 A.T.Co.R.E.	7/4/1919.
Lt.	WAKEFIELD.	P.H.	- do -	To 552 A.T.Co.R.E. DIEVAL.	7/4/1919.
Lt.	HAMES.	W.M.	478 Field Coy.	To POPERINGHE.	
Lt.	DAVEY.	B.C.	Att. - do -	To 207 Fd.Co. Rhine.	1/4/1919.
Lt.	BATTEN.	S.A.H.	- do - do -	To 237 Fd.Co.	1/4/1919.
2nd.Lt.	RAY.	M.C.	- do - -do -	to C.E. 3rd.Army. FLIXECOURT.	5/4/1919.
2nd.Lt.	WARREN.	J.F.	479 Field Coy.	To C.E.1st.Army.	
2nd.Lt.	MACKINTOSH.	W.	" " "	To C.E.1st. Army.	
Lt.	RUBERY. M.C.	S.	Attached to 479 Field Coy.	To NIVELLES CHARLEROI	4/4/1919.

19. RELINQUISHMENT OF ACTING RANK.

The undermentioned relinquished the acting rank of Lieut-Colonel on April 6th.1919. on vacating his appointment as C.R.E. 61st. Division.

Major and Brevet Lt-Colonel G.E.J. DURNFORD. D.S.O. R.E.

20. LEAVE.

The following officer has been granted leave to U.K.:-

2nd Lt. WARREN. J.F. 479 Field Coy. From April 5th to April 19th.

(Sd) G.H. SIMMONS. Capt.
Adjutant 61st. Div. R.E.

War Diary.
(ORIGINAL.)
for APRIL 1919
C.R.E. 61st DIVN.

APPENDIX 2

ORDERS

RECEIVED + ISSUED.

R.E. ORDER NO. 136.   Copy No. 6

1. The following animals will be retained temporarily for use with the Cadres. They will be handed in to Remounts, ABBEVILLE, when Cadres entrain for Port of Embarkation.

   R.E. H.Q. ... ... 1 Rider.
   Field Companies... ... ... 2 Riders
                                       5 Light Draught Horses.

2. All other animals will be handed in to No.2 Remount Depot ABBEVILLE on Saturday next, 5th inst.

3. An Officer will conduct each party and will hand over his animals at No.2 Remount Depot. He will take with him A.F.O.1640 or A.F.O.1640.a. He will obtain receipts for all articles handed over with his animals.

4. Each animal will take saddle blanket and rug (if in possession) and nosebag. These will be handed over. Remainder of equipment will be brought back by conducting parties.

5. R.E. H.Q. animals will proceed with the party from 479 Field Coy. The Officer i/c of this party will be in possession of a separate A.F.O.1640 for R.E. H.Q. animals and will obtain separate receipts for articles handed over with them.

6. Parties will march as follows :- Starting point X roads in AILLY.

   476 Field Coy... ... ... 08.00 hrs.
   478 Field Coy... ... ... 08.30 hrs.
   479 Field Coy... ... ... 09.00 hrs.

7. Lorries will be at No.2 Remount Depot at 11.00 hrs. to bring personnel back to units.

R.E. H.Quarters, 61st. Division.
   Issued at 14.00 hrs.
   April 3rd. 1919.

                                                 Capt. & Adjutant.
                                            For C.R.E. 61st. Division.

Distribution.

Copy No. 1. 183 Inf. Bde. H.Q.   Copy No. 4. 479 Field Coy.
        2. 476 Field Coy.   5. War Diary.
        3. 478 Field Coy.   6. War Diary.
              Copy No. 7. File.

SPECIAL ORDER OF THE DAY.
By LIEUTENANT-COLONEL C.E.J. DURNFORD. D.S.O.
Commanding Royal Engineers, 61st. Division.

On vacating my appointment after having had the honour to Command you for two and a half years in the field, I wish, for the last time, to place on record my high appreciation of your services.

I thank each Officer, Non Commissioned Officer and Man for the loyalty, co-operation and support on which I have always relied and which has never failed me.

The manner in which you have carried out your special duties has earned high approbation.

As soldiers you have displayed those qualities of of good Comradeship, determination to succeed, stubbornness which refuses to admit defeat and cheerfulness under all conditions which have ever been associated with the British soldier.

It is with many regrets that I relinquish my Command, but I shall always carry with me the remembrance of your fine spirit and your loyalty.

I take with me too my pride in your achievements.

Good bye.

Durnford.

R.E. Headquarters,   Lieut-Colonel,
APRIL 7TH. 1919.   C.R.E. 61st. Division.

BOARD OF OFFICERS

Copy No..........

A BOARD OF OFFICERS will sit in the C.R.E. Office AILLY-LE-HAUT-CLOCHER at 10.30 hrs. on the 16th. inst. in accordance with K.R. para.666.

President.   Major E. LONG. M.C. 479 Field Coy.
Members.   Capt. G.S. RIGDEN.   476 Field Coy.
     "   Lt. L.W.H. BEST. M.C. 478 Field Coy.

To enquire into certain deficiencies in the Mob. Store Equipment of the 61st. Div. R.E.

R.E. H.Q.
12/4/1919.   (Sd) H. HUMPHREYS. Major.
                              Commanding 61st. Div. R.E.

Distribution.

Copy No.1. H.Q. 183 Inf. Bde.   Copy No.2. 476 Field Coy.
  "   3. 478 Field Coy.   "   4. 479 Field Coy.
  "   5. War Diary.   "   6. War Diary.
  "   7. File.   "   8. File.

WO 37

CONFIDENTIAL

WAR DIARY of

C.R.E. 61st DIVISION

MAY 1919.

VOL. XXXVII

ORIGINAL

Army Form C. 2118.

ORIGINAL WAR DIARY
or
INTELLIGENCE SUMMARY.

(Erase heading not required.)

Instructions regarding War Diaries and Intelligence Summaries are contained in F. S. Regs., Part II. and the Staff Manual respectively. Title pages will be prepared in manuscript.

HEADQUARTERS,
61st. DIVISIONAL ROYAL ENGINEERS
Vol. XXXVII.
Page 1.

MAY 1919.

ABBEVILLE SHEET 14. 1/100,000.

Place	Date	Hour	Summary of Events and Information	Remarks and references to Appendices
AILLY-LE-HAUT-CLOCHER.				
	7th.		Adjutant. Capt. G.H. SIMMONS. M.C. departed for leave to U.K.	
	8th.		Received 61st.Div. No.D.B. 8/13 d/- 6/5/1919. Cadres are to be reduced from 50 O.R. to 40 O.R. and surplus Personnel sent for dispersal as soon as possible.	
	16th. 17th.		Issued Routine Orders Nos. 21, 22 and 23. G.O.C. 61st.Division visited R.E. AILLY-LE-HAUT-CLOCHER.	APP 1 (1).
	18th.		Church Parade at 10.00 hrs. Issued R.E. ORDER NO. 137. Ref. Shakespearian Recital in the Theatre, AILLY-LE-HAUT-CLOCHER, on May 20th.	A.PP. 2. (2)
	19th.		26 N.C.O. and men proceeded to Comcamp ABBEVILLE for dispersal in accordance with reduction in CADRE Establishment. 61st.Div.No.D.B.8/13 of the 6/5/1919.	

Army Form C. 2118.

ORIGINAL
WAR DIARY
of
INTELLIGENCE SUMMARY

(Erase heading not required.)

HEADQUARTERS,
61st. DIVISIONAL ROYAL ENGINEERS.
Vol. XXXVII.
Page 2.

Instructions regarding War Diaries and Intelligence Summaries are contained in F. S. Regs., Part II. and the Staff Manual respectively. Title pages will be prepared in manuscript.

MAY 1919.

Place	Date	Hour	Summary of Events and Information	Remarks and references to Appendices
AILLY-LE-HAUT-CLOCHER.			ABBEVILLE SHEET 14. 1/100,000.	
	20th.		Shakespearian Recital given in Theatre at AILLY-LE-HAUT-CLOCHER, by Lt. HAWKEN.	
	21st.		Received 61st.Div.No.A.104/122. dated 19/5/1919. allotting period 27-30th. May for Officers and O.R. to visit LE TREPORT.	
	22nd.		Adjutant Capt G.H. SIMMONS. M.C. returned from leave.	
	24th.		Received 183 Inf.Bde. Order No. S.C.2/1/2.d/- 23rd. Return all Horses on charge to No. 2 Advanced Remount Depot, ABBEVILLE. Received wire No.Q.X. 87. from 61st.Div that period 27th May to 30th. May altered to May 30th. to June 2nd. to visit LE TREPORT.	
	25th.		Issued R.E. ORDER NO. 138 re Handing over of remaining Horses to No. 2 Advanced Remount Depot, ABBEVILLE.	APP. 2 (6).

Army Form C. 2118.

ORIGINAL.
WAR DIARY
or
~~INTELLIGENCE SUMMARY~~
(Erase heading not required.)

Instructions regarding War Diaries and Intelligence Summaries are contained in F. S. Regs., Part II. and the Staff Manual respectively. Title pages will be prepared in manuscript.

HEADQUARTERS,
61st.DIVISIONAL ROYAL ENGINEERS.
Vol. XXXVII. Page 3.

ABBEVILLE SHEET No. 14. 1/100,000.

MAY.
1919.

Summary of Events and Information

Place	Date	Hour	Summary of Events and Information	Remarks and references to Appendices
AILLY-LE-HAUT-CLOCHER.	26th.		All remaining Horses, total 22 handed over to No. 2 Advanced Remount Depot, ABBEVILLE. Received 61st.Div.Order No. A.57/1/17 dated 24th. 61st.Divisional R.E. will be transferred from 183 Inf.Bde. Group at 12.00 hrs on 26th inst. Lt-Col. SUTTON A.A.&Q.M.G. 61st.Division. visited AILLY-LE-HAUT-CLOCHER. ref moving R.E. into ABBEVILLE.	
	27th.		Major HUMPHREYS and Adjutant visited ABBEVILLE area H.Q. ref moving into No.5 veterinary Hospital and afterwards visited the Hospital and inspected the accommodation.	
	30th.		27 NcC.Os and men departed to entrain at ABBEVILLE for 3 days leave to LE TREPORT.	
	31st.		R.E.Personnel Demobilized during the month of MAY previous to " "	Officers. W.O. O.R. - - 27. 8 3 338. 8 3 365 Total to Date.

Capt.
Adjutant 61st. DIV. R.E.

War Diary.
(ORIGINAL.)
for MAY 1918.
C.R.E. 61st DIVn.

Appendix 1

ROUTINE

ORDERS

BY

C.R.E.

ROUTINE ORDERS.

Issued by Major H. HUMPHRYS.

Commanding 61st. (South Midland) Divisional Engineers.

R.E. H.Q. May 10th. 1919.

───

§1. POSTINGS.

Rank.	Name.		Unit.	Posted to:-	Date of Leaving Unit.
Lt.	MALLINSON.	R.	478 Field Coy.	50th.Div.R.E.	19/4/1919.
Lt.	HOWARD.	S.R.	479 Field Coy.	" " "	19/4/1919.
Lt.	KING.	R.W.	478 Field Coy.	" " "	19/4/1919.
Lt.	HAMER.	W.H.	478 Field Coy.	G.H. No.5.Area.	19/4/1919.
2/Lt	WARREN	J.F.	479 Field Coy.	58 Artizan Works Co	3/5/1919

§2. CHURCH PARADE.

There will be a Church Parade for 61st.Divisional R.E. at 10.00 hrs. on Sunday May 18th. at the Theatre, AILLY-LE-HAUT-CLOCHER.

§3. LEAVE.

The following Officers have been granted leave to U.K. :-

Lt. WOOD. D.S. 478 Field Coy. From May.6th. to May.20th.
Capt. GIBSON. G.M. Adj. R.E. H.Q. " May.6th. to May.22nd.

(Signed) L.W.H. BEST. Lieut.
a/Adjutant 61st.Divisional
R.E.

War Diary.
(ORIGINAL.)
for MAY 1919.
C.R.E. 61st DIVN.

APPENDIX 2

ORDERS
RECEIVED & ISSUED

R.E. ORDER NO.137.   Copy No...4....

1.   Lieut.HAWKENS will deliver a SHAKESPEARIAN
        Recital in the Theatre AILLY-LE-HAUT-CLOCHER on Tuesday
        May 20th. at 11.00 hours.

2.   Companies will parade in the Theatre at 10.55 hours.

R.E. Headquarters, 61st.Division.   Major,
    Issued at 14.00 hours.   61st.Div.R.E.
    May. 18th.1919.

Distribution.

Copy.No.1. 476 Field Coy.   Copy No. 4. War Diary.
        2. 478 Field Coy.   5. War Diary.
        3. 479 Field Coy.   6. File.

R.E. ORDER NO. 138.   Copy No. 5

All horses will be returned to No.2. Advanced Remount Depot, ABBEVILLE tomorrow under authority 183 Inf.Bde. S.O.2/1/2 of the 23/5/1919.

Lt. D.S. WOOD 476 Field Coy will be in charge and will leave "X" roads AILLY-LE-HAUT-CLOCHER at 09.00 hrs where 478, 479 and H.Q. animals will rendezvous and follow.

Coys. will prepare A.F. 0.1640a in duplicate and receipt forms for Articles to be handed over and hand same in at C.R.E. Office today where Lt. WOOD will obtain them before starting.

Each animal will take nose-bag, hay net and horse rug (if in possession).

Lorry will be at No. 2 Remount Depot at 11.00 hrs to bring personnel back.

R.E. Headquarters, 61st. Division.
Issued at 14.00 hrs
May 25th. 1919.
                                             Capt.
                                   Adjutant 61st.Div.R.E.

- - - - - - - - - - - - - - - - - - - -

Distribution.

Copy No.1. H.Q. 183 Inf.Bde.   Copy.No. 4. 479 Field Coy.
        2. 476 Field Coy.   5&6. War Diary.
        3. 478 Field Coy.   7. File.

98 38

CONFIDENTIAL
WAR DIARY OF
CRE 61st Div.
JUNE 1917
VOL. XXVII

Army Form C. 2118.

WAR DIARY
or
INTELLIGENCE SUMMARY.
(Erase heading not required.)

Headquarters, 61st Divn. Royal Engineers
VOL. XXXVII   Page 1

JUNE. 1919

Place	Date	Hour	Summary of Events and Information	Remarks and references to Appendices
AILLY-LE-HAUT-CLOCHER (ABBEVILLE SHEET 14)	1st		Driver DOLLING proceeded on leave to U.K.	
	4th		Division D.A.A.G. visited R.E. H.Q., and left prior to move into ABBEVILLE, and reducing numbers down to Equipment Guard. Rcd. H.Q. British Troops in France Letter C.R. 8938(Md) 61st Divn A 184/15/1 re Cadres less equipment Guards to go for demobilization. Rcd. 61 Div. Div. Q.X 107, Field Coys. to move into ABBEVILLE forthwith.	
	5th		R.E. Order No. 139 issued, containing movement orders for Three Field Companies, 2/2 Field Ambulance, and No. 3 Coy. Train to move. Major Humphreys and Adjutant inspected Signal Depot and allotted accommodation.	Appx 1.
	6th		Cook houses erected in Signal Depot.	
	7th		2/2nd Field Ambulance moved into Signal Depot, ABBEVILLE.	
	8th		Major G.S Williams proceeded on leave to U.K.	
	9th		476 Field Company moved into Signal Depot, ABBEVILLE	
	10th		478 " " " " " " " Major Humphreys proceeded on leave to U.K. (terminating then.)	
ABBEVILLE	11th		Q.M. Brand proceeded on leave, will return to report to Rhine Army (62nd Divn) on termination thereof. R.E. H.Q. moved into Signal Depot, ABBEVILLE	
	12th		479 Field Coy. " " " " " Men now complete except for Potsdam and Tortille Waggons still left at AILLY.	

WAR DIARY
INTELLIGENCE SUMMARY.

(Erase heading not required.)

Army Form C. 2118.

JUNE 1919

Headquarters 61st Divn. Royal Engineers
Vol. XXXVII Page 2

Place	Date	Hour	Summary of Events and Information	Remarks and references to Appendices
ABBEVILLE (ABBEVILLE, SHEET 14)				
	15th		Lt BEST returned from leave to U.K.	
	16th		Inspection by G.O.C. 61st Divn. of men being demobilized as cadres. The cadres of the Three Field Companies and Divnl. DAVIES of R.E. M.G. and off to concentration camp, ABBEVILLE for dispersal. Capt. G.H. SIMMONS M.C. left for dispersal. Lt. L.W.H. BEST M.C. took over as A/Adjutant.	
	17th		Divnr DOLLING returned from leave.	
	19th		Divisional D.A.A.G. visited R.E.H.Q.; discussed moving of Troutt and Pontoon Wagon into ABBEVILLE, and preparations for moving Equipment to U.K.	
	22nd		All Troutt Wagons moved into Signal Depot, ABBEVILLE from AILLY	
	23rd 24th		Major LONG M.C. detailed on loan to BRUSSELS. Major WILLIAMS attached to Divn. for U.K. his relation in Capt. Stephenson telephoned from Division that MAJOR HUMPHREYS would be demobilized from leave.	
	29th			
	30th		R.E. personnel at this: now 1 O.R. int. 1 Officer and 1 O.R. attached.	

L.W.H.Best
Lt
A/Adjutant 61st Divn. R.E.

R.E. ORDER. NO. 139.   Copy No. 9

1. The three Field Coys. 2/2 (S.M.) Field Ambulance and No.3 Coy. Train will move into the Signal Depot ABBEVILLE.

2. The 2/2 Field Ambulance will move on Saturday the 7th. inst. under the Orders of O.C.

3. 476 Field Coy. transport will move on Monday the 9th.inst. 478 & 479 Field Coys. following immediately after as horses become available.

4. No. 3 Coy Train will move after the Field Coy transport has been moved.

5. Accommodation for transport is satisfactory and will be allotted by an R.E. Officer who will be at the Signal Depot on Saturday.

6. Horses can be stabled at A.H.T.Depot.

7. Rations will be drawn from detail issue store ABBEVILLE.

8. O.C. No. 3 Coy Train will find the animals to move the transport of all Units above mentioned and will arrange starting times direct with O.C. concerned.

9. Base Commandant ABBEVILLE is providing one lorry on Monday and daily until R.E. Transport is moved, to haul the trestle wagons etc. This lorry is reporting at C.R.E. Office AILLY-LE-HAUT-CLOCHER at 09.00 hrs. on Monday the 9th. inst. where O.C. 476 Field Coy. will arrange to meet it. This arrangement is xxxxxxxxx allowing for the 3 trestle wagons of each Coy to be moved in one journey.

10. Personnel of Field xxx Amb. and Train Coy. will move under Orders of their Commanding Officers.

11. Field Coy. Personnel will march under orders of respective O.C. as soon as possible after their transport.

12. Units will get the usual " NO CLAIMS " certificates signed.

R.E. HEADQUARTERS, 61st. DIVISION.
Issued at 16.00 hrs.
June 5th. 1919.

                                                        Capt.
                                              Adjutant 61st.Div.R.E.

Distribution.

Copy No. 1. Base Commdt. Abbeville.   Copy No. 6. 479 Field Coy.
         2. 61st.Division "G".   7. No. 3 Coy. Train.
         3. 61st.Division "Q".   8. 2/2 Field Amb.
         4. 476 Field Coy.   9&10. War Diary.
         5. 478 Field Coy.   11. File.

WD 39

CONFIDENTIAL.
WAR DIARY OF C.R.E. 21 Div.
JULY 1919.
Vol. XXXIX

ORIGINAL

WAR DIARY
or
INTELLIGENCE SUMMARY.

Army Form C. 2118.

HEADQUARTERS 61 DIV. R.E.
VOL. XXXIX Page 1.
JULY 1919.

Place	Date	Hour	Summary of Events and Information	Remarks and references to Appendices
ABBEVILLE SHEET 14	1/7/19		Rec'd 61 Div. Q.78/4 re reduction of 61 Div Train to Cadre "A"	App. 1.
	2/7/19		Rec'd 61 Div. A.Q.52. re Returns	"
	3/7/19		MAJ. WILLIAMS departed for DOULLENS Area	
	4/7/19		Company transport ready to move awaiting Lenval no. Destination	
	5/7/19		ditto	
	6/7/19		ditto	
	7/7/19		ditto. Rec'd 61 Div. A.59/39 re discipline on leave	App. 1.
	8/7/19		ditto. Having received sanction from 61 Div. Dermot papers forwarded to MAJ. HUMPHREYS on leave.	
	9/7/19		C.R.E. Documents etc. Also property etc. for preservation prepared for despatch.	
	10/7/19		Rec'd 61 Div. A.184/11 & Q.3.662 giving Serial No. Destination of C.R.E. Companies C.R.E. F.43 Destination not known. 476 F.A.O. AINTREE W. 478 F.A.1 D/COL.479 F.A.2. Depot.	App. 1.
	11/7/19		Wagons Packages marked accordingly.	
	12/7/19		ditto	
	13/7/19		ditto	

Army Form C. 2118.

WAR DIARY
or
INTELLIGENCE SUMMARY.

HEAD QUARTERS 61 DIV. R.E.
Vol. XXXIX Page 2
(Erase heading not required.)

JULY 1919

Place	Date	Hour	Summary of Events and Information	Remarks and references to Appendices
ABBEVILLE	14.7.19		Continued marking wagons. Peace celebrations. Holiday.	
SHEET 14	15.7.19		Continued marking wagons etc.	
"	16.7.19		Wagons completed ready to move.	
"	17.7.19		Surplus stationery, Records etc. despatched per M.F.O.	
"	19.7.19		Companies engaged in clearing up generally. Sports. Tennis also ran. Peace celebrations	
"	20.7.19		ditto. Many recover from previous day	
"	21.7.19		ditto	
"	22.7.19		ditto	
"	23.7.19		ditto	
"	24.7.19		ditto LT. BEST (A/ADJT.) proceeds on Paris leave	
"	25.7.19		ditto	
"	26.7.19		ditto	
"	27.7.19		ditto	
"	28.7.19		A.O.O. from No. 1 Section Record Office for particulars of Infantry attached Records destroyed by fire. Replied nil.	
"	29.7.19		Sports. Clearing up etc.	
"	30.7.19		"	
"	31.7.19		"	

Blay Major
Cmdg. S. 61 Div R.E.

www.ingramcontent.com/pod-product-compliance
Lightning Source LLC
Chambersburg PA
CBHW080841010526
44114CB00017B/2348